The Three Skills of Top Trading

Founded in 1807, John Wiley & Sons is the oldest independent publishing company in the United States. With offices in North America, Europe, Australia, and Asia, Wiley is globally committed to developing and marketing print and electronic products and services for our customers' professional and personal knowledge and understanding.

The Wiley Trading series features books by traders who have survived the market's ever changing temperament and have prospered—some by reinventing systems, others by getting back to basics. Whether a novice trader, professional, or somewhere in-between, these books will provide the advice and strategies needed to prosper today and well into the future.

For a list of available titles, visit our web site at www.WileyFinance.com.

The Three Skills of Top Trading

Behavioral Systems Building,
Pattern Recognition, and
Mental State Management

HANK PRUDEN

BICENTENNIAL
1807
WILEY
2007
BICENTENNIAL

John Wiley & Sons, Inc.

Published by John Wiley & Sons, Inc., Hoboken, New Jersey.
Published simultaneously in Canada.

Wiley Bicentennial Logo: Richard J. Pacifico

For general information on our other products and services or for technical support,
please contact our Customer Care Department within the United States at (800) 762-2974,
outside the United States at (317) 572-3993 or fax (317) 572-4002.

Wiley also publishes its books in a variety of electronic formats. Some content that appears
in print may not be available in electronic books. For more information about Wiley
products, visit our web site at www.wiley.com.

Library of Congress Cataloging-in-Publication Data:

Pruden, Hank, 1936–
    The three skills of top trading : behavioral systems building, pattern
recognition, and mental state management / Hank Pruden.
        p.   cm.—(Wiley trading series)
Includes bibliographical references and index.
ISBN 978-0-470-05063-7 (cloth)
    1. Stock price forecasting.   2. Stocks.   3. Futures.   4. Speculation.   I.
Title.
HG4529.P78   2007
332.63'2042—dc22

                                                              2006036653

10   9   8   7   6   5   4   3   2   1

*To Sarah—my precious wife,
lifelong love, and best friend*

Contents

Preface

This book gives the trader, the investor, and the analyst a true competitive advantage in the challenging markets of the twenty-first century. Today, there are powerful agitations in the United States and globally to shift responsibility for investing onto the shoulders of the individual. But, just as responsibility moves away from corporations and the government, the individual faces conflicting advice as to how to manage financial investments. The efficient market hypothesis is riddled with false assumptions that lead to wrong results. Equally mistaken are brokers who advise their clients to buy and hold. The real behavior of markets, what the data show in numerous markets over many time frames, is that "Market 'timing' matters greatly. Big gains and losses concentrate into small packages of time." (Benoit B. Mandelbrot)

Some of the most successful traders are the ones who got their market timing right. Take, for example, George Soros, who during two months in 1992 profited about $2 billion by betting against the British pound sterling. Although few traders are in the same league as George Soros, most can profit from market moves concentrated in time.

This book aims to equip the trader with a balanced set of skills for capturing the "packages of time" that make for big gain opportunities in the market. It will also help the trader sidestep the timing pitfalls stemming from superficial data analysis and erroneous interpretations of market indicators.

To compete successfully the trader must become a Complete Trader. As you can see in the Three-in-One Trader Model (Figure P.1), three mutually reinforcing elements form the Complete Trader. This book will help you develop skill within each of the elements of systems building, pattern recognition, and mental state discipline, giving you solid footing well along the path to becoming a Complete Trader.

This book brings together the three skills of top trading: behavioral models for systems building, pattern recognition, and mental state discipline.

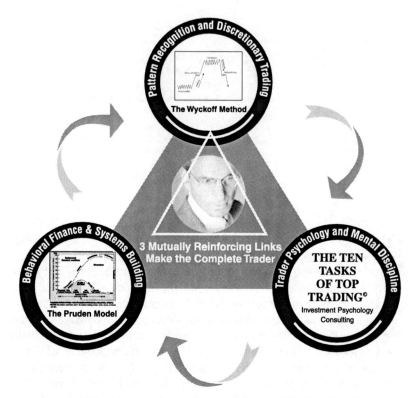

FIGURE P.1   Three Mutually Reinforcing Links Make the Complete Trader

These three key skill areas work together to move the art and science of technical analysis and trading to the level of sophistication required in the twenty-first century. This book integrates elements of trading that are often treated separately into a mutually reinforcing analytical package that makes intuitive sense.

Part One of *The Three Skills of Top Trading* addresses systems building and behavioral finance. There are three chapters devoted to this skill area.

Chapter 1, "Systems Building for the Three Skills of Top Trading," focuses on the building of decision-support systems. It introduces the right-brain/left-brain idea. Several schematics show the relationships of the Life Cycle Model of Crowd Behavior, the Wyckoff Method of Technical Analysis and Speculation, and the tools for mental state discipline found in the Ten Tasks of Top Trading.

Chapter 2, "Behavioral Finance," serves as a resource chapter for the trader. It defines the field of behavioral finance, gives a brief historical review, and explains how behavioral finance can be subdivided into individual behavior and mass psychology.

Chapter 3, "The Life Cycle Model of Crowd Behavior," explains how and why a trader can build a technical decision-support system. The Life Cycle Model defines the four key dimensions of price, volume, sentiment, and time. It also shows how indicators that measure these parameters are integrated into a mutually reinforcing decision framework. The S-shaped and bell-shaped curves of the Life Cycle Model's visual schematic are complemented by an analytical checklist for weighting indicators.

Part Two covers pattern recognition and discretionary trading, with a focus on the Wyckoff method of technical analysis and speculation. There are four chapters devoted to this skill area.

Chapter 4, "Wyckoff: The Man, the Method, the Mystique," shares tales of Richard D. Wyckoff, reveals the history behind Wyckoff's time-tested pattern recognition method, and proposes that his principles are increasingly relevant to the trader of today. In addition, it introduces the five steps of the Wyckoff method of technical analysis and speculation.

Chapter 5, "The Basic Elements of Charting for the Wyckoff Method," defines and illustrates the usage of the basic vertical line or bar chart and the construction and usage of the figure or point-and-figure chart. It also includes the proper procedures for drawing trend lines, trend channels and support and resistance lines within a trading range. In addition, charts show comparative strength and weakness, the role of price spread, volume, and divergences. Finally, you will learn how to coordinate bar and figure charts.

Chapter 6, "The Wyckoff Method of Technical Analysis and Speculation," defines and illustrates the application of Wyckoff laws, tests, and schematics. This chapter describes the three basic Wyckoff laws: supply and demand, effort versus result, and cause and effect. The nine Wyckoff tests are crucial for enabling the trader to identify and enter a trading position that has very favorable reward-to-risk odds. The analytical checklists of the three laws and tests are complemented by visual schematics of trading ranges for accumulation and distribution. Even though Wyckoff's method is a judgmental method and not a mechanical system, these laws, tests, and schematics are designed to give the trader a logical, systematic approach to chart analysis.

Chapter 7, "Anatomy of a Trade," offers concrete and complete examples of the diagnosis of a trading range and the identification of chart locations to take high-reward, low-risk trading positions. The second half of the chapter shows step by step how an expert Wyckoff-oriented trader entered, followed through, and exited trading positions using options on an energy company's stock. In addition, this chapter introduces nine new tests for reaccumulation as a supplement to the nine classic buying tests for accumulation.

Part Three covers trader psychology and mental state discipline. There are three chapters devoted to this skill area.

Chapter 8, "Trader Psychology and Mental Discipline," transitions us into Part Three by drawing on Wyckoff's observation that the mastery of a sound methodology is only half of the trader's battle; the other half is the mastery of one's emotions and mental state. At the center of this chapter is a model, the Ten Tasks of Top Trading, which provides the trader with a system for accessing the appropriate mental state for each key task of a trading campaign from diagnosis to action to exiting a trade.

Chapter 9, "The Composite Man," introduces the concept of the Composite Man, a powerful tool for mastering trading methodology, unique to the Wyckoff method. In addition, the concept of the Composite Man serves as a useful device in the quest for mental state control. This chapter explores in depth the nature and use of the Composite Man and introduces several other complementary techniques to capture the proper mental state for effective trading.

Chapter 10, "Putting It All Together: Ten Principles for a Trader to Live By," is at once an introduction to *The Three Skills of Top Trading* and a summary and conclusion to the book. The chapter concludes with an example of a three skills trader, Weylin Canada, foreign currency trader. The case study of Canada's trading reveals his growth as a trader, his adoption and application of the Three Skills of Top Trading, and examples of his technical analysis and trading actions using charts of currency pairs. Most important, it illuminates the three key skills: (1) He works with a *behavioral model*, a theory, an idea about how the world works that helps him gain profits. (2) He applies both *pattern recognition* and quantitative technical analysis tools. (3) He pays attention to his *mental state control*, which galvanizes him when he needs to take action and extract gold from the veins of ore that his system helps him spot on his price charts.

The Three Skills of Top Trading speaks to both the astute and the aspiring trader who wishes to sustain or gain an edge in trading to meet the challenging markets of the twenty-first century. The competitive edge is going to those traders who embrace skill sets reminiscent of the old-time traders and technicians who lived and worked on Wall Street in the early decades of the twentieth century. This book reveals how the new science of behavioral finance accelerates and enhances these skills and helps to make them accessible to traders of all levels.

In addition, this book addresses the needs of a wide variety of traders. Almost all traders can capitalize on at least one of the elements of the Three Skills model. For example, I believe that systems traders will find the message of Part One, "Systems Building and Behavioral Finance," to be quite rewarding; the Life Cycle Model of Crowd Behavior is especially versatile and rigorous. On another front, swing traders who use pattern recognition can benefit from the Wyckoff laws, tests, and schematics offered in Part Two. Finally, tape readers, and indeed all traders, can benefit from studying three sections located in Part Three: "The Ten Tasks of Top Trading," "Chart Reading in the R-Mode," and "A 'Sealed Room' and 'Only One Client.'" However, this book is truly greater than the sum of its parts, and the trader who integrates every facet of The Three Skills of Top Trading should have the decisive competitive edge in the twenty-first century.

The Three Skills of Top Trading is designed both to stand alone and to supplement and complement other books currently available on technical analysis and trading. I encourage you to read it carefully and to return to it often. Let it be your guide as you forge ahead along the path to better trading and expanded profits.

Acknowledgments

I wish to acknowledge the important contributions of several individuals to both the content and the processing of this book.

I have enjoyed the support of many editors and colleagues over the years. In particular, I want to thank Jack Hutson, editor in chief of *Technical Analysis of Stocks & Commodities*, and Charles D. Kirkpatrick, editor of the *Journal of Technical Analysis*, for their early, ongoing encouragement and publication of many of the ideas put forth in this book and for the access they provided. Many thanks also to Dr. Van K. Tharp of the Van Tharp Institute, who served as both a mentor and a collaborator in the creation of the Ten Tasks of Top Trading, and to the members of the Technical Securities Analysts Association of San Francisco, especially Bruce Fraser, Audrey Lewak, and Jim Forte, certified market technician, for sharing their observations and practices.

My very deep thanks go to Craig Schroeder of the Wyckoff/Stock Market Institute for the provision of charts, concepts, and schematics depicting the Wyckoff method, and to Daniel Pink, whose *A Whole New Mind: Why Right-Brainers Will Rule the Future* provided insights and inspirations. Finally, my appreciation goes to Weylin Canada for candidly, openly, and thoroughly sharing his experience as a Three Skills trader.

With respect to the process of compiling, editing, and creating this book, I owe a great debt of gratitude to my daughter, Laura Pruden. Laura served as the key person behind the thorough, proper, and timely completion of this book. In addition, I appreciate the valuable input by my wife, Sarah Pruden, and the efforts of Goldie Aranha, Cassandra Dilosa, Jimmy Lam, Mukesh Punjabi, and Lynette Webb, all of Golden Gate University, San Francisco, California.

I want to acknowledge the guidance and support of my editors at John Wiley & Sons, Inc., namely Kevin Commins and Emilie Herman. Emilie worked hard and long with Laura and me in our team effort to deliver a book that meets Wiley's high standards.

About the Author

Henry Oliver (Hank) Pruden, Ph.D., is the author of dozens of articles on behavioral finance, trader psychology, and technical analysis. A full-time trader for his own account for two decades, he is currently a Professor of Business Administration and Executive Director of the Institute for Technical Market Analysis at Golden Gate University in San Francisco, California. He earned his Ph.D. (with honors) in Marketing at the University of Oregon in 1968, his M.B.A. from the University of California, Berkeley, in 1965, and his B.S. from California State University, Chico, in 1961. Formerly, he was a professor in the College of Business at the University of Texas at Austin and a visiting professor at Northwestern University's Graduate School of Management.

Hank is the president of the Technical Securities Analysts Association of San Francisco (TSAASF) and vice president, Americas, for the International Federation of Technical Analysts (IFTA), and previously served as editor of the *Market Technicians Association Journal* for 11 years. He gives seminars to individuals and businesses worldwide and in the past decade has been a speaker on every continent but Antarctica. Highlights of his international speaking include serving as IFTA's educational ambassador to Europe in 2004 and 2005 and circling the globe speaking on the Wyckoff method for Dow Jones Telerate in 1997.

Dr. Pruden received awards for teaching excellence at both the University of Oregon and the University of Texas at Austin, and for research and scholarship at Golden Gate University. He has been honored for excellence in education by the Market Technicians Association and for Outstanding International Achievements in Behavioral Finance and Technical Analysis Education by P.I. Graduate Studies of Kuala Lumpur, Malaysia. In

2006, his research was highly commended by the Emerald Literati Network Awards for Excellence.

Hank lives with his wife, Sarah, near San Francisco. His web site is www.hankpruden.com.

PART ONE

Systems Building and Behavioral Finance

CHAPTER 1

Systems Building for the Three Skills of Top Trading

E arly in my trading career I was a student of the Edson Gould philosophy depicted in his *Findings and Forecasts* of the early 1970s. Then later, in the late 1970s through the early 1980s, as a full-time trader for my own account and an avid student of technical analysis, I became an enthusiastic follower of Joseph Granville and his Granville method of technical analysis. Joe Granville's system comprised a "tree of indicators" so that all the weight of decision making did not depend on any one branch. In Granville's hands, this weight-of-the-evidence and tree-of-indicators approach worked like magic during the widely swinging trading ranges of the 1970s and early 1980s.

I was impressed by Granville's capacity to call intermediate trend reversals in U.S. equity markets, but I was disturbed by his subjective approach to technical analysis. My PhD education and professional research training led me to seek out a model from the behavioral sciences for a framework that would give structure and discipline to Granville's tree-of-indicators approach. The results of this research were tested both in my own trading and by the experiences of my students and my technical-trading colleagues in San Francisco. Ultimately, my research crystallized into a decision support system called the Life Cycle Model of Crowd Behavior. (See Figure 1.7 later in this chapter).

The Life Cycle Model of Crowd Behavior rests on a solid foundation of behavioral science theory. Hence, the trader-analyst can have confidence that her decision support system is logical and dependable. This system covers the main dimensions of price, volume, sentiment, and time; it shows how these elements fit together in a mutually reinforcing scheme or system. Because price, volume, sentiment, and time are dimensions of market behavior that are independent of each other, the trader-analyst has the scientific reason she needs to compile the indicator readings of these four elements of technical analysis to obtain a more comprehensive and accurate reading of a market's present position and probable future trend.

One beauty of a decision support system is its flexibility. The market itself is dynamic, which means that from one market juncture to the next, a different mix of market indicators may become dominant. Hence, you, the trader-analyst, will lean most heavily on price indicators and downplay sentiment at one juncture, while later, sentiment will become the focus of your attention. With a decision support system you are free to judge the relative weightings of indicators at different market junctures and respond accordingly.

You can make the choice to push this decision support system more toward the nondiscretionary pole and use it as a semi-mechanical trading system. Conversely, you can rely on behavioral finance simply as a setup for market timing decisions. In my judgment, this degree of flexibility fits the dynamic nature of the market, but you risk filtering away the advantage of flexibility with decision systems that are too mechanical or too rigid in their rules for decision making.

After several years of full-time trading, tracking technical analysis systems, and being involved in the technical-trading community, I graduated to a higher level of trading. I elevated my attention more and more to pattern recognition and discretionary trading. I had always backed up my indicator analysis with chart patterns, which I found helpful. However, I was also aware that my interpretations of chart patterns succeeded on a hit-or-miss basis.

One of my colleagues in the technical analysis and trading community in San Francisco used a pattern recognition and discretionary trading approach that he swore by and that he encouraged me to learn. It was the Wyckoff method of technical analysis and art of speculation. My friend had been an engineer working in Lebanon for Middle East Airlines before one of the many wars in that part of the world forced him and his family to flee. However, while he was living in Lebanon, he had good success applying the Wyckoff method to U.S. stocks. He, too, had progressed from indicator analysis to pattern recognition. As an engineer specializing in reliability testing, he carefully classified the Wyckoff method as a sound and reliable system of market analysis and a total trading philosophy, including money management.

Around 1980 I enrolled in the Wyckoff correspondence course offered by the Stock Market Institute. Soon thereafter it became my principal method for triggering trades. Over the years, the Wyckoff method grew to become a dominant part of my trading and professional life. I created and began teaching a university graduate-level course in Wyckoff and subsequently tested the Wyckoff method extensively in my own trading. These experiences stimulated me to refine some basic Wyckoff principles and to create new tools to add power to the trader who adopts the Wyckoff method.

Also in the 1980s I became friendly with Mr. Robert Prechter and adopted the Elliott Wave Principle as another way to validate my Wyckoff interpretations. During the 1970s and 1980s, I expanded my acquaintances among the older traders and technicians in the New York area, including Mr. Anthony (Tony) Tabell, grand-nephew of Richard D. Wyckoff, from whom we shall soon learn a vital lesson that links the style of the old-time traders to the style that will lead to success for the trader in the twenty-first century.

Another two big steps forward in my process of systems building took place around 1990. First, I created the Action Sequence method for the active learning of Wyckoff's approach. The Action Sequence is a simulation and a sequential case study with chart analysis and feedback. Second, I collaborated with Dr. Van K. Tharp, trader psychologist, to develop a mental state control system that evolved into "The Ten Tasks of Top Trading."

The Ten Tasks of Top Trading is a system that helps the trader follow through on her trades. Essentially, it is a behavioral/psychological system for proper mental state management. The ten tasks of top trading are at the heart of the third part of *The Three Skills of Top Trading*: Mental State Management.

In sum, I have enjoyed a happy combination of formal education, trading experience, and collaboration with professional colleagues, and have profited from the appearance of new concepts for systems building that led to the discovery and creation of the Three Skills of Top Trading and the design of the three-in-one trader model. (See Figure 1.1.)

SYSTEMS BUILDING

The complete trader for the twenty-first century will most likely look a lot like the old-time stock operator who lived and worked on Wall Street a century ago. Hence, in *The Three Skills of Top Trading*, the systems building tools are designed both to capture the essence of the old-time trader and to introduce you to the skills and new thinking needed to meet the challenges you face as a trader-analyst in the twenty-first century.

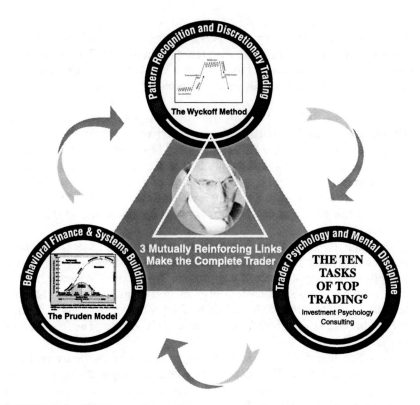

FIGURE 1.1   Three Mutually Reinforcing Links Make the Complete Trader

We begin with a human connection between the old-time traders and the trader of the future: third-generation technician and veteran of Wall Street, Mr. Anthony Tabell, who explains how the behavior of the old-time technicians and traders lines up with the latest thinking and theories of behavioral finance for trader-technicians of the twenty-first century.

This link between classic and modern eras leads us into the second section of this chapter: the story of Mr. Addison Cammack, a legend in his own time who operated on the New York Stock Exchange in the early 1900s. Cammack provides a model of a classic trader who captured all three of the skills of top trading, the type of old-time pioneer trader who is relevant to the new thinking about markets for this century.

The third section of this chapter introduces Daniel H. Pink's new and provocative book, *A Whole New Mind: Why Right-Brainers Will Rule the Future*, outlining its relevance to today's trader. I explore the power of capturing the essence of the technical-trader pioneers coupled with Pink's whole-mind approach in building your competitive edge in the twenty-first century, and I demonstrate the correspondence between Pink's "six senses" and the "new edge" tools for traders.

The fourth section of the chapter explores systems-building choices available to the trader. The systems-building approaches selected for you in this book are illustrated with the assistance of a series of schematic diagrams. You will discover a spectrum of systems building, from nondiscretionary to discretionary trading, with the Life Cycle Model of Crowd Behavior and the Wyckoff method of technical analysis and speculation spotlighted for further development.

This spectrum highlights the trader's need for self-discipline and mental state management. To gain the competitive edge in the twenty-first century, you will need to cultivate self-discipline and mental state management with the aid of conceptual frameworks like the Ten Tasks of Top Trading. This chapter also introduces the trader to conceptual schemes for decision support systems with the Life Cycle Model of Crowd Behavior, and a pattern-recognition and discretionary trading system with the Wyckoff method.

Appendix A offers the trader a trustworthy mechanical system, A Primary Trend Projector. Also included in this chapter is a more esoteric coverage of market facts and market research that argues in favor of methods that stress skill building and judgment. This rationale appears in Appendix B, where I recap survey, laboratory experiment, and case study research of market behavior and trading methods.

THE LEGENDARY TECHNICAL TRADER OF YESTERDAY FORESHADOWED THE TECHNICAL TRADER OF THE TWENTY-FIRST CENTURY

In an address to the Society for the Investigation of Recurring Events in 1992, Anthony W. Tabell, a third-generation technician and veteran of Wall Street, linked the behavior of the old-time technicians and traders to the latest thinking and theories of behavioral finance for trader-technicians of the twenty-first century. A dedicated lifelong student of the market, Tabell follows in the footsteps of his father as well as his great uncle on his mother's side, the legendary Richard D. Wyckoff.

For Tabell, the beauty of behavioral finance is its compatibility with the worldview of the old-time technicians and traders. Tabell anticipates that as the field of behavioral finance (for example, chaos theory) develops further, it will ultimately result in a view of the market similar to the way technicians and traders saw things back in the early days of the twentieth century. According to Tabell, the early technicians and first experimenters in the art of analytical speculation in the early twentieth century could be described as intuitive, deterministic, contrary, and apocalyptic.

Just how did those traders and technicians see things during the first quarter of that century? Tabell explained that the old-time technician had a hard-boiled world view that led him to buy and sell on the only thing he could trust, his *intuition*. Certain that there were larger forces at work in the market (for example, what Richard Wyckoff termed the "Composite Man," the sum of the interests that have an effect on the market) and that, though he could not *control* them, he could *detect* them, he was *deterministic*. A product of the era of the trading pool when the fix was always in, he was *contrarian*—the crowd, which was subject to the forces of the market, ultimately had to be wrong. Lastly, he had an *apocalyptic* worldview—no surprise, given the economic climate that eventually gave way to the crash of 1929.

Buying and selling on intuition resulted from skill and experience. It was a judgmental approach the trader and technician applied to his tape reading and to his chart analysis. Like having a sixth sense, the intuitive approach was a prized possession. Indeed, an archetype of the old-time trader was James Keene, a New York Stock Exchange floor trader who claimed to have no "rules" for trading but to buy and sell by intuition. Keene's skill at detecting market manipulation and, indeed, leading a pool operation of a stock made him sought after as an "operator." Keene and operators like him were also sought out by Richard Wyckoff, who observed and codified their best practices, which eventually became an integral part of his method of technical analysis and the art of speculation.

With respect to the old-timer's intuitive, deterministic, and contrarian attributes, Tabell reported that they were largely spawned by the *pools* of the pre-1929 era. These pools consisted of *investors* who would find an *operator* (for instance, Keene). Then they would enlist the help of *customers' men*, willing brokers who would put the word on the street that a stock was on the decline, going south fast. Then, when the value of the stock depreciated, the pool would scoop it up, running the stock price up again. They would then turn to their brokers (or the press) with doomsday news that would depress the stock anew, and the pool would purchase at bottom again.

"Then you could start a rumor that the company was going to cut its dividend—if your pool was close to the company itself, you might get them to *actually cut* their dividend!" related Tabell. "Finally, when you had accumulated all the stock you could possibly accumulate came the phase known as the *markup*, leading to the *breakout*, before the pool liquidated at tremendous profit."[1] Not surprisingly, this atmosphere prompted Humphrey Neill to coin the term *contrarian*.

You can tell a lot about a person by what she reads, and the old-time trader-technician's apocalyptic view of the world was betrayed by his book of choice: *Extraordinary Popular Delusions and the Madness of Crowds*, by Charles Mackay. In this classic, Mackay reports historical incidents when "whole communities suddenly fix their minds on one object and go mad in its pursuit . . . until their attention is caught by some new folly, more captivating than the last."[2] Mackay's book, first published in 1841, together with Gustav LeBon's book, *The Crowd*, are antecedents to my own analytical framework, the Life Cycle Model of Crowd Behavior, which is one of the cornerstones of *The Three Skills of Top Trading*.

Tabell concluded his address with the following observation: "If there is one concept that has fascinated technicians recently, it is the newly emerging science of chaos-fractal structures, if you will—that says that stock movements are not, in fact, linear. . . . There is no such thing as 'supply' and 'demand'—these occur when human beings are *willing* to buy or sell," he emphasized. In fact, chaos theory supports the notion that higher prices can produce more demand because of the herd mentality that leads people to follow a trend. Even in the midst of the madness of crowds, there are forces at work, and you can detect them.

But the true elegance of chaos theory, to Tabell, lies in its correlation and compatibility with the qualities of the old-time technicians. "You almost have to be intuitive because there are so many *possibilities*," he asserted. "You almost have to be deterministic because the new model tells you there are, indeed, *forces* out there that, through positive feedback, will gain a momentum of their own. You almost have to be contrarian, because under the new market mathematics, the crowd *can* be wrong; the best possible outcome—the perfect price—is not always the actual outcome. Finally, you have to be apocalyptic, because 1929 is the sort of thing that can happen in a chaotic market structure."

Tabell concluded, "I think the ultimate result [of chaos theory developing] will be a view of the market that is very similar to the way the old-time technicians perceived things back in the early days of this [the twentieth] century."

Traders and technicians using *The Three Skills* should note that the chaos theory mentioned by Tabell is associated with fractal analysis. Both chaos theory and fractal analysis are compatible with the new discipline of behavioral finance.

AN ILLUSTRATION OF THE OLD-TIME TECHNICAL TRADER

The story of Addison Cammack provides a historical example of the old-time technical trader Tabell described. I have selected excerpts from the

Cammack story as it appeared in *Reminiscences of a Stock Operator* by Edwin Lefèvre (New York: Wiley & Sons, 1994). As you read them, you will discover elements of the three skills: (1) an understanding of crowd behavior, (2) pattern recognition, and (3) mental discipline.

The story of Addison Cammack is told by Larry Livingston, the stock market operator and protagonist in *Reminiscences*. Livingston sets the stage for Cammack by describing what separated a professional trader like Cammack from the amateurs. This lesson from yesterday is a worthwhile lesson for the trader today.

> *A man can't spend years at one thing and not acquire a habitual attitude towards it quite unlike that of the average beginner. The difference distinguishes the professional from the amateur. It is the way a man looks at things that makes or loses money for him in the speculative markets. The public has the dilettante's point of view toward his own effort. The ego obtrudes itself unduly and the thinking therefore is not deep or exhaustive. The professional concerns himself with doing the right thing rather than with making money, knowing that the profit takes care of itself if the other things are attended to. A trader gets to play the game as the professional billiard player does—that is, he looks far ahead instead of considering the particular shot before him. It gets to be an instinct to play for position.*[3]

The following episode in the trading life of Addison Cammack illustrates the intuitive, contrarian, apocalyptic, and deterministic traits that Tabell identifies as distinguishing characteristics of the old-time traders and technicians. These same traits are important for the twenty-first century trader to consider. (It is my hope that *The Three Skills of Top Trading* will give you the tools to acquire these same distinguishing traits.)

> *I remember hearing a story about Addison Cammack that illustrates very nicely what I wish to point out. From all I have heard, I am inclined to think that Cammack was one of the ablest stock traders the Street ever saw. He was not a chronic bear as many believe, but he felt the greater appeal of trading on the bear side, of utilising in his behalf the two great human factors of hope and fear. He is credited with coining the warning: "Don't sell stocks when the sap is running up the trees!" and the old-timers tell me that his biggest winnings were made on the bull side, so that it is plain he did not play prejudices but conditions. At all events, he was a consummate trader. It seems that once—this was way back at the tag end of a bull market—Cammack was bearish, and J. Arthur Joseph, the financial writer and raconteur, knew it. The market, however,*

was not only strong but still rising, in response to prodding by the bull leaders and optimistic reports by the newspapers. Knowing what use a trader like Cammack could make of bearish information, Joseph rushed to Cammack's office one day with glad tidings.

"Mr. Cammack, I have a very good friend who is a transfer clerk in the St. Paul office and he has just told me something which I think you ought to know."

"What is it?" asked Cammack listlessly.

"You've turned, haven't you? You are bearish now?" asked Joseph, to make sure. If Cammack wasn't interested he wasn't going to waste precious ammunition.

"Yes. What's the wonderful information?"

"I went around to the St. Paul office today, as I do in my news—gathering rounds two or three times a week, and my friend there said to me: 'The Old Man is selling stock.' He meant William Rockefeller. 'Is he really, Jimmy?' I said to him, and he answered, 'Yes; he is selling fifteen hundred shares every three-eighths of a point up. I've been transferring the stock for two or three days now.' I didn't lose any time, but came right over to tell you."

Cammack was not easily excited, and, moreover, was so accustomed to having all manner of people rush madly into his office with all manner of news, gossip, rumors, tips and lies that he had grown distrustful of them all. He merely said now, "Are you sure you heard right, Joseph?"

"Am I sure? Certainly I am sure! Do you think I am deaf?" said Joseph.

"Are you sure of your man?"

"Absolutely!" declared Joseph. "I've known him for years. He has never lied to me. He wouldn't! No object! I know he is absolutely reliable and I'd stake my life on what he tells me. I know him as well as I know anybody in this world—a great deal better than you seem to know me, after all these years."

"Sure of him, eh?" And Cammack again looked at Joseph. Then he said, "Well, you ought to know." He called his broker, W. B. Wheeler. Joseph expected to hear him give an order to sell at least fifty thousand shares of St. Paul. William Rockefeller was disposing of his holdings in St. Paul, taking advantage of the strength of the market. Whether it was investment stock or speculative holdings was irrelevant. The one important fact was that the best stock trader of the Standard Oil crowd was getting out of St. Paul. What would the average man have done if he had received the news from a trustworthy source? No need to ask.

But Cammack, the ablest bear operator of his day, who was bearish on the market just then, said to his broker, "Billy, go over to

*the board and buy fifteen hundred St. Paul every three-eighths up."
The stock was then in the nineties.*

*"Don't you mean sell?" interjected Joseph hastily. He was no
novice in Wall Street, but he was thinking of the market from the
point of view of the newspaper man and, incidentally, of the general
public. The price certainly ought to go down on the news of inside
selling. And there was no better inside selling than Mr. William
Rockefeller's. The Standard Oil getting out and Cammack buying! It
couldn't be!*

"No," said Cammack; "I mean buy!"

"Don't you believe me?"

"Yes!"

"Don't you believe my information?"

"Yes."

"Aren't you bearish?"

"Yes."

"Well, then?"

*"That's why I'm buying. Listen to me now: You keep in touch
with that reliable friend of yours and the moment the scaled selling
stops, let me know. Instantly! Do you understand?"*

*"Yes," said Joseph, and went away, not quite sure he could
fathom Cammack's motives in buying William Rockefeller's stock. It
was the knowledge that Cammack was bearish on the entire market
that made his maneuver so difficult to explain. However, Joseph
saw his friend the transfer clerk and told him he wanted to be tipped
off when the Old Man got through selling. Regularly twice a day
Joseph called on his friend to inquire.*

*One day the transfer clerk told him, "There isn't any more stock
coming from the Old Man." Joseph thanked him and ran to Cammack's office with the information.*

*Cammack listened attentively, turned to Wheeler and asked,
"Billy, how much St. Paul have we got in the office?" Wheeler looked
it up and reported that they had accumulated about sixty thousand
shares.*

*Cammack, being bearish, had been putting out short lines in the
other Grangers as well as in other various stocks, even before he began to buy St. Paul. He was now heavily short of the market. He
promptly ordered Wheeler to sell the sixty thousand shares of St.
Paul that they were long of, and more besides. He used his long holdings of St. Paul as a lever to depress the general list and greatly benefit his operations for a decline.*

*St. Paul didn't stop on that move until it reached forty-four and
Cammack made a killing in it. He played his cards with consum-*

mate skill and profited accordingly. The point I would make is his habitual attitude toward trading. He didn't have to reflect. He saw instantly that was far more important to him than his profit on that one stock. He saw that he had providently been offered an opportunity to begin his big bear operations not only at the proper time but with a proper initial push. The St. Paul tip made him buy instead of sell because he saw at once that it gave him a vast supply of the best ammunition for his bear campaign.[4]

SYSTEMS BUILDING IN THE NEW AGE OF HIGH CONCEPT AND HIGH TOUCH

Science and art have progressed since the days of the old-time traders like Addison Cammack and the technicians described by Anthony Tabell. The trader who seeks success in the twenty-first century must absorb the best lessons from the past while embracing the newest thinking in the present. In this book, I attempt to help the trader reach those objectives by teaching the knowledge and judgment of the Wyckoff method of technical analysis and the art of speculation together with systems based on new thinking from behavioral finance.

To further deepen your understanding of the nature of the trading challenges that you will face in this new century, and to equip you with additional tools to deal with them, I wish to expose you to the ground-breaking thinking found in Daniel H. Pink's *A Whole New Mind: Why Right-Brainers Will Rule the Future.* The following introduction to Pink reveals his "high-concept, high-touch" attribute, one that the trader should cultivate for a competitive edge in the twenty-first century.

> *[T]he Conceptual Age also demands the ability to grasp the relationships between relationships. This meta-ability goes by many names—systems thinking, gestalt thinking, holistic thinking. I prefer to think of it as simply seeing the big picture.*
>
> *Seeing the big picture is fast becoming a killer app in business. While knowledge workers of the past typically performed piecemeal assignments and spent their days tending their own patch of a larger garden, such work is now moving overseas or being reduced to instructions in powerful software. As a result, what has become more valuable is what fast computers and low-paid overseas specialists cannot do nearly as well: integrating and imagining how the pieces fit together. This has become evident among entrepreneurs and other successful businesspeople.*

The narrowly focused specialists emphasize the L-directed or Left-Hemisphere (L-oriented) part of their brain, while the pattern recognition, big picture entrepreneur relies on the Right-Hemisphere (R-oriented) part of their brains.

> *[In Daniel Goleman's study of industry executives] Just one cognitive ability distinguished star performers from average: pattern recognition, the "big picture" thinking that allows leaders to pick meaningful trends from a welter of information around them and to think strategically into the future. . . . These star performers, he found, relied less on deductive, if—then reasoning and more on the intuitive, contextual reasoning. . ."*[5]

Pink's "new age" thinking creates some high-caliber ammunition for the trader-technician to use to gain the upper hand. Pink encapsulates this new thinking into "six senses" for the trader-technician to adopt—design, story, symphony, empathy, play, and meaning—that he believes will increasingly "guide our lives and shape our world."[6]

Introducing the Six Senses

Pink argues that in the Conceptual Age, you will need to complement your L-directed reasoning powers with R-directed aptitudes. In the following exploration I suggest how these right-hemisphere aptitudes can effect the trader-technician. Together these six high-concept and high-touch senses can help you develop the whole new mind-set that this new era demands. Table 1.1 provides a correlation between these senses and technical analysis tools.

1. Design. Pink contends that the new age calls for systems that are not only functional but also arresting, even beautiful. In technical analysis and trading, designing your systems to transcend function and engage you will lead to personal rewards both emotional and financial. One approach *The Three Skills of Top Trading* takes is to build dual systems that have both a visual, right-brained, component and an analytical, checklist component. These two approaches can help you capture the full benefit available from your whole mind.

2. Story. Welles Wilder, the creator of many technical indicators in use today, once told me that you have to have a "story" to get the message fully absorbed and appreciated. Pink's philosophy says that persuasion, communication, and your ability to understand yourself hinge on your capacity to understand and tell a compelling narrative.

TABLE 1.1 Traders' New Edge Tools Matched to Pink's New Age Concepts

New Age Concepts: The Six Senses	Traders' New Edge Tools
Design: Both right-brained and left-brained appeals	Schematics and checklists (for example, Wyckoff's Accumulation Schematic and Wyckoff's Nine Buying Tests).
Symphony	Interactive and independent systems (for example, S-shaped and bell-shaped curves of crowd behavior showing the interactions of price, volume, time and sentiment).
Story	The market tells its own story through the comparison of buying and selling waves. Chart reading and pattern recognition are important.
Empathy	Play the role of Composite Man. A trader should see, feel, and hear the market from the Composite Man's vantage point.
Play	Build skills through guided repetitions of market analysis. Gain empathy and enhance decision making with the Action-Sequence Method.
Meaning	Discern your purpose and gain a deeper meaning for your trading with practices inspired by the concepts found in "A Sealed Room" and "Only One Client."

3. Symphony. Pattern recognition, the old-fashioned way to read charts, is at a premium. Pink argues that now more than ever, in a global economy where specialized labor can be found all over the world, the real demand is for the individual who can put it all together. The great need is the ability to see the big picture, to perceive the interconnections of market themes—to take different pieces of the market puzzle and put them together in much the same way that a conductor pulls together the players and instruments to create the arresting sounds of a beautiful symphony.

4. Empathy. According to Pink, logic alone will soon be insufficient; we must be able to "feel" others, to intuit what motivates them. Assume that behind the stock screens on your computer, there dwells a market genie called the Composite Man. To understand him, you'll need to walk in his footsteps, and to walk in his footsteps, you'll need to cultivate that right-brained attribute called empathy. In Chapter 9, you will discover ways and means to cultivate your power and engage in empathy.

5. Play. You need to enjoy playing the game to extract the essence from the market and the best from yourself. Pink points out that both the health and professional benefits of laughter and games are well documented, and he contends that too much sobriety can actually be damaging for one's career and general well-being. Chapter 9 offers you opportunities to play in the "Chart Reading in the R-Mode" section and with the simulation I call the "Action Sequence." Taking pleasure in playing the market will also help you maintain the distance required to see yourself objectively and carry out the Ten Tasks of Top Trading outlined in Chapter 8, and to maintain the mental balance required for effective trading.

6. Meaning. Pink points out that the conveniences of modern life (mass food production and so on) have freed us to pursue fulfillment on a more profound level. To draw the best out of yourself and get the most out of your life as a trader, you need some greater purpose and meaning for yourself and your trading. This important attribute identified by Pink is addressed in Chapter 10 in the sections "A Sealed Room" and "Only One Client."

Although some of these concepts may seem foreign, they are attributes human beings have possessed since they dwelled in caves. To this day, we can see evidence of story and empathy in their drawings, of design in their tools. To some degree, Pink is encouraging us to return to the past in order to move into the future, a theme echoed by Tabell and evident in the technical analyst's return to Wyckoff and the Composite Man. As in the market, timing is everything. As Pink says, "Anyone can master the six Conceptual Age senses. But those who master them first will have a huge advantage."[7]

SYSTEMS BUILDING FOR THE TWENTY-FIRST-CENTURY TECHNICAL TRADER

Figure 1.2 shows a spectrum of trading systems available to the technical trader that range from extremely *nondiscretionary* systems to extremely *discretionary* systems. In my years as trader, editor, and professor, I have had ample opportunity to appraise the strengths and weaknesses of the various types of trading systems shown on this chart. I grew dubious of the reliability and accountability of the seat-of-your-pants, no-system approach, and equally skeptical of relying on an automatic black box that crunches mounds of data, often in an uninformed manner.

Between the extremes of mechanical and discretionary systems, the

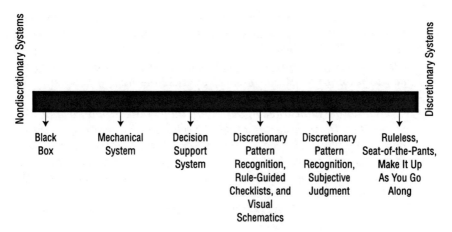

FIGURE 1.2 A Systems-Building Spectrum for Technical Traders, from Nondiscretionary to Discretionary Systems

trader-analyst can find a system that matches his cognitive-emotional makeup and that fits his goals and philosophy of trading. (See Figure 1.3.)

> *Professional traders always had some system or the other based upon their experience and governed either by their attitude toward speculation or by their desires. I remember I met an old gentleman in Palm Beach. . . . He was a very wise old codger who had gone through so many booms and panics that he was always saying that there was nothing new under the sun and least of all in the stock market.*

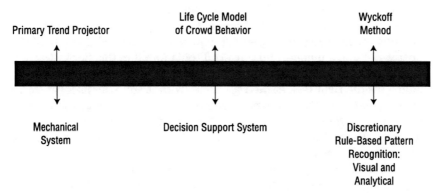

FIGURE 1.3 Systems Building for Technical Traders: Specific Technical Trading Systems for the Three Skills of Top Trading

The old fellow asked me a lot of questions. When I got through telling him about my usual practice in trading he nodded and said, "Yes! Yes! You're right. The way you're built, the way your mind runs, makes your system a good system for you. It comes easy for you to practice what you preach, because the money you bet is the least of your cares.

"Of all the thousands of outsiders that I have run across in Wall Street, Pat Herne was the only one who saw in stock speculation merely a game of chance . . . but, nevertheless, had the sense to stick to a relatively sound betting method . . . (yet) he did not stick to his own proved system. That's the trouble with most of them," and the old fellow shook his head at me.

—*Edwin Lefèvre*, Reminiscences of a Stock Operator[8]

As you move to the right along the spectrum of systems, the more subtle consolidation and reversal patterns are formed on charts and are valuable additions to the foregoing decision support system. Under the Wyckoff method of technical analysis these patterns provide triggers for buying or selling, together with money management rules. The Wyckoff method is clearly and admittedly a judgmental system, which is why it is definitely on the "discretionary" end of the spectrum.

Self-Discipline

The heightened pressures on the trader-analyst that are imposed by a discretionary system give rise to the need for systems of self-discipline and mental state management (see Figure 1.4). The Ten Tasks of Top Trading system for self-discipline and mental state management dovetails nicely with the Wyckoff method of technical analysis and speculation (see Figure 1.5).

The Ten Tasks of Top Trading system for self-discipline and mental management is described in Chapter 8. This system is one of the key methods for realizing the high-touch concept, and indeed it is one of the most well-honed, unique, and powerful tools found in this book. The Ten Tasks system is an important guide to making the appropriate emotional choice for the right task at the right time. With it you will discover that a powerful emotion like fear is not necessarily a negative thing. Rather, fear can be useful (for example, as a stimulus for getting out of a bad trade). At the right time and under the right circumstances, fear is a good thing for the trader to possess.

Two more concepts found in Figure 1.5 will be covered in Chapters 9 and 10. The concepts and tools for "Chart Reading in the R-Mode," given in Chapter 9, are a direct answer to Daniel Pink's call for the superior

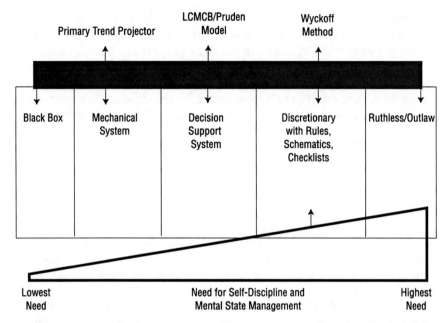

FIGURE 1.4 Systems Building for Technical Traders: The Need for Self-Discipline (Cognitive and Emotional)

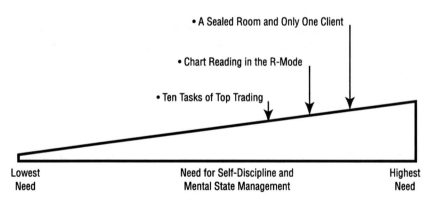

FIGURE 1.5 Systems of Self-Discipline and Mental State Management for Technical Traders

right-brained analysis that the trader needs in order to capture a competitive edge. R-mode thinking will help the trader see what is really there on the chart before him by showing him how to quiet the L-mode, which interferes with words and labels that distort the analyst-trader's perceptions. In Chapter 10, the topics of vision and purpose will help you mightily in your quest to pull the elements of the three skills together and to install them within you, the complete trader. Rounding out the mental control end of the spectrum, the trader-analyst will discover "Chart Reading in the R-Mode" and "'A Sealed Room' and 'Only One Client'" as supportive of high concept with high touch, or empathy.

Mechanical Systems

You need at least one unambiguous mechanical system to keep you on true course. Granville stressed that the Dow Theory of primary trend was paramount. Ned Davis added the 200-day moving average of the major equity indexes to give a cold, bloodless determination of the primary trend of the market.

The long history of the Dow Theory primary bull and bear market signals lends strong empirical support in favor of market timing. I have discovered that a true gauge of the primary trend of the market is indispensable to the trader. It serves as a powerful reference point upon which to anchor your estimation of the market. The Dow Theory's three phases of a bull market and three phases of a bear market help the trader follow and stick to the primary trend. Figure 1.6 provides a brief summary of primary trend analysis. A full description of how to use the primary trend appears in my "Primary Trend Projector" analysis package, in Appendix A of this chapter.

Primary Trend: **Bull Market**	Primary Trend: **Bear Market**
Three major market indexes above their respective rising 200-day moving average	Three major market indexes below their respective declining 200-day moving average

FIGURE 1.6 Systems Building for Technical Traders: A Mechanical Trading System, the Primary Trend Projector

In contrast to the relative simplicity of the "Primary Trend Projector" system, Figure 1.7 illustrates the complexity that can be involved in a comprehensive decision support system. In level one, a decision maker (trader-analyst) makes use of a model (showing how the world works) to gather and correlate data from the market environment. Market timing decision choices are offered to the decision maker by analytical models (sometimes statistical analysis packages), and a course of action can be selected by the decision maker according to an optimization rule.

Level two outlines the behavioral finance-based decision support system that is the subject of Chapter 3. This level illustrates that effective decisions result from a combination of visual (right-brained) activity using schematics and corresponding analytical/digital (left-brained) activity using in-depth checklists of indicators that measure price, volume, sentiment, and time. Since these parameters of the technical market analysis mix are conceptually independent of each other, they can be quantified and then added together to render more powerful and reliable buy or sell signals.

The trader-analyst who wishes to push the decision support system model approach toward the nondiscretionary end of the spectrum would be well advised to consult Charles D. Kirkpatrick and Julie R. Dahlquist's textbook, *Technical Analysis: The Complete Resource for Financial*

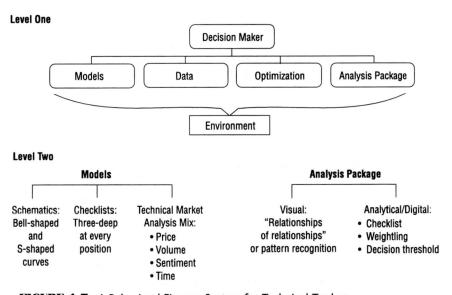

FIGURE 1.7 A Behavioral Finance System for Technical Traders

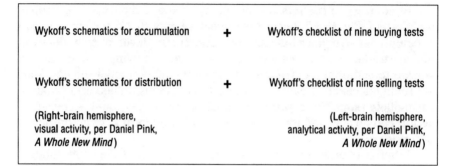

FIGURE 1.8 A Pattern Recognition and Discretionary Trading System for the Technical Trader: The Wyckoff Method

Market Technicians, specifically Chapter 22, "System Design and Testing." At the other end of the spectrum, trader-analysts who are intrigued by arguments favoring the necessity of discretionary systems and the concomitant reliance on skill and judgment are invited to consult Appendix B to this chapter, where they will discover a treatise on market facts and market research. The encouragement to cultivate skill and judgment to gain the competitive edge in the twenty-first century continues in Part Two, "Pattern Recognition and Discretionary Trading."

The Whole Brain

Figure 1.8 shows the Wyckoff method of technical analysis as comprising a combination of right-brained visual chart pattern-recognition functions coupled with left-brained calculation capacities. This whole-brain approach enables traders to make sounder market timing decisions and furnishes them with an edge nearly impossible to duplicate.

APPENDIX A: A PRIMARY TREND PROJECTOR

One of the very first rules of technical analysis is, "Trade in sympathy with the *primary trend* of the market." The primary trend is the tidal force, the major swing factor, the setter of important channel boundaries, the overarching movement within which all other time trends revolve. To ignore or to flaunt the message given by the primary trend is a folly.

Joe Granville acknowledged the folly of underemphasizing the primary trend in his book, *Granville's New Strategy of Daily Stock Market Timing for Maximum Profit*:

> *In my Strategy book I left much of the discussion of market phases until last, putting far too much stress on the day-to-day market action. It is of course important to get the day-to-day feel of the market, but being stretched out on the rack from time to time as a market loser, one at least respects the predominance at all times of the* big *picture, the main thrust of the market, what the Dow Theorists call the primary trend. That trend traverses all three phases of a bull market. It is the tide which sweeps one to fortune or disaster. Unless one swims with the tide, one will drown. The longer the game is played, the more one will come to respect the Dow Theory, the theory that always keeps things in their proper perspective, putting the primary trend first, the intermediate trend second and the day-to-day trend last. In the Strategy book, I championed the day-to-day trader, laying down the language of the market in day-to-day terms. While we had some brilliant successes, it was always the intermediate trend which surpassed the daily trend in importance and the primary trend that held sway over all. You can't beat City Hall. You must be in harmony with the primary trend of the market if you ever hope to crack the market maze and find your way through the hall of mirrors.*[9]

For the purposes of this exposition I am assuming that there are *three* primary trends: a bull market, a bear market, and a trading range market.

Ned Davis argued for using the 200-day moving average for a "cold, bloodless verdict of the market."[10] The moving average theory for the Primary Trend Projector, modified by the rules of Dr. Harvey Krow,[11] says that a bull market is in force when at least two of the three Dow averages (industrials, transportation, utilities) are above their rising 200-day moving average lines, and vice versa for bear markets. Anything in between is a trading range signal. These rules now also apply to the NASDAQ, S&P 500, and the Dow Industrials.

A Primary Trend, Updated: Something New, Something Old

According to classical Dow Theory, a primary bull market is signaled when the Dow Jones Industrial Average zigzags upward, confirming a similar upward zigzag in the Dow Transportation Average or vice versa. The bull market remains in place until definite evidence of a bearish reversal occurs when the industrials and the transports zigzag downward together.

These zigzag price movements are supposed to be of intermediate proportion, or upward and downward waves that endure from three weeks to three months. Accurately judging these intermediate waves is one of the more challenging tasks of a Dow theorist.

Another challenge to the Dow theorist is to use indexes that reflect the true state of economic affairs. A century ago the industrial stocks discounted the manufacture of goods while the railroad stocks discounted the shipment of those goods to the market. Now, a century later, we have evidence of both a new global economy that runs on information services rather than the rails, and an old economy that is composed of a tight linkage between manufacturing and logistics for the production and delivery of goods. According to the classical tenets of Dow Theory, the old and new economies need each other and should move together for reliable signals of the primary trend.

We can update the Dow Theory by substituting two readily available and broad market indexes that reflect the new economy and the old economy: the NASDAQ Composite in place of the Dow Transportation Average, and the S&P 500 in place of the 30 Dow Jones Industrial Average stocks.

To interpret the primary trend signals given by the NASDAQ and the S&P 500, the trader can rely on the tenets of Dow Theory and also on moving average theory. If the NASDAQ and the S&P 500 indexes are moving in tandem on the upside, a bull market exists. Moreover, if both indexes are above their respective rising 200-day moving averages, that gives further confirmation of the bull market. In sum, by using the current indexes, we can see the new economy and the old working together to give a valid and reliable definition of the primary trend of the market.

Rules for Trading in Harmony with the Primary Trend

First and foremost, of course, trade in *sympathy* with the primary trend of the market. During a bull market, this means concentrating on buying when intermediate to low junctures offer opportunities, or selling at intermediate peaks during a primary bear market, or going both long and short at the turning points of a protracted trading range, sometimes referred to as a *Dow Theory Line.*

Second, it is permissible to trade *contrary* to the primary trend of the market, but only when there are both very strong intermediate and strong minor cycle indications that a countertrend correction is imminent. These are the often-speedy downdrafts or updrafts that may retrace one-third to two-thirds of a prior uncorrected primary movement.

The third rule is to give yourself at least *three choices* by generating at least three alternative future scenarios of the market. This exercise provides the analyst with a *strategic premise* embracing the probable future rhythm of the market. Specifically, the first scenario should be based on the most compelling evidence of the primary trend indicators. With a confirmed bull market under way, the most likely scenario might call for an uptrending market containing shallow corrections. If this scenario came to pass quickly, the market would exhibit a parabolic acceleration to the upside. A more leisurely advance might evince a modest angle of ascent with frequent and perhaps relatively deeper corrections, as a second scenario. As a third, less likely scenario, the analyst might propose a reversal in trend or a sideways trading-range market in lieu of the two foregoing bullish options.

For each of these possibilities, the analyst should record in advance what events (things, indicators, and so on) would have to occur in order for it to come about. As the evidence arrives over time, the market will itself cut off the likelihood of one and then another option, leaving the trader free to concentrate on and exploit the most likely one. However, by keeping three options fresh and dynamic at all times, the trader-technician is psychologically positioned to modify, even to reverse his position.

Do not underestimate the importance of an accurate *strategic premise*: a proper orientation to the underlying rhythm of the market, which will enhance your ability to recognize and act on trading opportunities. To appreciate the importance of possessing the proper strategic premise, one can look at any number of scenarios from the field of military experience. The following passage describes how General Ulysses S. Grant's *feel* for the war led to his success in battle; a similar strategic premise can also lead to success in the market. (The emphasis added is my own.)

> *On a battleground like Donelson, and later in vast campaigns,* Grant had a remarkable sense of the whole of the event. *It was always changing, nothing was ever settled. His perception was not a single snapping of the shutter to give a brilliantly clear image of a battle stopped in full clarity. Instead, what he saw always included a dimension of time,* an awareness of the unfolding, evolving motion of the life of war. *He knew that each day and battle led to the next.* The way to ultimate victory was to develop a stronger sense of the war's rhythm than that possessed by the enemy. *As long as Grant could sense the movement of the battle, he could give explicit orders and get from his officers their best.*[12]

Bob Prechter confided to me that having what was essentially a strategic premise that the Dow was in a powerful bull market that could carry to 3,000-plus kept him in tune with the market from 1982 to 1987. Without that premise, and without a conviction in that premise, he doubted that he could have stayed in synch with the market for so long.

Primary Trend Projector Criteria

A *bull market* confirmation requires a Dow Theory "buy" signal, registered both by the S&P 500 Index and the NASDAQ Composite Index zigging upward, plus at least two of three standard averages (e.g., Dow Industrials) going above their respective rising 200-day moving average lines. (See *Investor's Business Daily*, www.investors.com.)

A *bear market* is confirmed by a Dow Theory "sell," signaled by the S&P 500 and NASDAQ jointly zigzagging downward, plus at least two of

---

Primary Trend Projector Decision Form

Dow Theory Evidence
What was the last *confirmed* Dow Theory signal, comparing the S&P 500 Index with the NASDAQ Composite Index? Circle one.

    Bull market   Bear market

What, if any, *divergences* have appeared between the S&P 500 and the NASDAQ? Circle all that apply. (UNC = upward nonconfirmation; DNC = downward nonconfirmation)

  UNC of industrials by transports   DNC of industrials by transports
  UNC of transports by industrials   DNC of transports by industrials

Moving-Average Theory Evidence
What are the positions of the averages with respect to their 200-day moving averages? Check one box for each index.

  Index above moving average   Index below moving average

INDEX	RISING	FLAT	FALLING	RISING	FLAT	FALLING
S&P 500						
NASDAQ						
DJIA						

Conclusion: The foregoing evidence shows that the primary trend is in a _____ market direction.

three averages (for example, Industrials) going below their respective declining 200-day moving average line.

A *trading range market* is defined by indexes showing mixed signals above and below moving averages and indexes moving sideways or even counter to the preceding prevailing primary trend.

Decision Forms

Use the Primary Trend Projector decision form in the accompanying box to analyze whether you are in a primary bull market, a primary bear market, or a sideways trading range market. To conduct your analysis, use charts that are available from *Investor's Business Daily* (www.investors.com) or a similar source. At the end of the form, be sure to write down the conclusion given by the hard evidence of the market. Then, finally, make a commitment to yourself to trade in sympathy with the rules of the Primary Trend Projector.

APPENDIX B: MARKET FACTS AND MARKET RESEARCH

In order to make sound decisions, the technically oriented trader or investor must have access to reliable facts about market behavior. Clearly, the more he bases his decisions on facts as opposed to guesses, the less likely it is that he will make incorrect market timing decisions. Proper research, such as the systematic collection of price, volume, or sentiment facts, helps eliminate the guesswork from decision making.

Market Facts

For the Wyckoff method, as in other aspects of technical analysis, the trader-analyst must have solid facts at his fingertips: facts about supply and demand, about effort versus result, and about cause and effect. He must have reliable and complete bar charts and reliable and accurate point-and-figure charts.

Over the years, various tools have been developed to help analysts and traders unearth hitherto unknown facts about markets. Statistical techniques based on central tendency and dispersion have been successfully brought to bear for the back-testing of market price data. Devices like oscillators and barometers have helped in evaluating the extremities of sentiment. Accumulated experience in the reading of patterns on market charts has helped to sharpen the skills needed to get honest and unbiased answers regarding continuation and reversal formations and the probable future direction of trends.

Few would disagree that, as far as the gathering of market facts is concerned, technical market research has become increasingly scientific. Nevertheless, it requires a long stretch of the imagination to conclude that technical market analysis has thus become a science. No one would deny that having the facts is important, but knowledge of the facts is by no means a substitute for judgment and skill in handling those facts in order to make sound market-timing decisions.

You, as a technical trader, must exercise judgment and skill in the interpretation of facts that compose charts and facts that enter into the indicators. And you must exercise further judgment and skill in translating these findings of fact into effective technical-market decisions. To date, no reliable and complete scientific technique has been developed to replace such intangible and essentially personal elements as judgment and skill. All the facts in the world, if poorly handled and/or inappropriately interpreted, can only lead to poor decisions.

For the trader, the *use* of charts takes priority. For example, with point-and-figure charts, you need to emphasize their use and not just look at the data they contain. This book pays attention to both sides of the coin—not only the problems of obtaining good facts to create point-and-figure charts, but also, and more importantly, the problems of interpretation once the point-and-figure charts have been obtained. The charts included in Chapter 5 will help you gain some familiarity with the kinds of tools and techniques that are available to the user of point-and-figure charts. By repeatedly conducting chart analysis, reaching decisions, and taking actions, I am certain that you will develop proficiency in the handling and interpretation of point-and-figure charts.

Market Research

There are several aspects to the term *market research*. First of all, good technical market analysis research does not involve the haphazard accumulation of market facts; rather, it implies a systematic approach to the collection and display of market facts. Furthermore, it implies that the facts gathered have some potential usefulness in the making of market-timing decisions. It is at this point that judgment enters the process and that models showing the interrelationships among different types of facts about market behavior prove their usefulness. The helter-skelter accumulation of numerous facts that have only a remote possibility of being useful is both expensive and wasteful. Finally, since the back-testing of indicators of market action implies the systematic gathering of facts and the application of statistical tests appropriate to the nature of the underlying behavior of the market, then the terms *market research* and *back-testing* clearly apply to a wide variety of techniques, tools, and approaches.

Obviously, there can be appropriately designed and well-conducted or "good" market research and back-testing, as well as poorly designed and conducted or "bad" market research and back-testing. Research reflecting the nonlinear dynamics and scaling effects of the market can produce results that are accurate portrayals of the market—or, poorly handled, research (including back-testing) can produce dubious or fallacious results. Relying on conclusions developed by poor research can be as dangerous and misleading as the absence of facts and the use of guesswork. Hence, an important aspect of the technical trader's job is the ability to differentiate between good and bad market research and back-testing.

Even accurate facts about a market, when poorly handled or misinterpreted, can lead to disastrous timing decisions. Not only must the technical market analyst be able to distinguish good research from bad, but he must also be skillful in handling the facts that are developed by sound market research. Knowledge of a variety of research techniques (for example, central tendency and probability, power laws, typologies, multivariate analysis, and so on) enables the technical market analyst to readily identify poorly designed and badly conducted market fact gathering and testing. In addition, common sense, good judgment, and practice in handling the results of research are essential ingredients for skill in making sound market-timing decisions.

Multimethod Research

As technical analysts strive to raise their body of knowledge and discipline to higher standards, the canons of the scientific method and empirical testing become more and more commonplace. In general, there are two polar approaches to conducting empirical research in the social sciences, hence also in behavioral finance and technical analysis. These two poles can be characterized as *survey research* findings across a large number of instances to establish statistical validity and reliability on the one extreme, and the *individual case study* on the other pole. The individual case study illustrates numerous variables and contingencies operating together in a real-life situation.

Following is a brief description of three different types of market research methods that I have used: the survey, the experiment, and the case study.

The Survey During the early 1980s, I conducted a survey using past price and volume on charts of the Wyckoff Wave index for price and the Wyckoff optimism/pessimism barometer (an on-balance volume type of indicator). The data were given to me by the Wyckoff Stock Market Institute. The purpose of the survey was to test the proposition that volume precedes price at market turning points. A study of 82 turning points that were followed by 5 percent or greater price moves yielded a mixed bag of results. In that data set covering 12 years, the proposition that volume precedes price was shown to be reliable only at market tops.

The Experiment   Using the cusp model from catastrophe theory as a framework, I interpreted the research data from a Caltech experiment on irrational exuberance that was produced by WGBH television and shown on PBS (*The MacNeil/Lehrer NewsHour*) in 1997. The Caltech experiment furnished empirical data to test the proposition from the cusp catastrophe model that a market would start to tip over before it tumbled. The experiment likewise offered an opportunity to extract and highlight several nominal rules or indicators of technical analysis that fit with the logic of the cusp model. The indicators of technical analysis that fit were then also applied to the data of the experiment in an effort to anticipate and profit from the catastrophic decline in price that followed the bursting of the speculative bubble created during the experiment.

The cusp catastrophe model itself and the application of it to the Caltech experiment on irrational exuberance spotlighted the efficacy of five principles of technical analysis and trading that are well known but often overlooked or underappreciated by technicians and traders:

1. Fear versus greed juxtaposed.
2. Trading range channels along tops and bottoms.
3. Descending price peaks: dissipative gradient.
4. Catastrophic panics causing price gaps.
5. Mental discipline needed to win the "greater fool" game.

These five principles could play an analytical role alerting a trader, a participant in the Caltech experiment, when to abandon playing the "greater fool" game. These principles of technical analysis and trading were instrumental in the diagnosis of the "dissipative gradient" and thus the prognosis of the decline. My report on the study was published in *Managerial Finance Journal*'s fifth issue of 2005. The article, titled "Catastrophe Theory and Technical Analysis Applied to a Cal Tech Experiment on Irrational Exuberance," was commended at the Literati Network Awards for Excellence in 2006.

The Case Study   The individual case study illustrates numerous variables and contingencies operating together in a real-life situation. Most technical analysis research studies for trading rely on the survey technique, which is appropriate and excellent. However, the execution of trades remains an art form, and the complexity of interacting indicators and decisions is better revealed through the story of a case study. For an example of an exposition of a trade based on a case study of a Wyckoff expert, see Chapter 7.

CHAPTER 2

Behavioral Finance

Philosophy, whether the thoughts of Karl Popper or anyone else, was not supposed to be a road map for making money in the real world. Yet for George Soros, philosophy would serve just that purpose. In time, he would go from the abstract to the practical; he would develop theories of knowledge, of how and why people think in certain ways, and from those theories he would spin new theories about the way the financial markets functioned.
—Robert Slater, *Soros: The Unauthorized Biography—The Life, Times & Trading Secrets of the World's Greatest Investor* (New York: McGraw-Hill, 1997)

Behavioral finance is in essence the study of how people really behave in markets, not as they are theoretically supposed to act according to the random walk hypothesis. Psychology and the social science disciplines of sociology and anthropology provide models for studying how real people really behave in markets. Scientific research using these disciplines reveals predictable patterns to human behavior.

What can a trader hope to gain from behavioral finance?

- More and better information. Models of market behavior based on behavioral finance economize the number of indicators employed and help extract more information from each indicator and from the interrelationships of indicators.

33

- A scientific basis for testing and diagnosis. Behavioral finance models provide sound, scientific logic for understanding how and why markets work, and therefore a sound guide for the selection, integration, and interpretation of market indicators.
- Creativity. Behavioral finance models help usher forth new ways to view markets and can spotlight overlooked indicators and techniques of great value.
- A confident edge in trading. A scientific rationale underlying a trade can give the trader greater confidence in entering trades, exiting trades, and following trends.
- Self-improvement. Behavioral finance is the solid ground upon which to build an understanding of trader psychology and mental state control.

What obstacles can behavioral finance help traders avoid?

- Too many technical indicators to select from. "There is nothing more practical than a good theory," goes the saying. Behavioral finance models can help the trader pare down the myriad indicators available on most software programs to a manageable if not ideal number of indicators.
- Systems that look good when back-tested but blow up when implemented in real time, using real money. Behavioral finance helps traders create more reliable, enduring trading systems based on proven patterns of human behavior.
- Infinite possibilities. There are endless possible combinations of indicators. Behavioral finance offers models to help you identify the key combinations and shows how they interrelate.

Behavioral finance can also help shed light on dilemmas confronting the trader:

- Complexity versus keeping it simple.
- Setup versus trigger versus follow-through.
- Mechanical versus judgmental.
- Right-brained, big-picture thinking versus left-brained, analytical thinking.
- Individual psychology versus mass behavior.
- A life-cycle-of-crowd-behavior model versus data mining.
- Fun versus discipline.
- Tight stop-loss orders versus wide stops.
- Short-term trading versus intermediate-term trading.
- Methodology versus mental/emotional discipline.

This chapter is designed to serve as a resource to you, the trader. You can return to this chapter for deeper insights into the nature and motivation of individuals and crowds as you progress through Parts One and Three of *The Three Skills of Top Trading*. You are advised to acquaint yourself now with its contents because this chapter continues the themes of Anthony Tabell and of Daniel Pink that were introduced in Chapter 1.

This chapter is divided into three sections. The first is an overview of the field of behavioral finance and gives you a general resource for systems building. The second and third sections of this chapter explore the two main subjects of behavioral finance that are of substantial importance to the trader and technician: individual behavior and mass psychology. The second section of this chapter, concerning individual behavior, serves as both a general resource about behavioral finance and as a particular resource for Part Three of this book, "Mental State Management." Finally, the third section of this chapter offers you the behavioral science basis for mass psychology and mass behavior.

In Chapter 3 the amorphous subject of mass psychology is translated into a system and a set of tools usable by the trader-technician. Chapter 3 introduces the Life Cycle Model of Crowd Behavior, a model that on the one hand is helpful for integrating technical indicators for setting up trades and, on the other hand, furnishes a logical behavioral science discipline that undergirds the bull-bear cycle of accumulation, markup, distribution, and markdown central to the Wyckoff method of technical analysis, which is the subject of Part Two of this book.

AN OVERVIEW OF BEHAVIORAL FINANCE

In 1969, Dr. Harvey Krow defined technical analysis as "behavioral finance" in his book *Stock Market Behavior: The Technical Approach to Understanding Wall Street* (New York: Random House, 1969). In the Preface, he identified three competing schools of thought: the fundamentals, the random walk, and the behaviorist.

Technical analysis fell within the behavioral or behaviorist school, according to Krow. Arguably, therefore, technical market analysis commanded the center stage of behavioral finance long before the arrival of behavioral economics shed light on decision making and there were studies of cognitive errors in finance—all of which has in recent years become generally known as *behavioral finance*.

Behavioral finance and technical market analysis are two sides of the same coin. Behavioral finance provides a sound, logical grounding in scientific models for understanding markets. Technical market analysis furnishes indicators for analysis and decision rules for taking action. Hence, the deeper and sounder the underlying theory about how markets work, the more reliable technical analysis can become.

Behavioral finance uses theories from psychology, sociology, and other behavioral sciences to explain and predict financial markets. It considers:

- Investor and money manager behavior.
- Attitudes toward risk.
- Cognitive errors.
- Lack of self-control.
- Regret in decision making.
- Mass or herd behavior.

Behavioral Finance: Some Recent History

Behavioral finance is in essence the study of how people really behave in markets, not how they are supposed to act in theory. Psychology, sociology, and anthropology provide models for studying how real people really behave in markets. Scientific research using these disciplines reveals predictable patterns in human behavior.

For the better part of the past 30 years, the discipline of finance has been under the thrall of the random walk and efficient market hypotheses, but enough anomalies have piled up in recent years to crack their dominance. As a consequence, the popular press has been reporting the arrival of new thinking and different methods to explain market behavior. The headlines herald the arrival of something known generally as "behavioral finance."

Here are some of the headlines that have appeared in recent years:

- "Efficient? Chaotic? What is the New Finance? Rational investors, beta, CAPM—everything they taught you in business school is now open to debate." (*Harvard Business Review*, March–April, 1993)
- "Frontiers of Finance: The idea that a financial market can be predicted is no longer confined to cranks." (*The Economist*, October 9, 1993)
- "Mind Over Matter: Psychology can help to explain the eccentric behavior of financial markets." (*The Economist*, April 23, 1994)
- "Financial Follies: Investors do the dumbest things. Now the budding science of behavioral finance seeks to figure out why—and how to benefit." (*Institutional Investor*, January, 1995)

- "Dismal Science Grabs a Couch: Psychonomics: If the old mathematical models don't work, you can always call a shrink." (*Newsweek*, April 10, 1995)

Do the provocative headlines appearing in the *Harvard Business Review* by the likes of Nancy Nichols and others signal a threat or opportunity to technical market analysis? The answer depends on your perspective, but before we can reach any conclusions, a more fully documented description of the field of behavioral finance is needed. The following sections provide a journalistic type of report on behavioral finance. A stanza of Rudyard Kipling's poem at the end of his story "The Elephant's Child" will help organize this discussion:

> *I keep six honest serving-men*
> *(They taught me all I knew);*
> *Their names are What and Why and When*
> *And How and Where and Who.*

What Is Behavioral Finance?

> *[A] burgeoning field of study called behavioral finance, which derives from behavioral economics, is attempting to identify and learn from the particular human errors that are characteristic of financial market places. Behavioral finance strives to go beyond folk wisdom to detect distinct modes of market behavior. . . . Behavioral finance theories range from self-evident to bizarre.*
> —Debbie Galant, "Financial Follies,"
> Institutional Investor, January 1995

Samples of the theories found in the new behavioral finance field include *neurochemical,* to gauge people's propensity to take risk; the *hubris hypothesis,* which says CEOs who initiate takeovers are acting out of overweening pride and arrogance; *barn-door closing,* which means chasing a past trend; *disposition theory,* which explains how trades become investments after they fall below costs; *anchoring,* which means that once an investor makes a decision about a stock's prospects, that decision rules despite fresh evidence to the contrary; and the *cockroach theory,* which says that just as you never find just one cockroach, you never find just one earnings surprise. Then there are the familiar "next time will be different" and the "greater fool" theories.

As previously defined, behavioral finance is derived from behavioral economics. In his April 10, 1995, *Newsweek* article, "Dismal Science Grabs a Couch," Marc Levinson reports that economics is turning to psychology to help explain seemingly irrational behavior. Behavioral economics pays attention to such things as herd instincts, irrational fears, and poor self-control. But he notes that when it comes to application, "No behavioral economist has more than a smattering of grad-school psych [and] . . . the high-flying math required to do even basic work in finance is beyond the grasp of most psychologists."

Who Invented Behavioral Finance?

Daniel Kahneman of Princeton and Amos Tversky of Stanford are credited with creating behavioral economics three decades ago. Richard Thaler at University of Chicago is a leading behavioral economist, as is Joseph Lakonishok of the University of Illinois. Dr. Vernon Smith, who spoke to the 1993 Market Technicians Association conference in San Antonio, developed the University of Arizona's Economic Science Laboratory. Added to this list of early figures involved in behavioral finance are such academics as University of Texas professor Keith Brown; the editor of the *Financial Analysts Journal*, Van Harlow; Richard Roll of UCLA; Dean LeBaron and Werner DeBondt of the University of Wisconsin; and Howard Rachlin, a professor of psychology at the State University of New York in Stony Brook.

The nonacademics who are involved or at least dabble in behavioral finance include economist and investment manager Henry Kaufman, contrarian David Dreman, and money managers Russell Fuller and Arnold S. Wood. Although not pitched in the center of the behavioral finance movement, students of chaos theory are important influences. Important market chaos theorists are Doyne Farmer, Norman Packard, and Brian Arthur of Santa Fe, New Mexico; and author Edgar Peters. They were joined more recently by Terrance Odean at the University of California, Andrew Lo at MIT, and Hersh Shefrin at the University of Santa Clara.

How Does Behavioral Finance Work?

The chaos theorists make extensive use of nonlinear mathematics and the computer. Dr. Vernon Smith at Arizona conducts laboratory experiments. The duplications are often conjectures that seem to plausibly explain market behavior. But at least they are operating more closely to the real

world, for if you don't know psychology, they argue, successfully anticipating what people will do and hence how markets will behave is difficult.

In 2001 Dr. Vernon Smith shared the Nobel Prize in Economics with
Professor Daniel Kahneman.

Where and When Can You Learn about Behavioral Finance?

You can find out what the behaviorists are up to by reading the articles
mentioned previously, by consulting the *Journal of Behavioral Decision Making*, or by attending a conference devoted to the subject.
For example, in June 2007, the Chartered Financial Analyst (CFA) Institute will offer a conference in Boston, Massachusetts, titled *The
Efficient Market and Behavioral Finance*, featuring many top names
in behavioral finance. As interest in the subject grows, more confer-
ences, research, and articles become available. In addition, there are
sophisticated two-day seminars put on by the Harvard University
Kennedy School of Government and by the University of California at
Berkeley.

Why the Shift toward Behavioral Finance?

The fall of the random walk and the rise of behavioral finance reflect a
revolutionary change in the discipline of finance: What seems to be under way is a paradigm shift. What is taking place in finance is apparently
an ideal case application of the paradigm shift model promulgated in
the book by Thomas S. Kuhn, *The Structure of Scientific Revolutions*
(Chicago: University of Chicago Press, 1962). For technical market
analysis as well as for behavioral finance, the message of Kuhn's book
is heady stuff. It essentially says that when the dominant theory of a
discipline becomes beset by too many anomalies, a shift occurs in
thinking which ultimately embraces a radically different model to explain the world. The revolutionaries who spawn and nurture the radically different model typically come from backgrounds outside the
prevailing discipline.

In contrast to the theory of the random walk, behavioral finance rests
on the more realistic assumption of behavioral man or psychological man.
Just as behavioral economics may become the inheritor and the benefi-
ciary of a swing toward studying the markets according to how human beings really act and not how they are supposed to act, so too should
technical market analysis as applied behavioral finance share in the inher-
itance and the benefits.

Behavioral Finance: Friend or Foe?

Technical market analysis has existed as a practice in real-world financial markets for a long time. It also has theoretical roots in psychology and sociology, but the emphasis has been on practical application by practical men and women of action. If we envision a theory-application spectrum, we can see behavioral finance occupying the theoretical pole while technical market analysis occupies the practical application end.

Returning to the question of whether behavioral finance is a threat or opportunity for technical market analysis, the answer is that it is an opportunity if technicians act wisely, and a threat only if we are neglectful. Technical market analysis and behavioral finance are both rooted in the assumption that man acts for behavioral reasons that, by the standards of classical economics, may seem irrational. Both approach the study of markets to uncover opportunities for profits.

A real blockbuster article by Matt Ridley appearing in the October 9, 1993 issue of *The Economist* related to the linkage between technical analysis and behavioral finance. The purpose was to discover whether a combination of computer horsepower and mathematical brainpower had made it possible to find new sources of profit in the forecasting of financial markets.

> *What the new mathematicians are mining for is not inefficiencies in the flow of information but something entirely different. They have found new meat in the familiar fact that traders are a diverse bunch; by unearthing some of its previously unrecognized effects. . . . [T]he most popular idea for explaining it has to do with the heterogeneity of traders in particular, the fact that people reason differently about the information they receive, that they have different time horizons, and that they have different attitudes to risk. . . . The efficient-market theory is . . . right that efficiency will delete time-arbitrage opportunities based on who does not have information, but wrong to conclude that therefore the market cannot be beaten.*
>
> *Prices do contain hints of what they will do next. Computers have resuscitated Chartism.*
>
> —Matt Ridley, "Survey: Frontiers of Finance,"
> The Economist, *October 9, 1993*

Through the attempt to predict using computers to study nonlinear behavior, an appreciation of technical analysis has evolved. Moving average timing and breakout signals produce profits more than by chance. Why? Because technicians are studying the behavior of people who make markets run. As the article in *The Economist* put it, "Chartists—who prefer to be called technical analysts—justify their techniques with quite reasonable arguments about the behavior of investors. They do not claim to predict the behavior of the index so much as the behavior of the people who trade in the market . . . a rising price is a bandwagon."

INDIVIDUAL BEHAVIOR

For a proper perspective of human behavior in the stock market, it is useful for us to put on bifocals. In the foreground we see how the hopes, fear, greed, rationalization, and so forth of the individual investor affect her chances of success. At a distance we can observe how the great mass of investors and speculators shape the overall course of the market through their collective behavior. These two viewpoints are so closely interlinked that it is almost impossible to consider one without reference to the other, but for the purposes of initial clarity in this chapter we will separate the individual from the mass.

In his highly esteemed book, *Reminiscences of a Stock Operator*, Edwin Lefèvre observed:

> *The speculator's chief enemies are always boring from within. It is inseparable from human nature to hope and to fear. In speculation when the market goes against you, you hope that every day will be the last day—and you lose more than you should had you not listened to hope—to the same ally that is so potent a success-bringer to empire builders and pioneers, big and little. And when the market goes your way, you become fearful that the next day will take away your profit, and you get out too soon. Fear keeps you from making as much money as you ought to. The successful trader has to fight these two deep-seated instincts. He has to reverse what you might call his natural impulses. Instead of hoping he must fear; instead of fearing he must hope. He must fear that his loss may develop into a much bigger loss, and hope that his profit may become a bigger profit. . . . The speculator's deadly enemies are: Ignorance, greed, fear, and hope.*

Let us begin by amplifying the individual trader's shortcomings. We are, of course, referring to those attitudes and actions that stand in her path to greater and more consistent profits in the stock market. These attitudes and actions emanate from a person's basic makeup, her beliefs, and her contact with others. Though not readily apparent to the individual, these emotional pitfalls are largely avoidable or controllable once recognized.

Overcoming Ignorance

Example 1: Linda Raschke's Next Move

Linda says, "Some things never change in the markets, but some things do—and you need to know what they are to keep your edge. . . . I'll test an idea on many markets because I want to know if it's a principle of price behavior. The crowd dynamics of buying and selling are the same in all markets. . . . I only had to make the same mistake about 100 times before I learned (i.e., you can get overconfident, start trading too large, and make other mistakes). I didn't learn from making the same mistakes just twice. It can take repeated bashing of the head for something to sink into the skull."
—Mark Etzkorn, Active Trader Magazine,
October 2006, 46–50

Lefèvre names ignorance as deadly enemy number one. Bright, well-educated, and professionally successful businessmen and women are too frequently dismal failures in the stock market. Ironically, the very traits that contribute to their organizational or entrepreneurial success work against them in trading and investing. Ambition, drive, the will to succeed, can translate into stubbornness in the stock market. In the corporate world, perseverance is an admirable trait. But whereas perseverance can help a manager overcome obstacles in business, this same doggedness can trap a trader into a stubborn refusal to change position despite an alteration in the trend of the market. Letting go of ambition or drive may seem counterintuitive, but if you cling to these traits, they will separate you from your money. The moral is that you, the individual investor, are merely a ship on a sea of opinion. To survive in the market, you must adopt a seemingly more wishy-washy stance; in other words, be flexible.

However, flexibility is difficult when you have made a financial commitment. Once you've gone long or short, you're no longer an unprejudiced observer. If you're long, you tend to see new items, charts, and statistics in a bullish light; if you're short, you'll probably see the very same data in a bearish cast. Either way, you are cleverly rationalizing your position to your heart's (not your pocketbook's) content. During 2003–2006, I was bombarded with e-mails that argued the market should decline, but it kept on rising. Linda Rascke, a consummately good trader-technician, contends that a good trader must learn and relearn the principles of the market, and oftentimes the hard way.

Example 2: John R. Carter's Worst Trade

A STROKE OF GENIUS?

At the time I had been trading for a few years part-time and had built up a trading account to just over $150,000 trading options. My plan was to take $30,000 out of the account to use as a down payment on the house. . . .

Unable to resist this bargain, I went ahead and bought another 100 puts, putting my entire account into this one trade. I calculated that a move of just two points in the option price would get me my house money. Needless to say, Einstein would be impressed.

The next day the markets did an odd thing. They opened higher. Even more unusual, they continued to move higher through mid-morning and into lunch. And strangest of all, the markets closed at their dead highs on the day. I was a bit perplexed, but at the same time I had confidence that the trade would work out. . . . The markets screamed higher for the next four trading days in a row. Unable to take the pain any longer, I finally called my broker and begged him to close me out. I got an unimposing 75 cents for my puts, leaving me with $15,000. In just four days I had caused $135,000 to vanish into thin air. . . . I had just blown out my trading account.

—John R. Carter, "How My Worst Trade
Ever Turned Me Into . . . A Better
Trader," Stocks, Futures and Options
Magazine, *October 2006, 30*

Successful businesspeople fall prey to their prejudices because of another trait that leads them up the ladder of success: enthusiasm. Once committed to an objective, your enthusiasm helps you follow through, and along the way it infects others with an urge to join you in the accomplishment. But in the stock market, enthusiasm is apt to blind you to the obstacles and pitfalls that you cannot overcome or bypass. A person in a heightened emotional state is susceptible to suggestion and sensational information, and is likely to imitate the crowd—to be influenced by headlines, influenced by trader chat, and so on. Her reactions are liable to become even more visceral and less cerebral the more the market price moves negatively away from her original entry point. It is hard to turn your back on a stock that you were rah-rah about when you purchased it.

Ignorance starts by failing to understand how one is emotionally tied to the market and what the emotional requirements of successful market operators are. In a nutshell, it is necessary for an investor to invert her reasoning powers in order to survive, and then succeed, in the stock market.

One reason behind the need for mental inversion is confusion concerning the present versus the future shaping in the stock market's performance. If you base your reasoning and emotional reactions on today's news and issues, you're out of step with the market. The competitive nature of the market causes its sophisticated participants to constantly anticipate future developments. The first crude images of the future are quickly translated into current stock prices. If important elements of the market are uncertain, yet potentially threatening, the result may be a panic sell-off in advance of or culminating with the final arrival of the bad news. The visceral reaction of the uninitiated is to sell upon bad news, which often gives that seller the dubious distinction of being the one who sold at the bottom, just as the worst possible future scenario was being discounted. Only acts of God (unforecastable events) are excluded from the market's discounting function.

As soon as John R. Carter decided that the market should give him the down payment on his home, he fell prey to an enthusiasm that caused him to abandon good money management principles.

Example 3: Staff's Findings from Inside the Hedge Fund World

These traders are strongly opinionated. While they like to hear what everyone else is talking about and get a feel for the mood and the theme, very rarely do you see people copy each other. But it could spark a thought—if something is interesting, it might lead them to a completely different trade. . . . For every buyer there's a seller, and for every seller there's a buyer—and one of those guys might be on the other side of your trade.

—*Interview conducted by the* Active
Trader *staff,* Active Trader *Magazine,*
August 2006, 42–48

If the market discounts the future, then how should the trader respond to the tide of public sentiment? Here the trader faces a dilemma. On the one hand, she is instructed to go along with the major trend, not to fight the tape, and, in effect, to join the crowd. On the other hand, she is counseled to invert her thinking, to take a position contrary to the prevailing majority sentiment in the market. These maxims are, obviously, diametrically opposed, leaving the investor a mental wreck if they are taken at face value. The trick to mental health is not to take them literally but to follow the prevailing sentiment during the middle of the trend, and to go contrary to it at extreme tops and bottoms. Accomplishing this, of course, requires that you know what constitutes a top and what constitutes a bottom.

Unfortunately, ignorance about how to play the market leaves the trader open to all the gossip, rumor, sensationalism, deceptiveness, and pooled ignorance of Wall Street. Without a sense of how the market operates, she gives in to her fears and hopes at just the wrong times. She joins the general public in selling too soon, repurchasing at higher prices, buying more after the market has turned down and then liquidating on breaks. This is destructive to the trader's confidence as well as to her pocketbook. As a consequence, she is apt to attribute her losses to a mysterious "they" who manipulate prices, to the random walk, to the President, or to just about anything and everything except her own ignorance.

Those traders who survive to become hedge fund pros have cultivated the capacity to listen to, yet withstand, the siren call of the emotion-laden talk that surrounds markets. To succeed, they must become gifted contrarians.

The Dangers of Hope, Fear, and Greed

Hope, fear, and greed are emotional enemies that must be subjugated if you are to have a fighting chance to realize the 7 out of 10 profitable trades that your superior stock market knowledge should bring you. Obversely, if ignorance, hope, fear, and greed take command of you, then the odds are probably 7 out of 10 that you will lose. As Albert Haas Jr. and Don M. Jackson MD wrote in *Bulls, Bears and Dr. Freud* (Cleveland, OH: World Publishing Co., 1967):

> *Greed might be defined sardonically as a lust possessing people— other people—who cannot control a healthy desire to make money. Fear takes the other hand of the greedy, fear that what is wanted most can be lost or denied; greed and fear together can team up to make stock market activities a profitless torment. Greed, like an intoxicant, fogs the mind, and fear unsteadies the hand. Both of these basic human feelings are sometimes hard to recognize and difficult to tease apart. A victim of greed and fear presents a curious paradox, since he hopes for so much and expects so little.*

A criticism of greed in the stock market is not made on moral grounds. Greed should not be expunged as an investor's motivator, for it is quite natural to wish for gains—preferably sizable gains—in the stock market. Criticism of greed is warranted when it is excessive and when it becomes the dominant motive at the wrong time.

"Don't wait for the last eighth of a point" and "Don't overstay a bull market when you're long or a bear market when you're short" are two Wall Street axioms designed to guard against an excess of greediness. When you see a position advance 30 percent and then insist that it has to double, you are being greedy. But you could counter this point with another Wall Street aphorism that says "Cut your losses short and let your profits run," to justify hanging on to a rising security. Granted, but what you have to guard against is an unwarranted change in attitude once an advance (decline) is well under way. If you start to become more confident, complacent, even cocky as your paper profits pile up, you are liable to raise your profit targets to unrealistic levels. This raising of expectations, insisting on "the final eighth," is likely unintentional and unconscious. It is the emotion of greed gaining control over your intellect; it is your aspirations forever outrunning your grasp.

In that example, greed grows after the advance has occurred. We become bolder rather than more timid as we move further and further away from our original support zone and closer to the resistance level where we should logically expect a reaction. We seem to undergo some sort of a learning or adjustment process whereby we expect continuance of the trend (up or down), thus giving vent to our heart-of-heart's desire for more of a good thing. This same sort of operant conditioning appears to occur over the market cycle as well; we become very bold and confident (greedy) after the market has risen for months, whereas we are cautious and fearful at the inception of the rise.

In the worst cases, fear, greed, and hope feed one another to create a cycle of perpetual powerlessness and poor decision making. The consequences of fear and greed have been documented in studies of brokerage house customers' portfolios. One report showed the following telltale results:

- The average price at which each stock was bought was higher than the average price at which it was sold.
- The trading methods of each account had undergone a pronounced and obviously unintentional change with the progress of the bull market from one stage to another.
- Stocks that were purchased at a bear market bottom were sold soon after at a moderate profit, even though in a few months these starting prices looked ridiculously cheap.
- As higher levels were established, the same stocks were repurchased at prices considerably higher than those at which they had previously been sold.

- At this stage, larger-percentage profits were the rule (evidence that what was considered a "reasonable gain" had been upped).
- Stop-losses were not in general use at this level, whereas they had been freely placed when prices were lower.
- The acquired confidence of the buyers seemed to have caused them to buy extensively on the first major reaction from the extreme highs.
- These were later liquidated at substantially lower prices.

—Don Guyon, One Way Pockets,
Fraser Publishing Company,
1965 (first published in 1917)

Fear gives way to greed and then returns. Hope leads us into a land of reverie where we can construct an imaginary world of fame and fortune. Hope transports us to the door of Lady Luck, whom we beseech to turn the tide in our favor. Hope helps us to overlook our losses while we wait for a favorable run of events, or even a sunny day. If we're long the market, we hope for a further advance; if we're short the market, we hope for a further decline.

Hope is a sort of daytime reverie that fogs our perception and clouds our reasoning. Our anxieties arise at night to keep us awake. We can combat hope as an enemy through the judicious use of stop-loss orders, for hope at its most debilitating makes us hang on to a sick position until it becomes so critical that we must undergo an amputation without an anesthetic.

Hope has two handmaidens: rationalization and denial. These are psychological defenses with which we can cope with the unpleasantries we encounter in life, either by reasoning them away or by pretending that we do not know what we do know.

Rationalization has hold of an investor when she habitually takes action or avoids it for reasons that appear perfectly sound, objective, and acceptable to her, though the real reasons are entirely different. When a stock that she has identified as a potential winner starts to move ahead, she invents numerous logical excuses not to act: the put/call ratio; some Department of Commerce statistics; the next quarterly earnings report will confirm the desirability of the stock; and so on. When she does take the plunge and her stock declines, she ignores the first few points and rationalizes away the next two or three as due to a sluggish market. If an unexpectedly poor earnings report is published and the stock retreats further, she rejoices that the bad news is finally out. She might even compound the error by averaging down through purchasing additional shares as the price declines, to show the courage of her convictions.

MASS PSYCHOLOGY

Example 4: Shiller's Insights on Social Dynamics

A great deal of evidence is presented here that suggests that social movements, fashions, or fads are likely to be important or even the dominant cause of speculative asset price movements; but no single piece of evidence is unimpeachable.

The most important reason for expecting that stock prices are heavily influenced by social dynamics comes from observations of participants in the market and of human nature as presented in the literature on social psychology, sociology, and marketing. A study of the history of the U.S. stock market in the postwar period suggests that various social movements were under way during this period that might plausibly have major effects on the aggregate demand for shares. Must we rely on such evidence to make the case against market efficiency? Yes; there is no alternative to human judgment in understanding human behavior.

> —*Robert J. Shiller, in* Richard H. Thaler,
> ed., Advances in Behavioral Finance
> *(New York: Russell Sage Foundation,
> 1993), 206–207*

There is a tremendous tendency toward convergence and conformity on Wall Street. Current appraisals of the market, estimations of the future, favorite industrial groups and their major stocks, all reflect moves toward consensus. This is a mindless conformity in as much as the crowd usually exaggerates a trend and ultimately underperforms the market averages. As a stock market operator, you must keep your own counsel. It is vital that you avoid being swept up by the emotions of the crowd.

Mindlessness is one of the hallmarks of crowd thinking. Singularly, a group of investors may be rational businessmen, lawyers, doctors, and Indian chiefs. As a group seeking profit on Wall Street, they will be unwitting, sometimes irrational, members of an unconscious groupthink. They share rising and sinking feelings with the tape; they are attracted to the same stocks at the same time and are apt to sell them in unison. As Gustave Le Bon wrote in *The Crowd*:

The gathering has thus become what, in the absence of a better expression, I will call an organized crowd, or, if the term is considered preferable, a psychological crowd. It forms a single being, and is subjected to the law of the mental unity of crowds.

> *The substitution of the unconscious action of crowds for the conscious activity of individuals is one of the principal characteristics of the present age.*
>
> *We see, then, that the disappearance of the conscious personality, the predominance of the unconscious personality, the turning by means of suggestions and contagion of feelings and ideas in an identical direction, the tendency immediately to transform the suggested ideas into acts; these we see, are the principal characteristics of the individual forming part of a crowd. He is no longer himself, but has become an automaton who has ceased to be guided by his will.*

A crowd does not reason; it is controlled by its sentiment. Is it any wonder, then, that the investor's deadly enemies are ignorance, greed, fear, and hope!

A deeper discussion of the crowd phenomenon is beyond the scope of this chapter, but you can find more information on the topics of panic, craze, imitation, anxiety and uncertainty, images, leadership, impulsive action, exaggeration, illusions, and intolerance of deviation in the sociological literature. Social psychology—including writings on selective perception, social comparison, reference groups, goal displacement, ambiguity, anxiety, collective misjudgment, stress—may also help explain why mass psychology has such a firm grip on Wall Street.

Example 5: Sir Cassell's Wisdom

> *When I was young, people called me a gambler. As the scale of my operations increased I became known as a speculator. Now I am called a banker. But I have been doing the same thing all the time.*
> —*Sir Ernest Cassell, banker to Edward VII*

Professional money managers, analysts, brokers, and opinion molders of Wall Street cannot escape the crowd phenomenon—quite the contrary. The performance of mutual funds, bank trust departments, and other institutions has been abysmally poor when compared to the market averages. They went headlong after the go-go performance concept in 1967–1968, only to see it collapse in 1969–1970; then they were in the thrall of the "one-decision stock," "two-tier" craze of 1970–1973, only to see their "nifty fifty" stocks (Avon, Xerox, Disney, International Flavors and Fragrances, etc.) come smashing down in 1973–1974 and 1976–1977. More recently, many were sucked into the Internet bubble of the late 1990s, only to suffer when it popped in the early 2000s. Rather than being cold, steely eyed, scarred veterans of Wall Street who withstand its periodic panics and crazes, we find that the pros are often leading the charge to catastrophe. Their favorite stock recommendations outperform the market for only a short term and to a limited extent. Over a longer term, stocks they shun outperform the stocks they favor!

The pros seem to suffer from their own version of crowd insanity, or groupthink. Under pressure to satisfy bosses and clients with current performance, dealing with data that are limited and difficult to define objectively, and facing major uncertainty over the future, professional money managers (unconsciously and consciously) turn to other people both for clarification and for benchmarks against which to measure their own opinions. Meeting and then beating the S&P 500 index becomes a sacred cow. Reality for the pros becomes social reality. What the larger group perceives as reality reflects a combination of objective and subjective criteria.

The moral of the story for the trader is clear: Be tough-minded so that you can take positions contrary to prevailing, majority opinion.

The Fashion Cycle Analogy

[T]he action of the stock market is nothing more nor less than a manifestation of mass crowd psychology in action.
                                                    —*Edson Gould, Market*
                                                    Guru of the 1960s–1970s

As I observed earlier in this chapter, Matt Ridley argues that "a rising price is a bandwagon" and that this bandwagon effect is largely due to the "heterogeneity of traders." Later, I mentioned Shiller's contention that "in social movements, fashions or fads are likely to be important or even the dominant cause of speculative asset price movements." To understand human and crowd behavior in the stock market, it is vital that the trader possess a deep and firm grasp of social movement over a fashion cycle.

The role of mass psychology in the evolution of a market cycle can be revealed by examining another, familiar cycle: that of women's fashion. The fashion world follows a pattern of innovation adoption similar to that of the stock market—from innovators to early adopters, to the mass market, to laggards—and results in the inevitable exhaustion of potential buyers.

A new fashion is seldom, if ever, adopted by everyone everywhere at once. Rather, it follows a trickle-down pattern. For example, the style, say a lower hemline, may initially be adopted only by high-status, fashion-conscious women. These ladies have traits of wealth, cosmopolitan surroundings, contacts in fashion circles, an awareness of what the creative designers are making, and so on. A new fashion may never reach beyond this level, as was the case with the midi skirt in the 1960s, if not adopted by a wide cross section of the population. To succeed, the fashion must trickle down to the greater masses of skirt wearers.

The trickle-down process is one of diffusion and adoption, aided and abetted by opinion leaders, advertisement, retail merchandising, word-of-mouth, imitation, contagion, convergence, and conformity. Let us explore each of these factors one at a time. *Diffusion* in this context means a spreading out, a broadening of usage. The concept implies that the diffusion starts from a center and works outward over time in concentric circles, capturing those nearest to the center first and converting those farthest away last. So we would expect the new hemline to be adopted by high-status women in large cities first, then by fashion-conscious younger women, and only later will longer hemlines appear on women who live in outlying areas, who are older, of lower status, and less fashion conscious.

The dissemination of information is needed to effect this diffusion. Fashion magazines display the new hemline in feature articles, women's magazines show key personalities dressed in the latest styles, and popular fashion editors lead opinion by advising what should be worn. Concurrently, advertisements appear in the national press while retail merchandisers are cajoled into placing orders for the new design. Meanwhile, among these fashion innovators and early adopters there will be considerable word-of-mouth discussion about appropriate style, color, texture, designer, and so forth, a communication network that tends to reinforce convergence toward a few accepted looks.

Imitation and emotion aid and abet the diffusion process. The greater the number of women seen in the new fashion, the greater the pressure to convert. Without anything being said to her directly, a non-adopter is apt to feel psychological discomfort—she feels awful because she perceives that she looks awful. Underlying her feelings are basic drives like fear and vanity. She fears that she may appear old-fashioned, unattractive, and undesirable. Her self-image, her vanity, tells her that she deserves a better reward than this. But she agonizes between the serviceability of her old wardrobe and the cost of a new one. Then, one day someone close to her (friend, enemy, neighbor, relative, etc.) appears in the new fashion and/or tells her about the bargains that Macy's now has in long-hemline ensembles. That does it. She goes on a buying spree, taking advantage of the great sale prices.

When at last Suzy Q. Perkins of Bonner's Ferry, Idaho, trades in her pantsuit for a long-hemline dress at the local Good Value shop, the fashion cycle is complete. For all intents and purposes there are no more buyers—the market has become saturated. Meanwhile, the original fashion innovators back in New York and Los Angeles have long since abandoned this look. At the same time that Suzy Q. is adopting it, the leaders are moving on to something diametrically opposed, like a shorter hemline. In effect, Suzy Q. has just purchased what is out of style. And so it goes, cycle after cycle.

The Stock Market Cycle

Many of the processes and motivations we observed in the fashion cycle are reflected in the stock market. It is most instructive to read back over the fashion example, inserting where appropriate such stock market elements as specialists, traders, financial press, advisory services, retail brokerage firms, fear and greed, glamour stocks, herd effect, panic and craze, hot groups, odd lotters, boardroom gossip, institutional sponsorship, fear and depression, greed and euphoria, and so on.

Analysis of the stock exchange reveals two underlying processes, one at the individual or psychological level, the other at the group or sociological level. These two processes are:

1. The motivation of fear and greed (individual level).
2. The cycle of diffusion and adoption (sociological level).

Fear and Greed

In this context, *fear* is defined as an unpleasant, often strong emotion caused by the anticipation or awareness of danger. *Greed* is an excessive desire for requiring or having. Fear and greed are not single-state variables; rather, they lie along spectrums of greater or lesser degree. The fear spectrum ranges from euphoria to confidence, to hope, to concern, to apprehension, to panic; in short, from optimism to pessimism. The greed spectrum ranges from headlong covetousness—leading to overbuying and overvaluation—to headlong parsimoniousness, leading to overselling and undervaluation.

Why don't fear and greed simply cancel each other out, leaving a stable, neutral market index? It is because the interaction between them is one of dynamic tension. At market bottoms when values are great, investors *should* be optimistic. After all, they should be greediest and most optimistic when the greatest bargains exist; this would be consonant, consistent, rational behavior. But what we discover at market bottoms is the opposite: When values are great, investors are pessimistic. This is manifestly dissonant, inconsistent, and irrational behavior. At market tops we find the opposite but equally irrational state of optimism versus low values. Is it any wonder, then, that when fear declines while greed rises at market bottoms we see explosive up-moves, or when fear overcomes greed at the tops we observe catastrophic declines?

SUMMARY

This chapter was designed to serve as a resource of ideas and procedures for the study of the human aspects of traders. Since behavioral finance is the study and practice, in financial markets, of concepts from the behavioral sciences and psychology, these were discussed under the headings "Individual Behavior" and "Mass Psychology."

The next chapter moves the concept of mass psychology in action beyond an amorphous notion. The crowd is brought into a manageable design that is both a picture and a checklist. This is accomplished through the application of behavioral finance, namely the "Life Cycle Model of Crowd Behavior." With this model, the trader will have an excellent opportunity to engage her whole brain: the left hemisphere for examining a digital checklist of the indicators, and the right hemisphere for visualizing how the elements of price, volume, time, and sentiment are combined and interrelated at different stages of the market cycle. Together these two analytical forms supplement and complement each other to furnish the trader with a *conceptual* edge.

APPENDIX A: BACKGROUND ON BEHAVIORAL FINANCE—SOURCES TO UPDATE THE TRADER

There are several sites worth looking at. First is the pretty interesting finance discussion group on Yahoo: http://finance.groups.yahoo.com/group/Behavioral-Finance/. Most of the concepts in that site are also considered at www.behaviouralfinance.net/. A great depth and breadth of writing on the topic can be found in the Financial Economics Network (FEN) behavioral finance articles: www.ssrn.com/link/behavioral-experimental-finance.html.

The web site of the *Journal of Behavioral Finance* is www.psychology andmarkets.org/. Robert Shiller's workshop in behavioral finance can be found at http://econ.yale.edu/~shiller/behfin/index.htm.

Further interesting sites for software include:

www.nag.com/index.asp
www.hoadley.net/options.html
www.decisioneering.com

For information and news:

www.fenews.com
www.financialengines.com
www.ssm.com

CHAPTER 3

The Life Cycle
Model of
Crowd Behavior

T his part of the book is designed to provide you with a big-picture framework into which to fit the various key indicators of technical analysis. This chapter is built around the distinct theme that stock market action follows the life cycle of other living organisms and so exhibits distinguishing patterns and phases. To convey this clearly, a model of adoption/diffusion is borrowed from sociology and communications theory as a framework for interrelating and interpreting indicators of market behavior. This Life Cycle Model of Crowd Behavior is an adaptation of the product life cycle model often used in business, forecasting, and planning. In marketing, the life cycle model has proven its usefulness time and again for understanding and guiding new products and other innovations.

The model developed in this chapter will show you how to organize and synthesize the technical market analysis of price, volume, sentiment, and time into a meaningful yet efficient system for market analysis. In addition to helping you organize and synthesize branches of technical analysis in this book, the Life Cycle Model of Crowd Behavior can be used as a supplement and complement to other textbooks on the subject of technical analysis. It is my hope that this chapter, and indeed this book as a whole, will become a useful reference and serve you well.

The trader gains a further advantage using the Life Cycle Model of Crowd Behavior because it employs both sides of his brain. A digital checklist analysis of price, volume, time, and sentiment engages the left hemisphere of the brain (L-directed thinking); a pictorial, graphic schematic that shows price, volume, time, and sentiment operating simultaneously and all together activates the right hemisphere of the brain (R-directed thinking).

Of course, L-directed plus R-directed thinking creates the winning combination—the whole new mind.

In this chapter you will learn about the analytical frameworks of the Life Cycle Model, namely a bell-shaped curve defining various categories of investors and traders, and indicating at which phase of the market cycle you can expect them to enter or exit the market. Next you will study an S-shaped curve showing the impact on price as the various categories of traders and investors join a bull trend or depart the market during a bearish trend.

The second section of this chapter features an application of the Life Cycle Model by two trader-technicians. Based on my experience and my observations of other traders, I have created two stereotypical characters, Wright and Lefty, who tell the story of their trading and the impact of the Life Cycle Model.

The third and final section of this chapter offers a mini lecture on the details of technical analysis, covering the parameters of price, volume, sentiment, and time as they are organized and synthesized by the Life Cycle Model.

INTEGRATING TECHNICAL INDICATORS

Conceptual models stemming from behavioral finance can help the trader-analyst construct and test systems of technical analysis. Further, the technician's intuitive grasp of crowd psychology for practical application can be harnessed through the use of a modified version of a life cycle framework.

The life cycle framework I have in mind is the *adoption/diffusion* model of crowd behavior, illustrated in Figures 3.1 and 3.2. These figures show how a society adopts an innovation over time, like a bandwagon of buyers chasing a desired stock. The graph takes the shape of a bell curve when representing the number of people adopting the innovation each period and looks like an S-curve when representing the number of people on a cumulative basis.

For dramatic examples of crowd behavior in action, we can look at such classic cases as tulipomania, the South Sea Bubble, and the Mississippi Scheme. More recently, we've seen kamikaze capitalism and cowboy capitalism, which are expertly outlined by Edward Chancellor in *Devil Take the Hindmost*. The herd instinct of financial markets found in these cases can be explained and predicted using the adoption/diffusion model. This bandwagon-like crowd phenomenon is also observable in market cycles of much shorter duration and smaller magnitude.

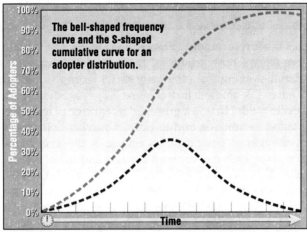

The bell-shaped curve shows the number of people in a society that adopt an innovation in each period, while the S-shaped curve represents the cumulative number of people over time.

FIGURE 3.1 Adoption of an Innovation
Source: From "Life Cycle Model of Crowd Behavior," by Henry Pruden, *Technical Analysis of Stocks & Commodities* 17, no. 1 (January 1999), 77–80. Copyright © 1999, Technical Analysis, Inc. Used with permission.

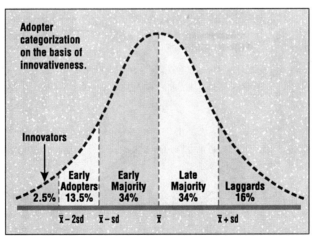

The innovation dimension, as measured by time at which an individual adopts an innovation, is continuous. However, this variable may be partitioned into five adopter categories by laying off standard deviations from the average time of adoption.

FIGURE 3.2 Adopter Categorization
Source: From "Life Cycle Model of Crowd Behavior," by Henry Pruden, *Technical Analysis of Stocks & Commodities* 17, no. 1 (January 1999), 77–80. Copyright © 1999, Technical Analysis, Inc. Used with permission.

Curves, S-Shaped and Bell-Shaped

The cumulative nature of the herd instinct is reflected in the S-shaped curve of the life cycle model (Figure 3.1), while the counterpart bell-shaped curve shows how groups of market participants are positioned and interrelated, ranging from the early smart money to the "odd-lotters," those who enter the market last (Figure 3.2). Together, the two curves form a life cycle model that is a powerful integrator of indicators to gauge technical market conditions and to predict market behavior. In fact, the life cycle concept is so powerful that economic theorist Theodore Modis argues that such models can forecast the rise and fall of almost anything.[1]

The foregoing adoption/diffusion life cycle model, which is widely used in social science and in marketing research, fits the stock market with ease. Using this model, Figure 3.3 shows how the four major parameters of technical analysis—price, volume, time, and sentiment—are interrelated.

Four Elements: Price, Volume, Sentiment, and Time

The four major technical parameters of the Life Cycle Model of Crowd Behavior are distinct aspects of the technical condition of the U.S. stock

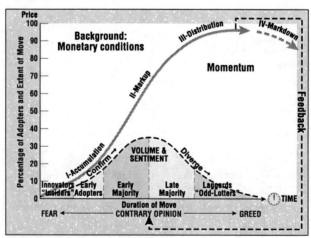

The adoption/diffusion life cycle model is modified here to fit the stock market. Here, we see the four technical analysis parameters used in the decision-making process—price, volume, sentiment, and time.

FIGURE 3.3   The Pruden Model
Source: From "Life Cycle Model of Crowd Behavior," by Henry Pruden, *Technical Analysis of Stocks & Commodities* 17, no. 1 (January 1999), 77–80. Copyright © 1999, Technical Analysis, Inc. Used with permission.

market. Since the data for each parameter are independent from that of the others, the indicators representing them can be combined. This additive feature of price, time, volume, and sentiment is very important; together they provide a more complete and binding conclusion regarding a market's present position and probable future trend.

Indicators that represent each parameter can be arranged to provide a more in-depth and reliable understanding of each parameter, as suggested in Figure 3.4. Furthermore, this grid can be used as a worksheet to aid in model development and testing. As the figure shows, each element is broken down into three levels of analysis. The analyst enters data into the "Indicators" and "Weighting" columns according to the market being analyzed and time frame selected. (See the last section of this chapter,

Indicators

Three deep at every position
Four elements: Price, volume, time, and sentiment
Three levels of analysis, or three units of analysis for every element

Element	Unit	Indicators*	Weighting
			Bullish—Bearish +4 +2 +1 −1 −2 −4
Price	Momentum Extent Form		
Volume	Total Upside/downside On-balance		
Time	Cycle Duration Season		
Sentiment	News Opinion Speculation		

This form shows each element broken down into three levels or units of analysis. Entries under "Indicators" and "Weighting" depend on the market and time frame being analyzed.
*Indicators are chosen by the analyst. Depending on the time frame used and the market studied, each technician can systematically select an array of specific technical indicators to represent each element of the model.

FIGURE 3.4 Three-Deep at Every Position
Source: From "Life Cycle Model of Crowd Behavior," by Henry Pruden, *Technical Analysis of Stocks & Commodities* 17, no. 1 (January 1999), 77–80. Copyright © 1999, Technical Analysis, Inc. Used with permission.

the "Mini Lecture," for in-depth expositions of price, volume, sentiment, and time.)

A *tree of indicators* concept comes into play during the building and testing of complex models. With this notion, rather than simply relying on price trend and sentiment, the analyst can add together indicators such as price pattern, Elliott Wave count, point-and-figure proportion, on-balance and total volume, and put/call ratio to fully exploit the technical information possibilities of the model. Using the adoption/diffusion model, analysts can make sense of how these various parameters are tied together.

Depending on the trader-analyst's time horizon and his confidence level with certain indicators, he can select, judiciously, from an arsenal of specific technical indicators. If, for example, he is an intermediate-term options or futures trader, then he might wish to examine the price parameter using stochastics or relative strength index (RSI) to study momentum, an hourly Dow Jones chart to count Elliott Waves, and a point-and-figure chart of the Dow Jones Industrial Average (DJIA) to measure the potential extent of moves. These price indicators can be seen positioned along the S-shaped curve.

With respect to volume, the analyst might include total daily New York Stock Exchange (NYSE) volume, a measure of overall upside versus downside volume, and perhaps also a further refinement of an on-balance volume study of the 30 stocks in the DJIA. Volume is appropriately viewed on the bell-shaped curve under the S-shaped curve of price.

Sentiment measures both the opinion and the behavior of various market participants. Sentiment indicators of opinion are captured by the feedback loop (see Figure 3.3), and behavior fits into the bell-shaped adoption curve. Here, the analyst might choose to evaluate market opinion by using the Investors Intelligence ratio of bulls to bears (www.investors intelligence.com). Moreover, he might evaluate the prevailing public sentiment with the headlines and leading stories from newspapers and magazines. He can appraise speculative behavior by calculating option put/call, open interest, and volume ratios.

Finally, the intermediate-term investor might utilize the fourth major parameter, time. This might be achieved by analyzing a 10- to 13-week trough-to-trough cycle, the duration spent in a given up- or downtrend, and the significance of seasonal influences.

Framing the indicators into the model shown in Figure 3.3 empowers the trader to better judge when the odds are optimal to buy an upside breakout. The combined picture of price-volume-sentiment-time appears different in the lower-left quadrant (accumulation) of the model than in the upper right (distribution). One would want to buy every high-volume upside breakout in the former case, but not when the latter circumstances appear to prevail.

The model also gives the trader grounds for establishing numerical benchmarks for entry and exit signals. These benchmarks can come from back-testing and real-time experience. Certain indicators might be given more weight, and the threshold levels between bullish, very bullish, bearish, and very bearish will depend on the analyst's choice of indicators, beliefs about the market, and experience.

The adoption/diffusion life cycle model allows the technical trader to use the rich array of indicators available in software packages, yet at the same time avoid being overwhelmed by data. As shown in Figure 3.5, small S-shaped life cycle curves build into larger ones. Thus, the model provides a systematic way to view and interrelate the daily, short-term, intermediate, and long-term trends of a market.

A general observation is that the field of technical trading has become too competitive for a trader to rely solely on a simple system of one or two indicators. Trading in the markets is rapidly approaching the levels of competition found in professional sports. Hence, you need something more complex yet intelligible to help you gain that extra edge. Behavioral finance models can help you frame your technical information to gain that advantage.

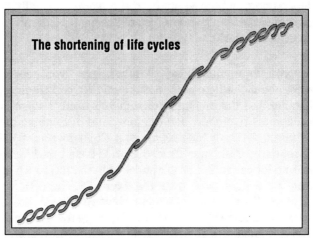

An overall S-curve pattern may consist of a long series of smaller S-curves. The life cycles indicated by the smaller S-curves become longer in the middle of the overall curve, then become shorter again. A successful technology will have a longer life cycle within the natural growth curve of a family of technologies. Toward the end of that family's natural growth, new products will come and go quickly. The shorter life cycles combine to form a larger cycle.

FIGURE 3.5 The Shortening of Life Cycles
Source: From "Life Cycle Model of Crowd Behavior," by Henry Pruden, *Technical Analysis of Stocks & Commodities* 17, no. 1 (January 1999), 77–80. Copyright © 1999, Technical Analysis, Inc. Used with permission.

THE SAGA OF TWO TRADERS: WRIGHT AND LEFTY

Sometime in the year 2005 in a major U.S. city, Wright met his long-time friend Lefty at a café near the stock exchange building. Wright strode in with the confidence of someone who had just won a challenging tennis match. He was eager to tell Lefty about the profitable result of his first-ever trade based on scientific logic and a forward plan. Wright hoped his good fortune would encourage Lefty, who purchased common stocks, attended trading seminars focusing on mechanical technical trading systems, and even installed a complete software program with end-of-day data feed. Despite all the time, talent, and treasure he devoted to trading, Lefty's experience was a hit-and-miss trail of losses and lost opportunities.

Wright described the three big things that helped him and that he thought could also help Lefty:

1. A change in attitude, a change in how he looked at the world: a conceptual, empathetic, twenty-first-century view.

2. A true scientific logic to guide his interpretation of stock market action through charts and indicators, using models from crowd behavior, behavioral finance, and the life cycle.

3. A balanced and integrated study of the market, visually and analytically, through the simultaneous use of schematic diagrams and checklists to evaluate market data.

"Before you do anything else," Wright began, "you need to get your head straight about the demands that the market and trading put on the technical trader and the mental approach you need to develop to attain and keep a competitive edge, like the new kind of thinking described by Daniel H. Pink in *A Whole New Mind: Why Right-Brainers Will Rule the Future*. Essentially, Pink says that while rule-based trading remains important, it is no longer sufficient. To succeed in the future we have to take a page from the distant past, from the days of Richard D. Wyckoff and Jesse Livermore. We need to regain our chart reading skills, to get a feel for the market, and to be able to listen to the story the market is telling us. These skills are lodged in the right hemisphere of the brain, what Pink calls R-directed or R-mode attributes. They enable us to put the pieces of the market puzzle together, to discern patterns, to really get a feel for a person, for people, and for the crowd.

"This R-directed approach appealed to me immediately," Wright explained. "I've always been a visually oriented person. When somebody is demonstrating a new concept to me, I like to see the big picture, to see it mapped out so that I can relate parts one to another. When I'm traveling somewhere new, I like to get a map *and* written directions. That works. For me, one without the other is less than half the plan. I can trust the life cycle market model because it gives me a schematic to look at and a checklist to fit the pieces together. But you need to start with accurate geography; otherwise no number or combination of turn-by-turn directions and detailed maps will get you to your destination. That's the problem with trading 'maps' based on the efficient market hypothesis—it's like believing that the earth is flat, not round.

"The efficient market, for sure, is a bad map of the stock market world because it's built on the faulty assumption that people who invest and trade all fit the 'economic man' model. By contrast, the market models from behavioral finance start with the assumption that market players are motivated by fear, greed, and other characteristics of human behavior identified in psychology, sociology, and anthropology. Anyone who lived through the Internet boom and bust of the 1990s knows in their bones that the markets are emotional and not efficient."

Wright went on to explain why he was particularly drawn to the Life Cycle Model of Crowd Behavior. From practical, real-world experience it made sense to him; he had observed the impact of the four seasons of the year, and the birth-growth-maturity-harvest cycle of plants and crops. Wright recollected a high school history class where he learned that the ancient Greeks used the life cycle model from nature to describe and explain the rise-and-fall of nations, other man-made institutions, and even the panics of crowds. Later, when he read that market guru Edson Gould had described crowd behavior as the "open sesame" to studying the markets, Wright was hooked.

Wright went on to tell his friend Lefty: "The two sides or two faces of the Life Cycle Model—the pictures and the checklist—gave me both the flexibility and the discipline to put things together and reach a compelling decision regarding the future or the next stage of the market. For example, I saw the base forming. The base showed me that the innovative smart money or 'strong hands' investors were preparing a new bull market cycle. Of course, I'm not a deep-pockets, deeply informed investor like the smart-money innovators, but I can keep an eye on them through technical analysis and follow in their footsteps.

"I came in as an early adopter. I bought the breakout from the base. The gradually expanding volume as prices advanced confirmed that buyers were entering the market, creating a bull-market bandwagon. I'm not an expert on time cycles," Wright went on, "But there are times when the big four- to four-and-a-half-year business cycle and the presidential cycle tell us that we are in the vicinity of a top or a bottom. Like in late 2002, a four-year cycle was heading for a bottom. Knowing that an important cycle low had clocked in gave me greater confidence to enter the market as the bull unfolded during early 2003. Also around that same time, there were scary news reports concerning Iraq and a falling economy, plus the market letters were bearish. All in all, price and volume were now joined by time and sentiment to create a bullish quartet.

"With the help of the Life Cycle Model, I pieced together the elements of time, price, sentiment, and volume into a mosaic that looked like a bull. The pattern grabbed me, but, since I am a guy who likes to wear suspenders as well as a belt, I was glad to have the analytical checklist half of the Life Cycle Model—what Pink would call the L-directed half—to compare it to. One good thing about the checklist is that I can choose my indicators and then add them up. I can have more confidence in the picture I see of the market if these indicators add up to the same bullish conclusion.

"If the indicators taken one at a time fail to add up to a bullish conclusion—in other words, if they are out of sync with the picture—I grow suspicious and back away from the market. On the other hand, sometimes the picture is so clear and persuasive that it pulls one or two indicators that were a little short of a full-blown bullish reading over the hump.

"The 'three-deep at every position' proposition that is built into the indicators checklist helps increase the validity and reliability of my market diagnosis. It's also good at giving the technically oriented trader ample opportunity to cherry-pick his indicators. It all adds up; it all ties together to give a more scientific basis for decision making.

"At the same time, the Life Cycle Model simplifies the trader's world by placing a cap of 15 indicators on the basic system. One could automate these readings and create a 'black box' or mechanical decision-making system, but adding the right look to the indicator array, as profiled on the Life Cycle Model, acts as a terribly important control filter. Insisting on the right overall look may not be a true fail-safe system, but it sort of acts like one.

"A really important hurdle to becoming a complete trader is learning to identify and accept your own limits. There are limits to how frequently you should trade, how much money you should place at risk, how many different stocks or commodities you should invest in, how many technical indicators you should use, and so on. The Life Cycle Model is a great help in regards to placing limits.

"According to the logic of the Life Cycle Model graph and the 'three deep at every position' notion, I discovered that it's best for me to restrict myself to 15 indicators. I like to trade in two time frames: the intermediate, or 13-week to 26-week cycle; and the major, or four-year cycle. I select 15 indicators for each of these two different time frames and an array of indicators that are sufficiently different from each other that I can add them together.

"I used to believe that more was better. I would build trading systems composed of stochastics, RSI, rate of change (ROC), and moving average convergence/divergence (MACD) in various time frames and think that I really had something significant when they confirmed one another. But once I appreciated that you need independence among items before adding them together, I realized I'd been looking at fool's gold. It finally dawned on me that all of those indicators were momentum indicators— they were all tapping the same underlying dimension of market behavior, and so of course they would be highly correlated. Since they didn't tap separate, independent dimensions of market behavior, the additional momentum indicators didn't add much to the reading given by a single momentum indicator!"

Wright concluded, "Mindless number crunching to try to identify predictors of market behavior is a primitive state, an information age nothink to which I simply cannot return."

Lefty Learns from Professor Hank

By late June 2006, Lefty felt that he had at last realized a decisive breakthrough in his trading. That month, Lefty attended a two-day conference in San Francisco, California, conducted by Professor Hank Pruden that was devoted to the concepts central to *The Three Skills of Top Trading*, specifically the Life Cycle Model of Crowd Behavior, the Wyckoff method of technical analysis, and the Ten Tasks of Top Trading. Lefty enjoyed the "contrarian" flavor of the conference and was delighted to participate in putting the pieces of the technical jigsaw puzzle together in real time. Lefty believed, too, that he experienced and finally felt the balanced usage of Pink's left-brain/right-brain or whole-mind approach in market analysis and implementation.

When Lefty finally recognized the paramount importance of the primary trend of the market, he got solid traction under his trading. Underlying everything at the conference was the fact that the U.S. markets were in a primary bull trend. The Primary Trend Projector (see Chapter 1, Appendix A) indicated that the major market averages still pointed upward in early June 2006. Hence, until there was a decided downside movement in prices that would cause the 200-day moving average to turn downward and prices to remain below declining 200-day moving averages, a bull market would remain in force. Until that confirmed reversal in the primary trend, the trader could expect hesitations and reactions in the market to be corrections and buying opportunities. To Lefty's thinking, things were shaping up into a buying opportunity.

Rather than being frightened by the sharp decline in share prices during the week that had gone by, Lefty now knew that traders should focus on the opportunities that can make money during the months ahead. As of this writing, we are most likely nearing an outstanding buying juncture in U.S. stocks and maybe the last good bargain juncture of the current bull market. We should not miss this opportunity. We should prepare ourselves to profit from the next up-leg of this bull market. Profit opportunities can be great during a final leg of a bull market, but risks are also commensurately high. We'll need to play smart and apply the best principles we can learn about trading.

Setup, Trigger, and Follow-Through   Lefty applied one of these principles when he recognized that in late June, sentiment was bullish as the total put/call ratio was the highest in history on May 29, 2006.

A classic approach to trading, popularized by Jake Bernstein, is to think of it in terms of *setup, trigger,* and *follow-through.* The setup signals are given by the Life Cycle Model of Crowd Behavior. One of the four big elements in that model is sentiment (shown both on the graph and in the checklist). An extreme reading of the current put/call ratio gives a +4 bullish reading. A +4 reading on sentiment comes at market lows when fear becomes the dominant mood and the rankest speculators are betting on the downside. Market movements end with exhaustion, and exhaustion is in part revealed when the laggards come into the market, buying puts late in the downswing (see the bell-shaped curve). Record levels of put buying in late May and early June 2006 showed strong evidence that the odd-lotters were aggressively joining the bear bandwagon. Such extreme put/call ratios usually occur after prolonged and scary declines. But in June 2006 we have evidence of these laggard types already joining the downside bandwagon and expressing a degree of fear that is out of touch with the price and volume evidence of the market index.

The trigger is given to us by the Wyckoff elements of price and volume. The Wyckoff method has been giving evidence of the proximity of a low point. Often the price and volume readings are sufficient and do not need strong corroboration from the sentiment indicators. However, in this instance the sentiment readings are a powerful cross-validation of the Wyckoff price and volume signals and further argument that an important low is at hand.

The third step is the follow-through. This is where most people miss the boat because they are too afraid to buy. They want more confirmatory information to convince them to act. Their insistence on receiving this additional evidence tends to make them laggards on the bull side. To overcome this psychological handicap and follow through intelligently, the trader-analyst needs to invoke the Ten Tasks of Top Trading, outlined in Chapter 8.

In general, magazine cover stories fall under the heading of sentiment indicators. At the conference Lefty learned about that first-hand, as a bear had appeared on the cover of the *Economist* magazine's May 27–June 2 issue. Good technicians are aware of the *contrary opinion* implication of the Economist's cover story and know that sentiment is definitely bullish! Nevertheless, many traders don't fully grasp the contrary opinion implication of a bear cover story. Rather, they are apt to be persuaded to sell after seeing a bear on the cover of the Economist, which is just what the Wyckoff Composite Man wishes them to do.

The bear on the cover of the *Economist* is another +4 reading for sentiment in the Life Cycle Model decision support matrix.

Price and Volume Give Bullish Indications   In addition to the sentiment indicator's bullish reading, Lefty learned that the price and volume activity confirmed the bullish trend. On June 8, 2006, a large expansion in volume relative to the preceding days, coupled with a large spread in the price range and a closing price near the top of the day's range, denoted a probable selling climax. As is discussed in Part II of this book, the Wyckoff method classifies such a climax as a temporary or permanent stopping of the preceding downtrend in price from the recent high of 11,680 to the June 8 low of 10,760.

From the summary figures of price and volume on selling climax day, we can infer that the smart-money, strong buyers (demand) overwhelmed the sell offers being pressed upon the market by frightened investors. The on-balance volume index failed to confirm the new low price by the Dow during the decline. The price and volume readings set up a positive divergence and the anticipation of a turning of price trend to the upside; however, the ultimate confirmation or rejection of this bullish hypothesis would require a test that should occur within a few days or a week. A successful test of the selling climax would be a price sell-off following the automatic rally that would hold at or near the selling climax price lows, preferably on relatively light volume. Since that test is not yet complete, we give an overall bullish rating of +2 for price and for volume.

During the second day of the conference Lefty heard the story told of the senior market trader-technician (see box), which helped him put all the pieces together. Lefty resolved to study and to use the technical parameters of price, volume, sentiment, and time spelled out by the senior market trader-technician.

Gaining an Edge: The Senior Market Technician/ Technical Trader

It is the job of the senior trader and market technician to see that all elements of technical analysis—price, volume, time, and sentiment—are integrated into a whole. This often difficult task of integration must be performed regardless of the type of market under study, the complexity of indicators utilized, or the number of contributing data feeds and commentaries involved. These complex situations dictate that the technical trader employ some framework or model that includes and interrelates all the key elements of technical market analysis. The trader-technician needs a plan, a system that brings all the elements together into a meaningful mix.

There are four elements in the technical market analysis mix: price, volume, time, and sentiment. Most bar charts show only three components of the market mix: price on the vertical axis, volume on the vertical axis below the price, and time along the horizontal axis. Sentiment can be represented by the relationship between categories of buyers and sellers (for example, put/call, volume ratios) or by external expressions of opinion. These building-block elements are often combined to form more comprehensive patterns, such as continuation and reversal formations on the charts. Through the detailed study of charts, the interrelationships among these main functional elements of market analysis become readily apparent.

Coordinating these various elements of market analysis is among the most critical problems the senior technical trader will face. This is particularly likely to be the case in large and complex trading organizations or when the following of a large number of markets stimulates the need for the division of labor and specialization. You can imagine the combinations of talents that might be assembled to technically analyze a market: a flair for sentiment analysis; analytical skills in the price area; creative insight into volume behavior; a creative approach to the study of time; and finally, a great grasp of the whole.

The importance of the overall coordination of such specialization in an environment of mounting globalization of markets leads to an increase in the use of senior traders/technicians who supervise, coordinate, and integrate various specialists.

The need for integration of the technical market analysis mix should be obvious at this stage in the evolution of trading. Indicators and models of price, volume, and other elements of the market analysis mix are merely different tools in the senior technical trader's tool kit. These tools

(continues)

are used individually and in combination for the diagnosis and prognosis of market behavior.

The senior technical trader's challenge is to blend the elements of the technical market analysis mix so as to achieve the utmost accuracy in timing. In part, this is a matter of selecting the right tools from the sometimes conflicting recommendations of the various technical specialties. It is also a matter of recognizing patterns, thinking broadly, and seeing the full implications of a given recommendation. Basically, the key to effective coordination is balance: the right elements used in the wrong combination, or the wrong relative emphasis on primary versus intermediate versus minor market trends, may have disastrous results. Effectively and efficiently integrating the technical analysis mix to support trading is a challenging task.

Lefty spent the evening after the conference going over all the items mentioned in the handouts that were covered in the two days. He found the transcript from the mini lecture on technical analysis an especially helpful resource (see the next section). With the help of the S-shaped curve of the market model (Figure 3.3) and the analytical checklist of indicators (Figure 3.4), he weighted the price, volume, time, and sentiment indicators. Lefty went to bed that night with the comfortable feeling that he now knew how to build a compelling case of technical evidence to set up for a possible trigger based on a Wyckoff principle.

A MINI LECTURE ON PRICE, VOLUME, SENTIMENT, AND TIME

This mini lecture on the subject of technical analysis parameters should serve as a refresher on the basics of technical analysis for some readers and as a brief introduction of the elements of price, volume, sentiment, and time for others. Everyone should study this lecture carefully in order to grasp fully how technical indicators are integrated by the Life Cycle Model of Crowd Behavior.

Price

When you look at the surface of the market, what do you see? *Price*!

Gains and losses are registered by comparing the price of entry with the price of exit. Our sense of well being or our sense of frustration is often a direct reflection of whether prices are rising or falling in line with our present commitments and future expectations. It is little wonder then that price is the most important market parameter for most investors.

The Life Cycle Model of Crowd Behavior likewise gives an analytical position of prominence to price. In that model, price is the dependent or response variable reflecting the underlying struggle between supply and demand. But price is not a mere passive agent; it is not a blob which floats upward or downward with the rising and lowering tide of market forces. Rather, price is both a response function of supply and demand and a stimulator of supply and demand.

We can visualize price as an S-shaped curve recording the cumulative pressures of the supply and demand emanating from the bell-shaped curve of adoption. We can also visualize a "feedback loop" from price to the underlying control variables of volume and sentiment. After all, a change in price is news that gets communicated through the news media, impacting the attitudes and actions of present and potential investors. We classify this feedback nature of price under the parameter of sentiment (refer to Figure 3.3).

In this portion of the lecture we shall concern ourselves with the direction of price movements, the amplitude of price rise and fall, the speed of its movement, and the structure or form of price over various stages of expansion and contraction. These concepts will be referred to as *direction, extent, momentum,* and *form.* The tools we will use to examine these four dimensions of price behavior are trend analysis; measurement; thrusts, trend lines, and oscillators; and the Elliott Wave principle. Theoretically, these analytical concepts and tools are applicable to stocks, commodities, bonds, futures, and so forth (refer to Figure 3.4).

The trader should strive to assemble the building blocks of price behavior into a mutually reinforcing system of information. For example, when the trend has been down but is now in the vicinity of price objectives, losing downside momentum and in a third declining wave, you should conclude that you are approaching some sort of a market bottom. Then when you observe an upward price zigzag, preceded by a base count for higher potential prices, gathering upside momentum and a new Elliott Wave impulse, you should conclude that a new markup stage may have commenced.

Price Movement Logic in Perspective   Price movement addresses the "what" of the stock market. What are prices doing? Going up? Going down? Remaining unchanged? A key assumption is that what prices have been doing, they will continue to do. If price has been trending upward, it will continue to move up; if price has been moving down, it will continue to move down. In other words, price moves in trends. This tendency of

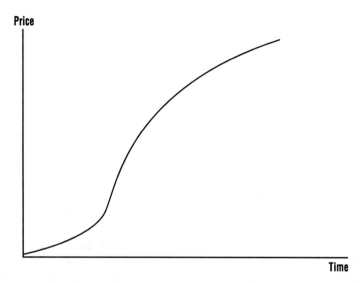

FIGURE 3.6   Price Movement Logic

price to continue to persist in the same direction is commonly known as
bull market trends or *bear market trends*. Prices therefore move up,
move down, or move sideways in trends. The general rule of conduct for
traders and investors is to invest in harmony with an established trend.
When the trend of the overall market is up, be a buyer and stick with your
long position. When the general trend is down, be a seller and stick with
your short position. We define the general trend with our Primary Trend
Projector (see Appendix A, Chapter 1).

Sticking with a position, adhering to a trend can be a difficult proposition because prices do not move in a straight line up, down, or sideways.
Rather, prices move in a zigzag pattern. Price movement occurs in alternating waves of buying and selling. Waves represent an imbalance between supply and demand. When demand exceeds supply, prices move
upward; when supply exceeds demand, prices move downward. In an upward trend in price movement, the buying waves are longer and stronger
than the selling waves, and vice versa for a downward trend. When demand and supply are in equilibrium there is a sideways zigzag of price
movement or horizontal trading range.

Waves of buying and selling come in various sizes (amplitude) and
ages (duration), and they occur in a hierarchy where small up-and-down
waves are the building blocks of larger up-and-down waves, which are
part of still larger waves. Waves range from intraday swings moving a few
points or fractions of a point, to giants lasting years and moving hundreds

of points. Dow Theorists have codified wave movements into three categories: primary, intermediate, and short-term.

The primary trend is the most important price movement. Reactions downward against a rising primary trend and rallies upward against a declining primary trend are expected to revert back in favor of the previously prevailing primary trend. The primary trend is the underlying tidal force; it defines the line of least resistance. Since all price movements (primary, intermediate, and short-term), evolve in a cyclic pattern of accumulation, markup, distribution, and markdown, it is inescapable that trends—up, down, or sideways—must come to an end.

Turning points in price movement trends are the most critical single phenomenon facing the technical trader. When the turn in price movement comes, traders and investors must alter their expectations, strategies, and tactics. Hence, it is not surprising that many technical tools and prescriptions are designed to identify turning points in the market (for example, trend line breaks, crossing of moving averages, Dow Theory non-confirmations between industrials and transports, price breakout above a key resistance level, and so on).

A limited number of things can happen to a price movement, or an S-shaped curve of price. These parameters of price and their characteristics, described in Table 3.1, can help you organize your thinking about price movement so that turning-point diagnosis may be accomplished in a systematic and exhaustive manner. Use all parameters together in making a diagnosis and prognosis. Do not rely too heavily on any one factor—it is the overall weight of the evidence that counts most.

The rhythm of the market is composed of alternating waves of buying and selling. Brief interludes of equilibrium between supply and demand (sideways or horizontal markets) frequently mark the turning point between bull and bear waves or between bear and bull waves. The underlying trend of the market is the line of least resistance. Despite rallies or reactions in the contrary decision, assume that the trend will reassert itself.

Long-term trends are the most important. Zigzags in the minor trends will tend to be resolved in the direction of the (underlying) intermediate trend, while zigzags representing buying and selling waves in the intermediate trend will tend to be resolved in the direction of the major trend. The violation of a major bull or bear trend carries much more weight than the violation of minor or intermediate trends.

Trend violations signal that a reversal of trend may be in the offing. A trend violation may first be ascertained by the breaking of a trend line. Bullish potential is recognized when the downtrend line connecting descending tops is violated by the price index moving through it to the upside. Bearish potential is recognized when the uptrend line connecting

TABLE 3.1 Parameters of Price Movement

Parameters	Technical Concepts	Examples of Technical Tools for Diagnosis
Direction	Trend up, down, or sideways.	Dow Theory, trend-lines, channels and moving averages.
Extent	Measurement of the extent of the probable price movement from bottom to top, top to bottom, time elapsed since the last comparable turning point, peak to peak, or trough to trough.	Horizontal and vertical point-and-figure figure chart counts. Vertical price projections and/or retracements using chart patterns, measured moves, or ratios.
Momentum	Momentum or the rate of change at which prices are moving, such as accelerating or decelerating.	Five-week, 13-week, and annual rate-of-change cycles. Overbought and oversold readings on the oscillator of stocks over or under their 10-week moving average.
Form	Cyclic phases or stages of birth, growth, maturity, and decline; the S-shaped curve of the price movement.	The Elliott Wave principle of three upward legs in bull moves and two downward legs in corrective bear moves.

ascending bottoms is penetrated to the downside by the current price. Trend line violations carry more authority (1) the longer the trend line has been in existence, and (2) the more turning points it connects. The stronger these two conditions are, the greater the likelihood that a trend line will act as a point of future support or resistance.

Juncture violations are key indicators of a trend reversal. The failure to make a new high following a period of advancing prices, followed by the downside penetration of the most recent bottom, defines a downside reversal. Similarly, the failure to make a new low after a period of descending prices, followed by the upside penetration of the most recent rally top, defines an upside reversal. Reversal signals that do not follow through (that is, they are soon cancelled by a reversal in the original direction) are identified as *whipsaws*.

Volume analysis can aid in determining the validity and reliability of trend line and juncture penetrations. Given the generalization that volume goes with the trend, especially during bull markets, look for confirmation of a trend violation (reversal) in the expansion of relative volume. Other price indexes also offer confirmation of the trend. The joint penetration of trend lines and/or junctures by the Dow Industrials, Transports, Utilities,

S&P, and NASDAQ carries substantially greater authority than does a single index movement. Furthermore, nonconfirmation of one index by other indexes is often an early warning signal of a possible reversal of trend. Dow Theorists give special credence to joint penetrations of important support or resistance junctures by both the Dow Industrials and the Dow Transports.

The failure of one index to join the other in penetrating an important price high or price low is a nonconfirmation and an early warning indication of a possible reversal in price trend. Also, buying climaxes and selling climaxes are early warning signals of an impending reversal of trend. A climax denotes the termination of a recent wave of intense buying or selling. At the termination, relative volume expands, but the price index does not advance (decline) commensurately, suggesting that opposite bull or bear interests are entering the market in force. Buying climaxes are often associated with *overbought* conditions, while selling climaxes are often associated with *oversold* conditions. These overbought/oversold conditions are invariably followed by a rally or reaction in price, often referred to as a *technical rally* or *technical reaction* (see Figure 3.7).

A climax (a) followed by a technical rally (b) or often a 50% countermove reaction, then by a test of the climax juncture (c), followed by a reversal (d) or continuation of trend (e) is the scenario frequently followed by the market.

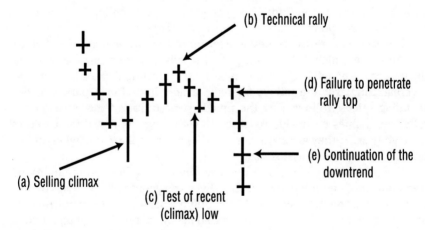

FIGURE 3.7 Market Action and Reaction

Diagnosis and Prognosis From the foregoing parameters, concepts, and tools, together with the diagram of price shown in Figure 3.8, the technical trader could make the diagnosis (prognosis) of an impending turning point from a bull move to a bear move. The trend direction had been up, as evidenced by the upward zigzag of prices. Eventually this price movement starts to roll over (lose momentum). The loss of momentum takes on critical significance when it occurs in the vicinity of the previously projected price target. Finally, if the form reveals an upward zigzag entering the final step of stage III, then the analyst can conclude that the upward trend is coming to an end and that an important down move is probable.

I have often found that the Elliott Wave structure of a market on a smaller time scale is a good clue as to the current health and probable future trend of a market. For example, if a rally occurs during a protracted decline that is composed of five subwaves, it is safe to assume that more rally efforts will be forthcoming.

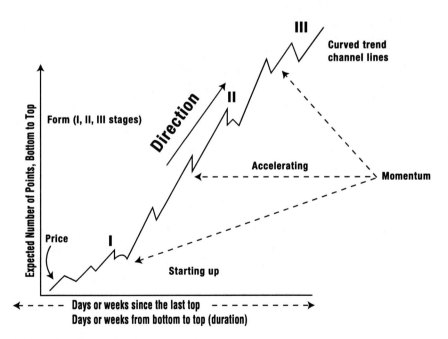

FIGURE 3.8 Idealized Diagram of Price Movement Parameters

Volume

*Is it volume which causes price changes, or do price changes cause
volume—the hen or the egg, which came first?*
—*H. M. Gartley*, Profits in the Stock Market
(Miami, FL: Lambert-Gann Publishers, 1935)

The relationship between the S-shaped curve and bell-shaped curve gives
an answer to the question of which comes first by showing that volume is
both cause and effect. The imbalance between supply and demand created by the volume of orders on the sell side or the buy side creates an adjusting response in the price level as the market seeks equilibrium
between the number of shares bought and sold. Volume of trading is in
turn influenced by the price index.

The Dow-Jones Industrials' price index is a widely disseminated and
repeated item of information. A rapidly rising Dow will draw people into
the stock market, causing a swelling of the volume of trading. This mutually reinforcing spiral of expanding volume and rising prices will persist,
or keep up the rising *momentum*, as long as the rally can continue to attract a following of buyers. When the rally is no longer able to attract a following, we can conclude that demand or the reservoir of potential bullish
adopters has become exhausted.

How can we reconcile the apparent contradiction between what was
said earlier about the cross-influence of price and volume and the assertion that cause and effect runs from volume to price? We can turn to the
adoption/diffusion model for a clue to overcoming this dilemma. Note that
the bell-shaped curve of adoption, which we measure by volume, reaches
its pinnacle before the S-shaped curve of price (volume) hits its peak. So
indeed the model shows that volume does precede or lead price in time.
This lead-lag relationship is tied up with the notion of momentum.

*To use a homely analogy, volume is to the price movement of stocks
as gasoline is to the automobile. If you step on the accelerator of
your car, giving the motor more gas, the car will start to travel
faster. The more gas you feed it, the greater will be its momentum.
Now, when your car has acquired considerable momentum, if you
throw the clutch out and coast, your car will travel a considerable
distance on the acquired momentum.*
—*The Stock Market Institute*[2]

Thus, if we liken volume to gasoline and price to the automobile, the
momentum concept explains how and why volume precedes price. In the

stock market, history shows that volume tends to precede price in the clear majority of cases. The market has thus handed us a very powerful tool for diagnosing, even anticipating, turning points in the stock market. Essentially, volume should hit a peak jointly with price, react, and then price moves onward to a higher high unconfirmed by volume. As long as price and volume are jointly making new highs, there is plenty of gas, push, or momentum to keep prices rising. Hence, we should wait patiently until prices rise to a higher high on less volume before concluding that a downward reversal in trend is imminent. There are exceptions to volume preceding price, to be sure, such as when price and volume terminate together in a huge blow-off climax.

One analytical approach to volume indicators is to classify them in a hierarchy from the grossest level to the more refined: from total volume, to upside versus downside volume, to refinements such as on-balance volume.

Volume/Price Relationships   Volume is the number of shares traded in a given period of time, such as an hour, a day, a week, and so on. Reported volume figures represent an equation between the number of shares bought and the number of shares sold—sell orders must always match buy orders. If there is an imbalance of demand to buy shares over sell orders at any time, equilibrium is restored by an advance in price to a level where enough sellers are attracted to restore the equilibrium. If there is an imbalance of sell orders (supply) over buy orders (demand) at any time, prices decline to a level where enough buyers are attracted to equal the number of shares for sale.

Price trends, up or down, tend to feed upon themselves, as rising prices attract more buyers and falling prices attract more sellers. In other words, buying waves and selling waves tend to snowball or follow a bandwagon effect. The bandwagon effect occurs because the stock market is a manifestation of mass/crowd psychology in action. Crowd behavior snowballs on account of contagion, imitation, suggestion, convergence, and a strong leader-followers relationship.

A bandwagon of crowd behavior tends to form a bell-shaped curve. A move starts out with a few innovative buyers or sellers, who are followed by a bulge of other buyers or sellers who join the move, after which activity tapers off as laggards are recruited from a shrinking number of remaining potential buyers or sellers. In broad, general terms, the model of mass/crowd psychology in action is a bell-shaped curve of volume. The start of a move is represented by the left-hand tail of the curve, the bulge of activity occurs around the middle, while the termination of the move occurs on lighter relative volume represented by the right-hand tail of the curve.

The major price/volume relationships are observable by integrating the bell-shaped curve of volume with the S-shaped curve of price, at three points: (1) At the birth of the markup or markdown phases, the volume expansion confirms the price movement; (2) the bell-shaped curve shows that the volume peak leads the price peak on the S-shaped curve; (3) volume diverges from price as price crowns over or rounds under as the move comes to an end. In sum, the bell-shaped curve reveals three useful generalizations regarding volume and price movement:

1. Increasing volume with increasing price spread on the upside means higher prices to follow.
2. Increasing volume with decreasing price spread indicates a price reversal is imminent.
3. Initial down thrust with wide price spread and heavy volume indicates lower prices to come.

Heavy volume with price not giving further ground following a protracted decline indicates that the decline is nearly complete—a selling climax has been reached; accumulation is probably commencing. Climactic volume following a long up move indicates that the termination of the up move is nearing, particularly if the heavy volume is not accompanied by further price progress; thus, the distribution phase is starting. A breakout from a trading range in either direction when accompanied by heavy volume and wide price spread indicates the validity of the breakout. Further movement is likely to take place in the direction of the breakout: markup or markdown confirmed.

Generally, large relative volume accompanies the terminus of a move. Small price advance on relatively large volume is evidence that smart money is moving counter to the trend—their sell orders or buy orders are overwhelming the less knowledgeable public participants. Turns occur when there is considerable volume effort and comparatively little price result. Alternatively, when small volume occurs at the bottom (top) of a considerable decline (advance), or at the bottom of a reaction or small slip (top of a small rally), it usually indicates a lack of pressure (power)—a drying up of selling pressure or buying power. However, price declines on small volume are frequently bearish. Whereas bear moves terminate in narrow price moves with the accompaniment of low volume and listless trading, bull moves terminate with relatively wide price swings accompanied by high volume and more or less feverish trading activity, although volume may be less at the end than in earlier stages of the bull market. It is the change from dullness to activity, or the reverse, that is important—perhaps more important than the absolute level of volume.

Some students of the stock market argue that volume plays a much more important role than simply corroborating a price movement. They contend volume takes precedent over price because it leads price. Key exponents of this philosophy are followers of the on-balance volume (OBV) system for predicting prices. This philosophy contends that volume acts as a momentum variable which carries over to subsequent price movement. Recall the earlier analogy that volume is to the price movement of stocks as gasoline is to the automobile. Remember that an increase or a decrease in volume is significant. Gradual or sudden increases or shrinkages in volume will assist you in detecting turning points, determining the trend, timing when to open or close a trade and when to change your stops, and identifying when a move may be culminating or about to culminate. Whereas price deals with the "what" of the stock market, volume deals with the "how." How are prices moving? Are they moving upward on comparatively light volume? Are they going downward on heavy volume? Are they going nowhere on massive volume?

Remember that changes in the market commence internally and work outward; internal volume behavior precedes external price behavior. In turn, volume and price precede external fundamentals and news. In my own trading I have found this on-balance volume information to be of value for obtaining a solid indication of the present position and probable future trend of a market.

Time

The ancient Romans visualized time with the aid of a series of stones stretched out to denote future dates. The focus of emphasis, indicated by large size, was devoted to those significant dates in the future toward which the Romans felt they were moving, like the Ides of March. When current time was far away from a significant date, the present day was of little import and so deserved nothing more than a small stone (see Figure 3.9). In our culture, we seem to invert what the Romans did; we emphasize the present, while continually shrinking the importance of dates that are farther and farther away in the future. This habit is so ingrained that our method of telling time seems natural, logical, and incontrovertible. But when it comes to Wall Street, I think we might be wise to do as the Romans did!

Speculation is the art of profitably discounting the future. What are significant in the future are those infrequent dates that commemorate top or bottom turning points, both large and small. Our analysis of and orientation to current data should be guided by those future reference points. With a proper focus on future junctures we can more readily

Series of Stepping-Stones

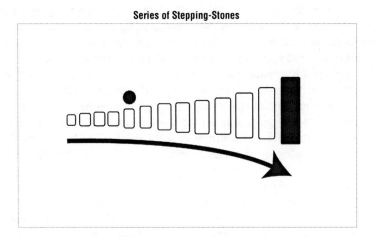

FIGURE 3.9   Telling Time the Roman Way

quell two of the great pitfalls of the Wall Street trader: impatience and lack of perspective.

Having some idea of where the future turning points might occur becomes an essential prerequisite to making this shift in our orientation to the future. Techniques purported to be valid and reliable for foretelling the future, though desirable, are questionable.

The three complementary tools for attempting to date future turning points are *cycles, duration,* and *seasonality.* Cyclic analysis promises the most in terms of comprehensiveness, and cycles give reasonable reliability and validity. One can argue that duration is really no more than a subset of cyclic analysis. However, I think predictive accuracy and our confidence in our predictions are heightened through separate attention to the expected duration of an advance or decline. Finally, there is the very impressive pattern of seasonal strength and weakness over a year's time. Seasonality says that days or weeks of strength or weakness in market price tend to repeat year-in and year-out at much better than chance odds. For seasonal signs we need go no further than Yale Hirsch's outstanding *Stock Trader's Almanac* (New York: Wiley, 2006).

Time is of the essence in stock market analysis. Purchases should be made when prices are low, in anticipation that at a later date sales will be made when prices are higher, and vice versa. Market fluctuations take place over time. That is why the control of market risk is called *market timing.* Time can be static or dynamic.

Static Time   Static time is the interval of (relatively) fixed periodicity that has been discovered by filtering through historical price data. Some key periods discovered are the four-year cycle, the 18-month cycle, and the quarterly or 12-week cycle. Fixed-period time cycles are more reliable when measured from bottom-to-bottom; top-to-top cycles have greater variability. When measuring a fixed time cycle, the analyst should take into account bottom-to-top time and top-to-bottom time as well as bottom-to-bottom or top-to-top time intervals. These measures are usually means and their deviations, but medians and modes are acceptable, too.

A *moving average* is an important time-cycle filtering technique. A moving average suppresses (filters out) all fluctuations that are equal to or shorter in duration than the moving average time span. Since moving averages contain only waves longer than the time span of the moving average itself, by judicious selection of two moving averages, and subtraction of one from the other, we can end up with a single isolated wave. This wave can then be studied in detail with neither longer nor shorter waves interfering with the clarity. The direction of the wave longer than the one under study sets the trend. When the trend is up, cycle peaks come late; when the trend is down, cycle peaks come early. Moving averages should be plotted back one-half their time span from the most recent day's data.

For example, the average, midpoint, or half span of a 200-day moving average of the Down Jones Industrials is 100 days. Hence, the last recorded point of a 200-day moving average should be placed back 100 days on the chart! Moving averages lag the market; their placement in current time on most stock charts is theoretically wrong. Moving averages on stock charts are future trend projections; they must be interpreted in a way similar to that of simple trend lines.

Dynamic Time   Typical primary market cycles last 50 months, plus or minus 6 months, bottom to bottom. They are ideally composed of three intermediate cycles. Typical intermediate market cycles last 17 months, plus or minus 3 months. They are ideally composed of six subintermediate, or twelve-week cycles. The typical subintermediate market cycle lasts 12 weeks, plus or minus 3 weeks. In turn, the intermediate cycle is composed of four three-week cycles, but these are extremely volatile. Since cycles are expected to repeat within the time frames of past precedent, the technical trader can venture predictions of when future tops and future bottoms should occur.

Prediction of future turning point dates is a static time manipulation. It is a fixed future prediction based on historical repetitions. Actual cycles can vary by their rate of change. A quickly rising market can reach its forecast destination in a shorter time span than a slowly rising market. This is the dynamic dimension of time cycles. The Elliott Wave principle can help analyze the dynamic dimension of time.

The Life Cycle   There is a correspondence between static form and the dynamic waves of time that helps describe the structure of time waves in the stock market, just as we describe the structure of time in a number of physical and biological sciences. The form or shape of the stock market is life cycle growth. A life cycle is divisible into stages of birth, growth, maturity, decline, and death. Life cycles may reflect any of several growth functions, including exponential, logistic, and logarithmic growth curves. The Elliott Wave principle rests upon the Fibonacci mathematical series of dynamic growth and decay. The Fibonacci series is the basis for three ascending and two descending legs in market cycles described by the Elliott Wave principle. It is also the basis for logarithmic growth curves. The stock market analyst can track the unfolding of a dynamic time-price cycle by (1) counting the Elliott Waves and (2) keeping in mind the perspective of (logarithmic) growth curves. Elliott Waves are arranged in a time hierarchy, ranging from hourly Dow Jones counts to waves spanning decades.

Theoretically, all waves unfold according to the same principle and thus are interpretable in a parallel fashion. The Elliott Wave principle of dynamic cycle analysis provides a goodness-of-fit test for static price-time projections. If the market has had three legs up into a time frame where you had expected an intermediate top, you may conclude that you have a validation of your original prediction. The subdivided Elliott Waves can help pinpoint where, within a static time frame projection, the actual turning point may occur. The static frame of reference likewise aids in the interpretation of the Elliott Wave.

Sentiment

Sentiment is one of the most intriguing areas of technical analysis. Presumably, sentiment (desire, fear, crowd behavior, emotion, etc.) can tell us why the stock market is behaving as it is today and, more importantly, how it will behave tomorrow. This rich, fascinating field of study is also very elusive, treacherous, and contradictory.

While sentiment data may help the technical trader separate a continuation pattern of price from a reversal pattern, it may also mislead him because sentiment is such an elastic indicator. What is normal sentiment behavior under one set of circumstances may quickly undergo a metamorphosis into something fantastic and seemingly irrational. For a classic example of extreme crowd behavior in a speculative bull market, see the section on tulipomania in Charles Mackay's book *Extraordinary Popular Delusions and the Madness of Crowds*. Why and how such a phenomenon as tulipomania develops can be attributed to the social psychology of crowd behavior. For analysis of crowd behavior, students of technical analysis have long looked to *The Crowd* by Gustave Le Bon. Writing in 1896, Le Bon observed that as crowds are ultimately composed of individuals, and individuals are driven by their sentiments, crowds are driven by sentiment. Many times you will hear reference to fear, greed, hope, reactions to news (stimuli), and expectation as factors that drive or limit investor behavior.

Ideas from psychology and the social sciences can help the trader analyze sentiment in the stock market. Here again we meet our old companion, the model of adoption/diffusion. Finally, we arrive at one of the most valuable, most widely used, and most widely abused areas of market analysis, popularized by Humphrey B. Neill: contrary opinion.

Elements of Sentiment Analysis Stock market analysis may be conveniently divided into trend analysis and sentiment analysis. The subjects of trend analysis are price, volume, time, and their interactions. When combined, these trend components adhere to the successive life cycle stages of accumulation, markup, distribution, and decline. This cycle repeats in the same manner as a fashion cycle. This life cycle curve is the S-shaped cumulative curve for adopter distribution, depicted in Figure 3.1.

In stock market analysis, sentiment refers to expectations, attitudes, and opinions on the one hand and adoptive behavior on the other hand. For example, an individual goes through a series of mental steps in reaching a decision to buy or sell. This is an individual adoption process of awareness, interest, belief, liking, and action. The individual adoption process is influenced by the person's prior attitude and behavior; a perpetual bear who is always shorting the market will have a different predilection than a perpetual bull who is always long the market.

The communication of relevant stock market information can be analyzed with the aid of a communications model (see Figure 3.10). The flow of communication may be either one-step or two-step. One-step communication goes directly from the mass media to the individual receiver. In two-step communication, mass data are first encoded by an opinion leader who then sends the messages to the individual receiver. Our stock market equivalents of the opinion leaders are the advisory services, news commentators, and institutional analysts.

Public optimism or pessimism is heavily influenced by feedback from the market tape—the Dow Industrials. The Dow Industrial Average is closely watched and widely disseminated. If it is in a rising trend, people accept that as evidence, an omen, of a rosy future. Commentators' interpretations and favorable prognostications further stimulate positive public opinion, and ultimately the positive price trend will attract all categories of buyers.

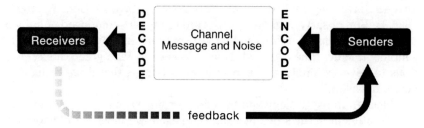

FIGURE 3.10 Communications Model

Persons of similar background and inclinations who are exposed to the same information, including the tape, are liable to converge on buying or selling actions at the same time. Buying and/or selling may be viewed as adoption (of an innovation). Stock market participants can be grouped into adopter categories according to the time at which they adopt (see Figure 3.2).

Market analysts seek to identify who makes up the adopter categories and at what levels their buying or selling behavior becomes significant. Since innovators and laggards are at the extremes, analysts tend to emphasize the behavior of one group or the other. Innovators are important because they account for initial levels of accumulation or distribution and their behavior influences later adopters. In the stock market, the innovators are the insiders, historically typified by NYSE specialists, corporate insiders, and major investment organizations.

Traditionally, the NYSE specialists were unusually significant innovators, due to their officially sanctioned roles of agent, trader, and investor, replete with privileged information in their book and the unique power of the short-sale. A specialist had the motives of a merchandiser; he accumulated an inventory of stock at bargain prices when the news was bad and other investors were pessimistic, then marked up the price, distributing his inventory when the news was good and other investors were optimistic. When the specialist had a negative inventory (net short position), he was prepared to handle a markdown in stock prices.

Bull markets and bear markets begin with imbalance between insider and institutional stock and cash positions. Advisory services taken collectively are an excellent focal point for the formation of contrary opinion. Historically, they are extremely bullish just before market declines; then they become extremely bearish just before a market advances. The speculative public is also a good focal point for the formation of contrary opinion. When the ratio of public short sales is high and the put/call ratio is high, the trader should be bullish. Conversely, when these ratios are low, the trader should be bearish. Historically, the odd-lot short seller has been a fine focal point for contrary opinion. He does most of his shorting at market lows. In addition, the mass media moves in concert with the crowd: News is positive and bullish at the price tops, while negative and bearish at price bottoms.

During recent years the specialist and the market maker roles have become diffused outward beyond the stock exchange floors. For example, major institutional trading firms such as Goldman Sachs now play a key role in making large markets for clients. The growth of the derivatives market has helped to neutralize the risk exposure stemming from the purchase and short-selling of large blocks of common stock.

Large institutions have come to dominate the stock market; nevertheless, the all-important last phases of market swings, intermediate and major, reveal the arrival of the less sophisticated public speculators. The participation of the odd-lot public becomes reflected in imbalances in traditional sentiment indicators, such as the ratio of put buying to call buying.

The trader-analyst is encouraged to familiarize himself with the advisory services that provide sentiment information. Some useful sources of sentiment data are the American Association of Individual Investors (http://www.aaii.com), Consensus, Inc. (http://www.consensus-inc.com), and Market Vane (http://www.marketvane.net). In addition, useful sentiment data are published each week in *Barron's* magazine.

To resist the pull of the crowd, the trader-analyst must cultivate contrary opinion. In general, the trader himself must get in step with the smart money, Wyckoff's Composite Man.

Pattern Recognition and Discretionary Trading

CHAPTER 4

Wyckoff:
The Man,
the Method,
the Mystique

Anyone who buys or sells a stock, a bond, or a commodity for profit is speculating if he employs intelligent foresight. If he does not, he is gambling.
—Richard D. Wyckoff

The October 2002 issue of *Stocks and Commodities* magazine featured an article in which staff writer David Penn went on "a not-so-random walk through the history of charting the markets." This walk through history led Penn to identify five historic figures as "titans of technical analysis." He included Charles Henry Dow, Ralph Nelson Elliott, William Delbert Gann, Arthur A. Merrill, and Richard D. Wyckoff. About Wyckoff he wrote, "Many of Wyckoff's basic tenets have become *de facto* standards of technical analysis: The concepts of accumulation/distribution and the supremacy of price and volume in determining stock price movement are examples."

Richard Wyckoff became a celebrity name on Wall Street during the early decades of the twentieth century, an epoch many observers believe was truly a golden age for tape readers, chartists, and speculators. Wyckoff earned a fortune from his *Magazine of Wall Street*, along with other publications and advisory services. The accuracy and power of his analysis and predictions gained him a titan-like status in the eyes of his 200,000 subscribers—an incredibly large following even by today's standards.

After retiring from his advisory services in 1928 due to failing health, Wyckoff felt compelled to make the insights he had gathered during his 40 years of experiences on Wall Street available to the serious public who were willing to study and learn. Around 1930 Wyckoff announced that he wanted to reveal the truth about what it took to gain or lose on Wall Street. He knew that industry reports, earnings, and the like were not the secrets to success many believed them to be; instead, he wished to offer a set of principles and procedures, "the real rules of the game." These rules became known as the Wyckoff method of technical analysis and stock speculation.

HISTORY LESSON: WYCKOFF, THE MAN

Wyckoff started as a stockbroker's runner at the age of 15, became a brokerage firm auditor a few years later, and at age 25 opened his own brokerage firm. The method he developed of technical analysis and speculation emerged from the keen powers of observation and communication skills of an unusually gifted man who spent a long and varied career on Wall Street during the golden era when much of the basis of technical analysis was first formulated. From his autobiography, *Wall Street Ventures and Adventures Through Forty Years*, we get a glimpse of Wyckoff's involvement on Wall Street, and we gather an appreciation of his powers of observation as he collected the "real rules of the game." The following sample is something he wrote about inside information, circa 1901:

> *In those days I used to go to great lengths to find out what important people were doing. Not having many good connections, but making the most of those I had, I could have surprised certain large operators by producing memoranda of what they had done in the market during the day. For example Charles M. Schwab was a tremendous buyer of Pennsylvania Railroad stock through a house on one of the lower floors of the Empire Building. I used to get a daily report of the number of shares he bought on balance and my clients were long on Pennsylvania. I watched Schwab buy it up to the 160s and then suddenly stop. I've never known whether this was a stock market move on behalf of Mr. Carnegie or whether Mr. Schwab was employed by other interests to do the buying and see whether control could thus be obtained.*[1]

From his many observations of the behind-the-scenes manipulations by the large operators, Wyckoff discovered time and again on the tape and from the charts that the best indicator of the future price of a security was the relationship between supply and demand. In 1910 under the pen name of "Rollo Tape" he wrote *Studies in Tape Reading* (Fraser, 1995; Cosimo,

2005). In this now classic book about how to read the market and how to conduct speculative operations, Wyckoff covered such basics as stop orders, volume indications, dull markets and their opportunities, and numerous other market techniques that would one day be incorporated into his Wyckoff method, which first appeared around 1931.

Wyckoff placed prime importance on the analyst's ability to judge the relative power of buying and selling waves and thus divine the intent of the dominant forces behind a market move. In essence, this pattern recognition approach predated what Daniel Pink labeled the "information age," and the talents Wyckoff deemed important for effective stock market diagnosis and prognosis foreshadowed what Pink asserts will become the dominant mind-set in the twenty-first century, the "conceptual age." Wyckoff, the man, was at once quintessentially classic and utterly modern.

WYCKOFF, THE METHOD

In the years following 1930, Wyckoff and his associates formulated a valuable set of laws, tests, and schematics (see Chapter 6). The basic elements of charting, particularly bar charts and point-and-figure charts, used in the Wyckoff method appear in Chapter 5.

The Wyckoff method is a five-step method of market analysis. This method is at the heart of Part Two of this book, and we delve further into the specific elements of this approach in Chapter 7. Meanwhile, here is a summary of the five steps of the Wyckoff method:

1. *Determine the present position and probable future trend of the market.* Then decide how you are going to play the game. Use bar charts and point-and-figure charts of market index.

2. *Select stocks in harmony with the trend. If you are playing the game long, select stocks which you believe are stronger than the market.* If you are not sure about an individual issue, drop it. Use bar charts of individual stocks.

3. *Select stocks with cause that equals or exceeds minimum objective.* Choose stocks that are under accumulation or reaccumulation. Use point-and-figure charts of individual stocks.

4. *Determine the stocks' readiness to move.* Rank stocks in order of your preference. Use bar charts and point-and-figure charts of individual stocks; apply the nine tests for buying or selling outlined in Chapters 6 and 7.

5. *Time your commitment with a turn in the stock market index.* Put your stop-loss in place and relax. Then follow through, until you close out the market position. Use bar charts.

The Wyckoff method has stood the test of time. Over 100 years of continuous development and usage have proven the value of the Wyckoff method for use with stocks, bonds, currencies, and commodities around the globe. This accomplishment should come as no surprise because, as explained in the previous section, the Wyckoff method reveals the "real rules of the game."

Before you can master the Wyckoff method, you must firmly embrace the fact that it is a judgmental method. To gain skill in making judgments, the trader needs experience in a variety of different case situations steered by accurate and intelligent guidelines. Remember, the market is more organic than mechanistic, and the artistry applied by the technical trader is important. Nonetheless, this five-step procedure can help the technical trader orient his thinking and organize his learning.

WYCKOFF, THE MYSTIQUE

They say that an individual's mystique cannot be defined. However, in an effort to understand this important element of Mr. Wyckoff, I consulted the *Random House Dictionary* for some insight. I have included the definitions I found below, together with a couple of my conclusions, which appear in brackets.

> **Mystique**—(1) a framework of directions, ideas, beliefs, or the like, constructed around a person or object with enhanced value or profound meaning: The mystique of Poe [or the mystique of Wyckoff]; (2) an aura of mystery or mystical power surrounding a particular occupation or pursuit: the mystique of nuclear sciences [or the mystique of technical trading according to the Wyckoff Method].

The mystique of Wyckoff is wrapped up with (1) his celebrity status as revealed earlier by Penn, who declared Wyckoff a titan of technical analysis; (2) the Wyckoff method's codification of the best practices used by the old-time trader-technicians, many examples of which are found in the famous book by Edwin Lefèvre, *Reminiscences of a Stock Operator*; and by (3) the Wyckoff concept of the Composite Man, which we take up presently.

WYCKOFF'S COMPOSITE MAN

The Wyckoff concept of the Composite Man envisions a trader as an almost mythical and sometimes mysterious super trader. As Wyckoff and his disciples have said:

> *In studying, understanding, and interpreting market action, we consider all market action as a manufactured operation in which the buying and/or selling is sufficiently centered and coming from interests better informed than the generally untrained individual investor/speculator. The many large interests which do have an effect on the market place (trust companies, banks, mutual funds, investment trusts, investment companies, hedge funds, specialists, position brokers, etc.) are best thought of as the Composite Man. This Composite Man causes the market to act and react. Or, what actually happens is the market responds to the ageless, natural law of supply and demand. The Composite Man and the effects of the law of supply and demand are really synonymous. It is the result of the motives, objectives, hopes, and fears of all the buyers and sellers whose actions produce the net effect upon the market.*
>
>
>
> *Other terms which may be thought to be synonymous with the Composite Man would be "the market," "the sponsor," "the operator," or "they." These terms are used interchangeably. . . . The selection of the terms is determined by what is most meaningful to the student. It should be your objective to think of the Composite Man as the primary force in the market place. Thinking of him in this light should enhance your analysis of the action resulting from the dominant groups operating within individual stocks and their total effect within the general market place.*[2]

Wyckoff based the Composite Man, and his own trading philosophy, on his observation and intimate understanding of such famous old-time professionals of the early twentieth century as James R. Keene, Russell Sage, Edward H. Harriman, and Jesse Livermore. Indeed, Edwin Lefèvre's *Reminiscences of a Stock Operator*, which is dedicated to Jesse Livermore, is an excellent model of the Composite Man or composite operator.

Wyckoff implored traders to follow in the footsteps of the Composite Man, to think like him. Wyckoff argued that "all the fluctuations in the market and in all the various stocks should be studied as if they were the result of one man's operations. Let us call him the Composite Man, who, in theory, sits behind the scenes and plays a stock to his advantage."[3] He went on to advise the trader to understand and play the market game as the Composite Man played the game. In fact, he said that it doesn't even matter if the moves were artificial.

In general, the Wyckoff philosophy accepted that:

- The Composite Man carefully plans, executes, and concludes his campaigns.
- The Composite Man creates a "broad market" by advertising his stock on the ticker tape.
- One must study charts with the purpose of judging the behavior of the stock and the motives of those who dominate it.
- One must look for the motives behind the action that a chart portrays. Wyckoff and his associates believed that the market behaves naturally in this very manner. If you learn to understand this market behavior of a so-called Composite Man, you can learn to make judgments, then conclusions, that should have a positive effect in your stock market operations.[4]

To attain the perspective of the Composite Man, we should ask ourselves such basic questions as "What is the motive of the Composite Man?" and "What would I do if I were the Composite Man?" In addition to these two basic queries, we can add such complementary questions as "What is it that the Composite Man is attempting to prepare or carry out or conclude?" and "What is the Composite Man attempting to do to the public and for what purpose?" You will be given an opportunity to create your own questions as you gain understanding through practice with the role of the Composite Man in Chapter 9.

To better interpret the motives and the methods of the Composite Man, students of the Wyckoff method can organize the information seen in market charts with the aid of an analytical model. I have organized the familiar action and test rhythm of Wyckoff seen on the charts, as a two-step analytical model of exchange between the Composite Man and the public. This model (see Figure 4.1) tracks how the Composite Man *initiates* action to attract the public and then *evaluates* the degree of the public's conformity to his initiatives. We assume that the Composite Man is forever attempting to attract a public following to help carry out his campaigns.

The Exchange

The concept of the Composite Man holds that the market is forever an exchange between buyers and sellers. Furthermore, someone always has ownership of a security. Since markets go up and down, one side of every

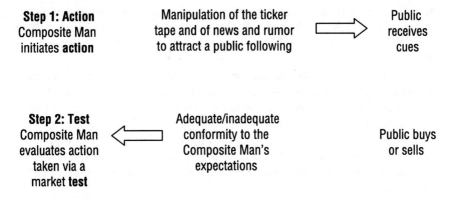

Step 1: Action
Composite Man
initiates **action**

Manipulation of the ticker
tape and of news and rumor
to attract a public following

Public
receives
cues

Step 2: Test
Composite Man
evaluates action
taken via a
market **test**

Adequate/inadequate
conformity to the
Composite Man's
expectations

Public buys
or sells

FIGURE 4.1 Two-Step Exchange between the Composite Man and the Public

transaction must have the prospect of profit, while the other side of the exchange has the prospect of loss (actual or opportunity).

Fundamentally, the manipulations (actions) of the Composite Man are possible because market participants are propelled by their own inner drives of fear or greed in an environment of risk and uncertainty.

Remember that for every buyer there must be a seller. The stock market is also known as a stock *exchange*. An exchange can occur if the public can be motivated to buy on balance or to sell on balance. A price trend will persist as long as the public can be attracted. And the public can be attracted as long as a reservoir of public buyers or sellers exists. Thus, a trend will persist until the exhaustion of public buying or selling.

Elements of the Exchange   We can capture the elements of the exchange phenomenon with the familiar questions of who, what, when, where, and why.

The *who* of the exchange includes the Composite Man as innovator, the floor traders and other professional speculators as the early adopters, the public as the majority, and the laggards. (See Chapter 3.)

The *what* is an exchange of securities for dollars, and vice versa, between the Composite Man (the "smart money") and the less well-informed and less skillful public. *Where?* It can take place on any organized exchange for securities (bonds, stocks, commodities, options, futures, etc.), be it the New York Stock Exchange or an electronically executed market in Europe. *When?* In any time frame that suits the Composite Man's desire and ability to conduct a campaign. In the classic

ideal, this time frame was envisioned as four to six good buying and selling opportunities within a calendar year. But that ideal time constraint
can be relaxed to include intraday, weekly, monthly, or other time
frames.

Another way to answer the "when" question is to view the exchange
phenomenon as the exhaustion of buyers or sellers. The Composite
Man attempts to attract a following on either the bull side or the bear
side of the market. He will continue to attract that following through repeated stimulations until the laggard buyers or sellers have committed
themselves and thus have exhausted the trend. (See the discussion of
Edwin Lefèvre's *Reminiscences of a Stock Operator* at the end of this
chapter.)

How? The Composite Man carries out his campaigns through the manipulation of the ticker tape and the spreading of news. For example, to
panic the public into selling its securities, the Composite Man conducts
his campaign on the bear side by pressing prices downward and spreading
bearish news. In short, the Composite Man sets out to exploit the emotions of greed and fear through market action and the news. Thus, he will
initiate an action and then later test to see if the action he initiated triggers the moves by the public that he desires. If he is successful in attracting a public following, then he can proceed with his bull (or bear)
campaign to accumulate and mark up prices, or to distribute and mark
down prices. If he fails to attract a following, he may be forced to reverse
sides or to postpone his actions until the necessary public behavior sets
up another opportunity.

Why? The Composite Man conducts market campaigns on the bull
side and the bear side for his own profit, and he fulfills these campaigns by
attracting a public following.

Illustrative Examples of the Composite Man's Motives and Methods

The two-step analytic model of exchange between the Composite Man
and the public becomes more meaningful when concrete people and
their trades are used to flesh out the model's analytical abstractions. It
has been my experience that the following vignettes, taken from the
same era and from the same people studied by Wyckoff, add greatly to
the trader's feelings of competence and confidence in handling the
Wyckoff method. Furthermore, these episodes are excellent background
reading for the trader who wants to gain the full benefit from the Wyckoff laws, tests, and schematizations presented in Chapters 6 and 7. All of
the studies below can be found in Edwin Lefèvre's *Reminiscences of a*

Stock Operator (New York: John Wiley & Sons, 1994). I recommend you look them up.

- Case Study 1: James R. Keene and the Distribution of the United States Steel Corporation's Common Stock or How a Composite Operator Attracts a Public Following (pages 240–250).
- Case Study 2: The Composite Operator Buying or Selling On-Balance While Manipulating the Public with the "Ticker Tape" and with "The News" (pages 246–258).
- Case Study 3: "Old Turkey" Sits with His Position or How a Smart Money Operator Employs Mental Discipline (pages 65–71).

Episodes in the Composite Man's Operations during a Trading Range

In my opinion, Richard D. Wyckoff deserves to be known as the master of the trading range. The Wyckoff method takes distinct advantage of the trading range for diagnosing superior entry positions and for prognosticating the probable extent of the future price trend. Once again, I consulted the Wiley edition of *Reminiscences of a Stock Operator* for ministories that can help the trader/analyst orient his thinking about trading ranges and give him insight into how Wyckoff organized his own thinking about trading ranges. These episodes add valuable flesh to the skeletal schematics of accumulation and distribution presented in Chapters 6 and 7.

Remember, the following phases refer to the phases of the Wyckoff Schematic of Accumulation or Distribution, while the page numbers point toward the corresponding passages in Lefèvre's *Reminiscences of a Stock Operator*.

- Phase (A) of a Trading Range, "Stopping the Trend" (pages 112–118).
- Phase (B), "Building the Cause" (pages 121–124).
- Phase (C), "Testing" (pages 85–89).
- Phase (D), "Defining the Trend" (pages 121–124 and 262–263).

CHAPTER 5

The Basic Elements of Charting for the Wyckoff Method

T he purpose of this chapter is to provide the trader-technician with a set of tools for conducting technical market analysis the Wyckoff way.

TRENDS AND TYPES OF CHARTS

The basic tools of the Wyckoff practitioner are the bar chart and the point-and-figure chart. Historically, students of the Wyckoff method have referred to these two types of charts as the *vertical line chart* and the *figure chart*. In addition, students of the Wyckoff method use a third type of chart, the *line chart*.

This chapter explores the construction, value and application of these different charts as they are used in the Wyckoff method. Throughout this chapter I incorporate a wide variety of real-life examples.

In addition to being introduced to the basic bar and point-and-figure charts, the trader-analyst will see how daily and weekly charts form into trends, and how trend-lines and trend channels can help the trader visualize trend continuation and trend reversal. The chapter also investigates the importance of price spread and volume, support and resistance, divergence, and Wyckoff's unique construction and use of point-and-figure charts.

The Bar Chart

The bar chart's graphic representation of price and volume on vertical bars, one above the other, makes it the most comprehensive tool available to the Wyckoff-oriented trader-analyst. The bar chart appears frequently in the *Wall Street Journal* and *Investor's Business Daily* and is used widely in software programs and technical analysis publications.

Figure 5.1 shows a vertical line or bar chart with the high, the low, and the closing price on the vertical axis, and the total volume appearing as a separate bar immediately below the price bar. Time (in dates) appears along the horizontal axis at the bottom of the chart.

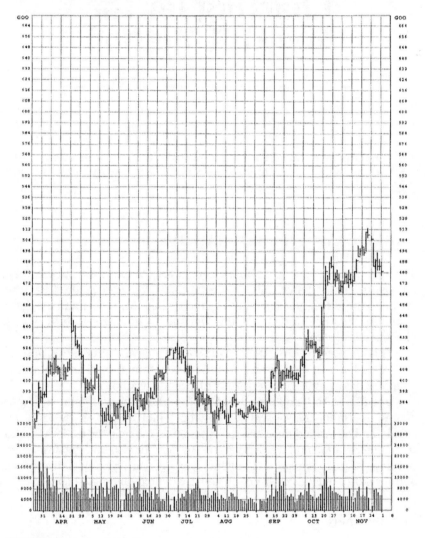

FIGURE 5.1   Vertical Line or Bar Chart
Source: SMI.

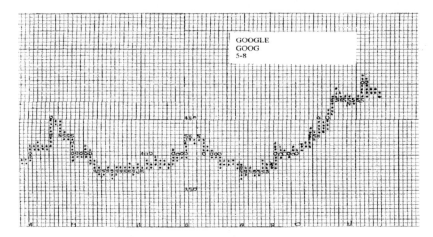

FIGURE 5.2   Point-and-Figure Chart
Source: SMI.

The Point-and-Figure Chart

Figure 5.2 shows a figure chart, or point-and-figure chart. Precise procedures must be followed to properly construct this type of chart according to the Wyckoff method. The figure chart is very useful, though considerably less popular than the vertical line or bar chart.

WYCKOFF MARKET CYCLE

Figure 5.3 shows two idealized representations of a stock or market movement over the four phases of accumulation, markup, distribution, and markdown. The upper diagram reveals that the action of a stock or the market fluctuates around a broad primary growth trend, in this case a primary bull market trend.

The lower graph is an artificial line chart that traces out the broad configuration of price movement within trends and trading ranges. For the analysis of actual trends, trading range, and turning points, the trader-analyst can construct charts or obtain charts from any of the numerous data feeds available, such as Commodity Quote Graphics (www.cqg.com), StockCharts.com, and Worden Brothers (www.worden.com).

The movements from one phase in an uptrend in a market cycle to the

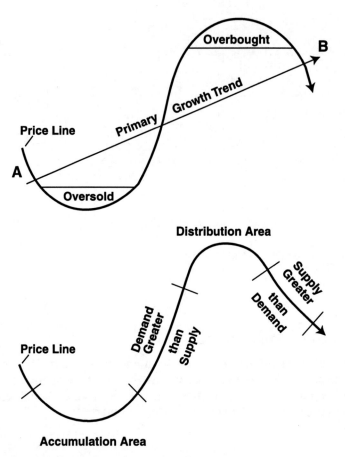

FIGURE 5.3 Idealized Four Phases of a Market Cycle
Source: SMI.

next phase of the market cycle can be likened to connecting the dots from point A to point B in Figure 5.4. Likewise, connecting A to C reflects a sideways movement and connecting the dots from A to D a downtrend. These connections might be made by drawing a simple straight line from A to B, A to C, or A to D. Alternatively, these connections might be made by drawing a more elaborate zigzagging line, a bar chart, or other styles of charts.

Figure 5.5 shows that a more elaborate bar chart could connect the

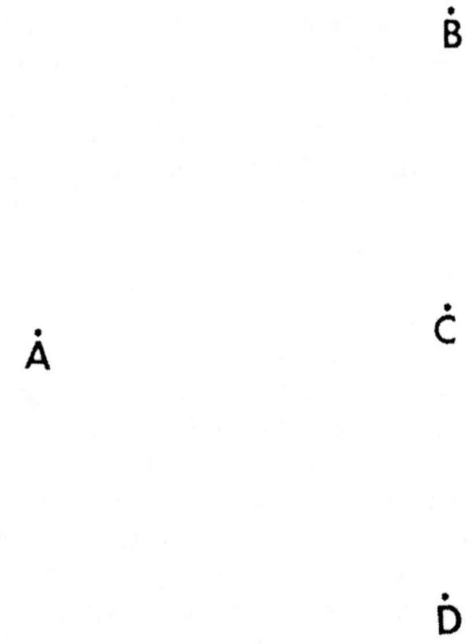

Ḃ

Ȧ   Ċ

Ḋ

FIGURE 5.4 Connect the Dots
Source: SMI.

FIGURE 5.5 Intraday Bar Chart
Source: Copyright 2006 Yahoo! Inc.

dots at points A and B. This upward sloping zigzag line defines an uptrending, bull market channel. As you can see, this charting method is equally applicable to long- and short-term time periods.

An even more elaborate line chart for connecting the dots appears in Figure 5.6. The large arrow on the left-hand side of the chart points along an interim uptrend that could have been used to connect points A and B. At a lower degree, a more detailed level, we see that the larger swing is composed of shorter-term upward, downward, and sideways trends. Finally, the larger up arrow in Figure 5.6 defines a swing that could now connect point A to point D in Figure 5.4.

A complex set of swings similar to those in Figure 5.6 is presented in Figure 5.7. The difference is that Figure 5.7 is a daily or daily-basis chart. The solid vertical bar shows the range of price recorded during that day (low to high), and the small crossbar appended to that day's price range indicates the closing price for the day. The price movement from A to B to C on the chart defines an uptrend while the movement C-F-G defines a downtrend. Note that the movement between points D and E denotes a brief upswing within the larger downtrend from C to G on Figure 5.7.

A third type of chart commonly used in the Wyckoff Method is the figure chart or point-and-figure chart. An example of the figure chart is given in Figure 5.8. From the lower left corner of the chart around the 50 level to the upper right corner around the 85 level, price is seen to move upward in zigzag fashion. This figure chart could be used to connect the dots between Points A and B on Figure 5.4.

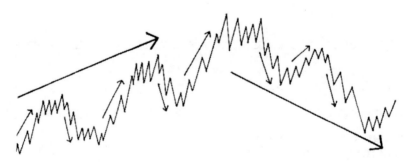

FIGURE 5.6 Elaborate Line Chart
Source: Courtesy of SMI.

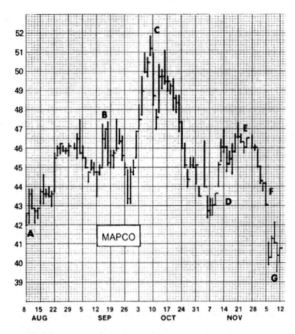

FIGURE 5.7 Bar Chart with Complex Swings
Source: SMI.

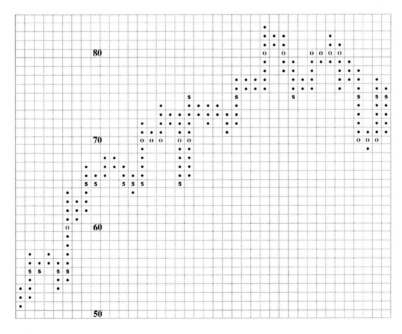

FIGURE 5.8 Figure Chart with Complex Swings
Data Source: SMI.

TREND LINES

We have now observed the use of line, bar, and figure charts in defining trends. We also observed there were transitions from up movement to sideways movement to downtrend and vice versa. The trend-line is a very helpful tool for defining trends and catching turning points.

The trend line is an artificial line that is drawn on the chart by the trader-analyst. In Figure 5.9, the uptrend between points A and H is more precisely delineated by trend lines. An uptrend is defined by the trend line drawn along the lower apexes of the zigzag line, at C and E.

Good judgment was used in the selection of points C and E. By contrast, poor judgment would have been used in the selection of points that would create a trend line that was too steep and would soon be broken, destroying its effectiveness as a definition of the future trend of price action.

Uptrend line C-E defines a nice line of ascending support points. The basic trend line or demand line, C-E, connects the ascending lows that appear in Figure 5.9. The line B-F-H is drawn parallel to the initial line C-E. This second parallel line is referred to as the *overbought* line. Together they define a trend channel.

Figure 5.10 highlights the support line and the overbought condition. In

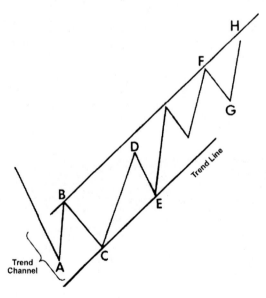

FIGURE 5.9 Trend Lines and Trend Channel
Source: SMI, with adaptations and modifications.

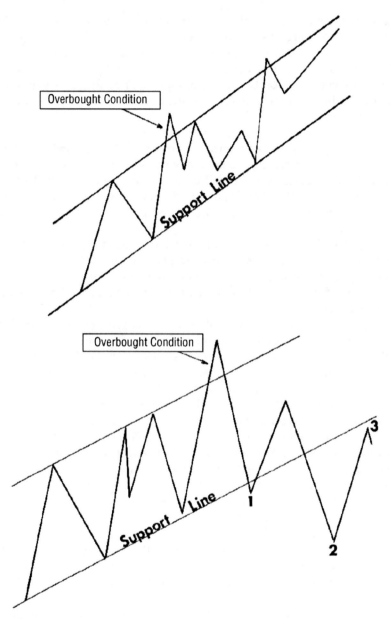

FIGURE 5.10 Support Line, Overbought Conditions, and Trend Reversal
Source: SMI.

particular the trader-analyst should be aware of the overbought conditions identified by the arrows. Students of the Wyckoff method identify these as *throw over* conditions, which are extreme and irrefutably overbought conditions. These are created by overexuberant buying and lead to the corrective action that carries price back to the level where buyers are willing to offer bids for the stock for sale—in other words, the line of support.

Points 1-2-3 in the bottom part of Figure 5.10 show a reversal in the trend from up to down, with lower price peaks. Points 1 and 3 are lower price peaks following the highest peak price to point 2. Another reversal is at point 2, and that reversal is used to define the parallel support line. That support line, once penetrated, reverses its role and becomes a line of resistance along which attempted price rallies will be turned downward.

Figure 5.11 is another example of the parallels that can be observed between line charts and bar charts. An uptrend channel is drawn and an overbought condition appears at points A and C. This is followed by a weakening of the trend at D and then a definitive break of the uptrend on the decline to E.

Figure 5.11 illustrates two additional Wyckoff principles to which the trader-analyst should become sensitive. One is the phenomenon of *action-test*. Point A appeared to have been a high-volume culmination of the sharp upward price movement from the 60 price level to the 76 price level. The analyst-trader would have marked this as a provisional *buying climax* to be proven or disproved on the subsequent *secondary test*. Point C was a successful secondary test. Note that the day-to-day price spread and volume on the rally from the reaction low at 71 back to 76 was considerably narrower and lighter than on the earlier rise from 60 to 78. We can conclude by the action from B to C that the buying power, the demand, had been used up in the violent upward push to point A. This comparison of "waves" to ascertain the waxing or waning of buyer or seller strength is a hallmark of the Wyckoff method.

The second Wyckoff phenomenon that appears in Figure 5.11 is the sideways price action from point A to point F and beyond. Later, after studying Figure 5.14 just ahead, I encourage you to return to Figure 5.11 and conduct an analysis of the sideways movement that formed after point A.

Figures 5.12 and 5.13 are the reciprocals of the previous exhibits that defined uptrending action on line charts. In these figures the supply line, the defining line, connects descending price peaks. The parallel trend line identifies oversold conditions. Throw overs are also present on a downtrend violation.

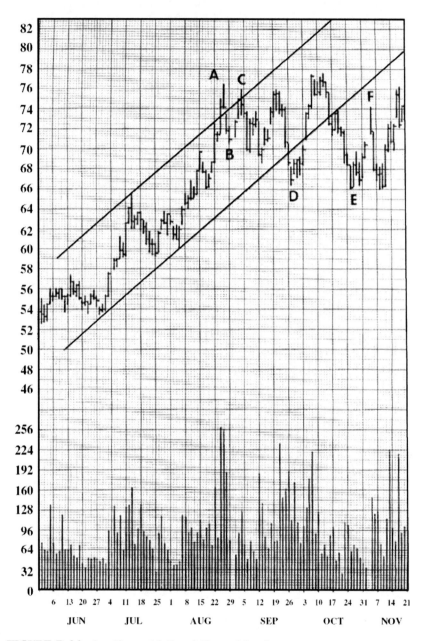

FIGURE 5.11 Bar Chart with Trend Channel Break
Source: SMI.

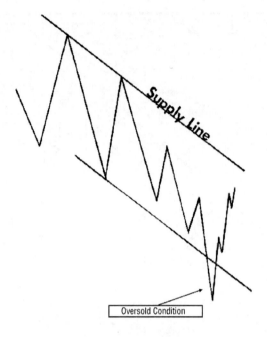

FIGURE 5.12 Supply Line and Oversold Condition
Source: SMI.

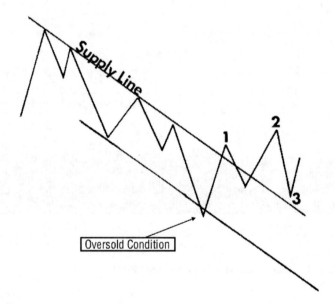

FIGURE 5.13 Supply Line, Oversold Condition, and Trend Reversal
Source: SMI.

Something new, however, appears in Figure 5.14. Here we discover the application of support and resistance to sideways price action. *Resistance* is the price level where repeatedly the sellers overwhelm the buyers and push prices down. On the other hand, *support* is the level at which the buyers enter the market to absorb the offerings, overwhelm the sellers, and push prices upward.

Point A on each of the two charts in Figure 5.14 marks the point where a prevailing trend was stopped and a sideways trend or trading range emerged. In general, the trader-analyst can assume that a trend,

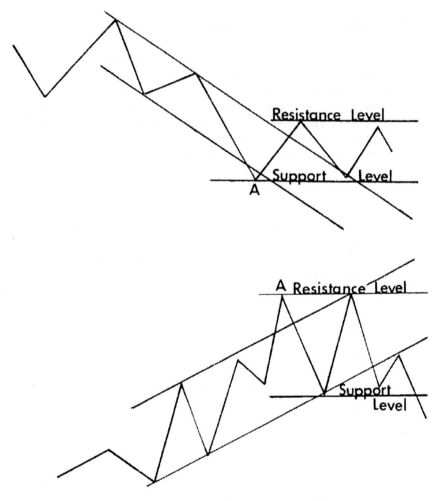

FIGURE 5.14   Resistance and Support Levels
Source: SMI.

once in force, will remain in force until there are definite signs that the trend is ending. Sometimes these endings become reversal points. More often, junctures like point A are the departure points for the emergence of a sideways trading range. And that trading range will then later be followed by either a resumption of the preceding trend or a reversal into a trend in the opposite direction.

The foregoing discussion of trend direction and the use of bar charts reflect the Wyckoff law of supply and demand. If demand exceeds supply, prices will rise; if supply exceeds demand, prices will fall.

POINT-AND-FIGURE CHARTS

I liken the use of figure charts to the stick shift transmission: easy, almost unconscious for the driver who has learned it well, but a grating, jarring, unnerving experience during the learning process. The Appendixes at the end of this chapter outline the unique Wyckoff philosophy and procedures for figure chart construction. The boxed sequence below takes the trader-analyst step-by-step through the creation of a one-point reversal chart, then shows how to convert a one-point figure chart into a three-point reversal chart.

Construction of a one-point reversal point-and-figure chart (box size = 1 point, three periods of data, for example, intraday or daily).

Assume 37 was the last point-and-figure posting. The data for posting to the figure chart are:

Period One:	36-37-35-36-35
Period Two:	34-40-35-36
Period Three:	35-36-35-36-35-40

Period One: The stock declines to 36, then reverses to 37. Then, it fluctuates between 35 and 36. Note that a "5" is placed at the 35 level and a "0" at the 40 level to make it easier to locate price levels.

Figure Chart Posting:

37	•	•	
36	•	•	•
35		5	5

(continues)

Period Two: The stock declines to 34, rallies to 40, and then drops to 35, followed by a rise to 36.
Figure Chart Posting:

40				O		
39				•	•	
38				•	•	
37	•	•		•	•	
36	•	•	•	•	•	•
35		5	5	5	5	
34			•			

Period Three: Price fluctuates between 35 and 36 before rallying to 40.
Figure Chart Posting:

40				O					O
39				•	•				•
38				•	•				•
37	•	•		•	•				•
36	•	•	•	•	•	•	•	•	•
35		5	5	5	5	5	5	5	
34			•						

Note: You will notice that no column has fewer than two entries. This is because the Wyckoff method requires that a column have at least two entries before the analyst moves to the next column to the right.

(continues)

Conversion of a one-point reversal point-and-figure chart into a three-point reversal chart.

Step One: Using straight lines, mark the three-point (or greater) reversals on the one-point reversal chart:

40				Ø					Ø
39				•	•				•
38				•	•				•
37	•		•	•	•				•
36	•	•	•	•	•	•	•	•	•
35		5	5	5	5	5	5	5	
34				•					

Step Two: Post the figures on a three-point reversal chart:

40		O		O
39		•	•	•
38		•	•	•
37	•	•	•	•
36	•	•	•	•
35	5	5	5	
34	•			

The figure chart is often called the *cause and effect* chart. The horizontal formations created on the figure chart measure the cause, or the bullish or bearish potential built up during the trading range. The subsequent trend emerging out of the trading range is the effect. There is a one-to-one correspondence between the cause and the resultant effect. To put it another way, for every effect there is a cause. These figure chart relationships are wrapped up in the Wyckoff law of cause and effect. Hence, figure charts are important and the trader-analyst ought to resolve to master the figure chart and its application.

Another Wyckoff law is the law of effort versus result. This law interprets the harmony or disharmony between price (the result) and volume (the effort). When the two indicators are out-of-gear with each other, the trader-analyst should be on alert for a potential reversal of trend direction.

Figure 5.15 illustrates an inharmonious relationship between volume and price. The Optimism/Pessimism (OP) Index is a Wyckoff/SMI generated index that is approximately equivalent to a chart of on-balance volume or an accumulation/distribution indicator. Figure 5.15 shows a case where considerable downside volume effort during June and July did not result in a commensurate degree of downside price weakness. This divergent action would put the trader-analyst on the alert for a possible (probable) price trend reversal to the upside. An upside reversal in the Wyckoff wave price index occurred during August and September 2006.

Figures 5.16 a and b demonstrate a procedure that is central to the Wyckoff method: the coordination of bar charts and figure charts. In general, the procedure is to first identify the completion of a pattern of horizontal accumulation or distribution on the bar chart. This first step is facilitated by the identification of an "action and test." The action is shown as the breakout above the recent trading range at $77 around August 15; the test is shown by the pullback to the breakout point at $72. This pullback ending point at $72 is referred to by Wyckoff as the *last point of support* (LPS). The LPS is the point of departure for measuring the cause on the figure chart as well as for entering a position on the long side of the market.

In the Merrill Lynch bar chart (Figure 5.16a), the trading range that occurs between $65 and $72 following the price advance or upward trend from $54 to $81 is a zone of *reaccumulation* because the breakout and the test proved that the uptrend was being resumed. The count along the $72 line in the figure chart (5.16b) generated an upside price projection (potential effect) of 27 points (one-point reversal chart) for an upside target of $92–$99. The upward trend action subsequent to the LPS at $72 confirms that the trader-analyst ought to sit tight in anticipation of reaching that price objective.

The Engelhard Minerals & Chemicals charts in Figure 5.17 are a case study of distribution and decline. The uptrend was halted first around $57 and then emphatically stopped at $62, from which point the horizontal resistance line is drawn. Following the halt at $62, Engelhard finds support at $49, from which point the horizontal support line is drawn. There is

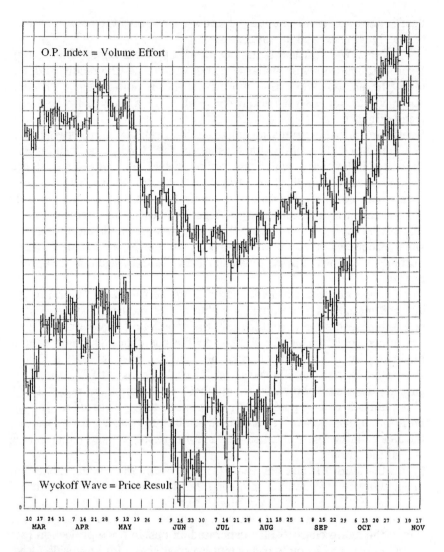

FIGURE 5.15 Disharmony/Divergence between Price and Volume
Source: SMI.

FIGURE 5.16a Coordination of Bar Chart and Figure Chart, Bar Chart
Source: Copyright 2006 Archer Analysis Pty Ltd (www.archeranalysis.com).

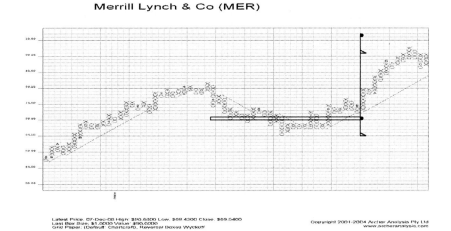

FIGURE 5.16b Coordination of Bar Chart and Figure Chart, Figure Chart
Source: Copyright 2006 Archer Analysis Pty Ltd (www.archeranalysis.com).

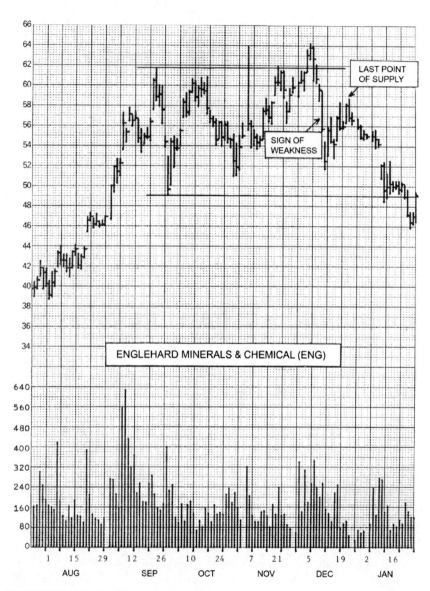

FIGURE 5.17 Distribution and Decline
Source: SMI.

another attempt to reestablish the uptrend from $49 to $64, but this is followed by the sharp price breakdown on expanding relative volume from $64 down to $52. This bearish action where supply is clearly in control is labeled as "Sign of Weakness." The subsequent rally on diminishing price and shrinking volume constitutes the test, the end of which is the LPS. A sale or short-sale could be made at that point. Also, a figure chart count can be taken from that point.

Figure 5.18 shows the downside potential (effect) generated during the distribution trading range. This effect reflects the cause measured along the $59 level on the figure chart. The flagged points A, B, C, D, and E on the downside are signal levels for the trader-analyst to stop, look, and listen for possible stopping price action on the downside as Engelhard reaches those targets. Note that here, too, in the case study of Engelhard we witness the importance of coordinating bar chart and figure chart action.

Stocks A and B in Figures 5.19 and 5.20 afford the trader-analyst an opportunity to apply the basic chart elements of Wyckoff. The trader-analyst

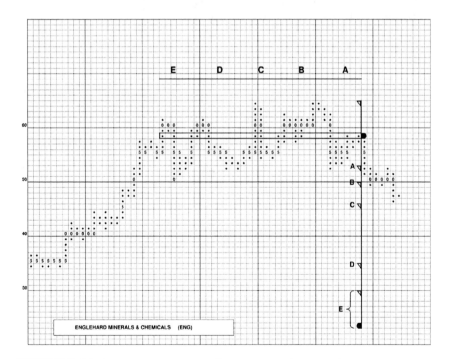

FIGURE 5.18 Downside Potential (Effect) Generated by Distribution
Data Source: SMI.

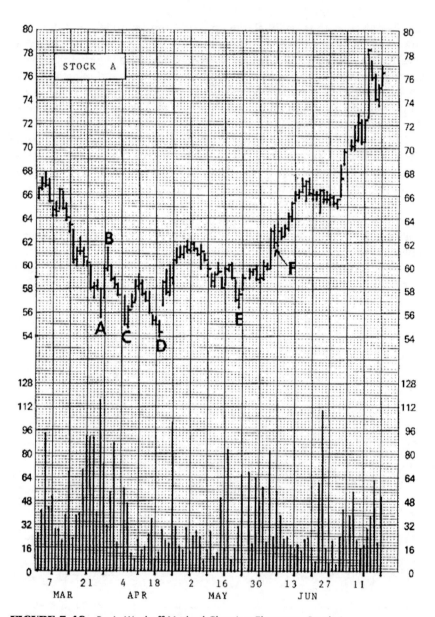

FIGURE 5.19   Basic Wyckoff Method Charting Elements, Stock A
Source: SMI.

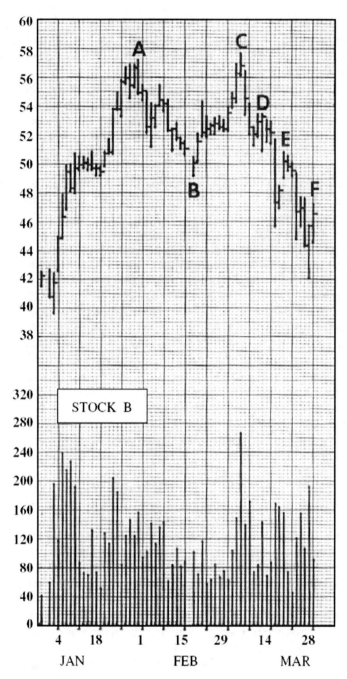

FIGURE 5.20 Basic Wyckoff Method Charting Elements, Stock B
Source: SMI.

should draw supply lines and oversold lines, horizontal support and resistance lines, and then coordinate the actions of the bar charts and the figure charts. Stocks A and B are fine opportunities to practice analyzing all four phases of the Wyckoff cycle.

Two more stocks appear in Figures 5.21 a, b, and c. But here the trader-analyst meets an entirely different Wyckoff principle: these figures are devoted to the principle of comparative strength or weakness. The principle states that the trader-analyst should purchase stocks that are stronger than the market and avoid stocks that are weaker than the market.

The market in Figure 5.21a is defined by the Wyckoff Wave (an index of eight stocks). By comparing each common stock to the Wyckoff Wave index, it becomes obvious which one is stronger than the market. The trader-analyst will want to purchase a stock like stock 1 for his portfolio.

The charts of Micron Technology (Figures 5.22 a and b) illustrate trading range and trend analysis. In these two cases the trader-analyst's attention should be focused on *exit strategies*. In Figure 5.22, the price failed to reach the target price of 28-32 before stopping and reversing. The Wyckoff trader-analyst would be wise to exit because of the light volume and narrow price spread on the second rally attempt to $18 after the breaking of the up trendline. By contrast, Figure 5.23 illustrates a case where the actual price overshot the price objectives on the downside. Rather than exiting at the "stop-look-and-listen" target point of $38, the trader-analyst could have remained with a short-sale of this stock because the price and volume rally at $38 was so feeble—there was no indication of a stopping of the downtrend nor of a selling climax at point B. Later on and $8 lower, at point C, the trader-analyst has the necessary evidence to exit the short sale.

Chapter 5 has introduced the trader-analyst to a set of tools for conducting technical analysis the Wyckoff way. The basic tools covered have been bar charts, point-and-figure charts, and line charts. In Wyckoff parlance, the bar chart and the point-and-figure chart are also known as the vertical line chart and the figure chart, respectively. These charts have been used to illustrate the construction of support and resistance, the definition of trendlines and trend channels, the reversal of trend direction, disharmony/divergence between price and volume, relative strength, and the coordination of bar charts with figure charts. The appendixes to this chapter demonstrate how the trader-analyst can interpret point-and-figure charts, and how to use them to make price projections. Taken together, this chapter provides the essential building blocks for the Wyckoff method.

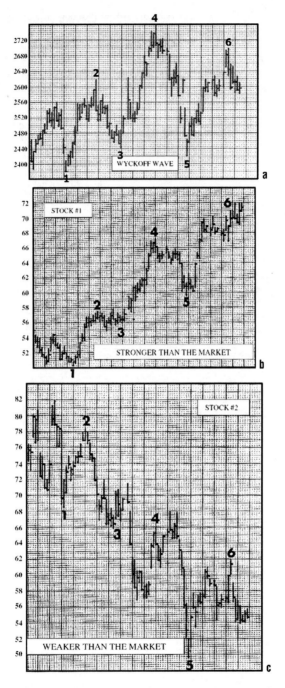

FIGURE 5.21 (a) Wyckoff Wave Index for Comparative Strength and Weakness; (b) Stock Stronger than the Market; (c) Stock Weaker than the Market.
Source: SMI.

FIGURE 5.22a   Trading Range and Trend Analysis, Bar Chart
Source: Copyright 2006 Archer Analysis Pty Ltd (www.archeranalysis.com).

Micron Technology Inc (MU)

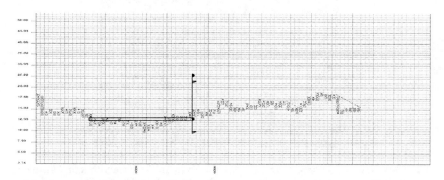

FIGURE 5.22b   Trading Range and Trend Analysis, Point and Figure Chart
Source: Copyright 2006 Archer Analysis Pty Ltd (www.archeranalysis.com).

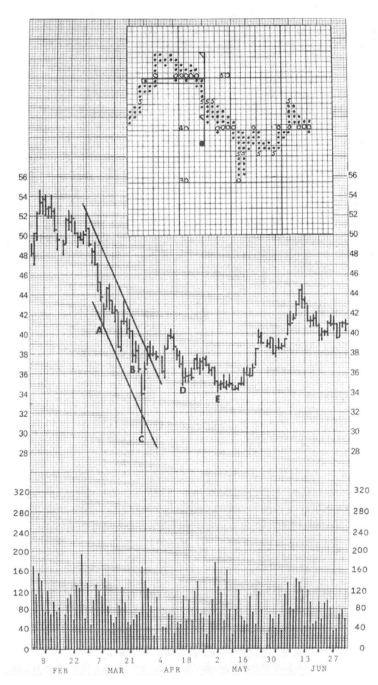

FIGURE 5.23   Trend Analysis: Overshooting Price Objectives
Source: SMI.

APPENDIX A: HOW TO INTERPRET WYCKOFF POINT-AND-FIGURE CHARTS

The procedures for the interpretation of the Wyckoff-oriented point-and-figure chart are listed below, outlined as six steps.

Start with a bar chart and a point-and-figure (P&F) chart covering the same patterns and time. Wyckoff prefers the one-point reversal chart—for example, the DJIA blocked in boxes of 100 points each. But Wyckoff insists that at least two entries must appear in each and every column. That leads to occasionally combining X's and O's or up and down price movements to meet the minimum standard of two entries per column.

The box size is important. For the DJIA the Wyckoff/Stock Market Institute uses 50 and 100 points. Please note that those are generated by the actual tape prints within a day. Hence, a very volatile day may produce many point-and-figure ups and downs.

1. Use the bar chart to identify one, or usually two or three, potential reversal patterns—for example, an inverse "head-and-shoulders" (H&S) bottom followed by a "cup-and-handle" on the same chart.

2. The point-and-figure count will be taken from the right shoulder or from the handle identified on the bar chart—in other words, from the last pullback before the price advance or markup stage.

3. On the P&F chart count the number of boxes across the accumulation formation (for example, inverse head-and-shoulders, from shoulder to shoulder).

4. Count the number of boxes (columns) and multiply that number by the value found in each box (for example, 50 points). Note that although some columns may have only two boxes, one after the other, and other columns contain several boxes, the same per box value applies. In our case, the 2002–2003 bottom had 72 boxes (columns) each worth 100 points, for a total of 7,200 points.

5. Add the total count to the lowest price on the P&F chart itself and to the count line itself. Thus, in the 2002–2003 example 7,200 points were added to the low price (the "head" of the inverse head-and-shoulders of 7,200) for an upside projection of 14,400.

6. *Conservative* is the guiding principle. Project the minimum price first; use the minimum projection to estimate the reward-to-risk ratio.

APPENDIX B: HOW TO MAKE PRICE PROJECTIONS USING A FIGURE CHART

> *The average ticker hound—or, as they used to call him, tapeworm—goes wrong, I suspect, as much from overspecialization as from anything else. It means a highly expensive inelasticity. After all, the game of speculation isn't all mathematics or set rules, however rigid the main laws may be. Even in my tape reading, something enters that is more than mere arithmetic.*
>
> *—Edwin Lefèvre,* Reminiscences of a Stock Operator

Cause and Effect

According to the Wyckoff law of cause and effect, the trader analyst measures the extent of the cause built up during a trading range on a P&F chart and then projects a price objective representing the potential effect of that cause. The relationship between the cause and the subsequent effect is one-to-one, which means that every unit of cause that is measured horizontally in a trading range translates into an expected one unit of vertical effect.

For readers who recall their high school physics lessons, the law of cause and effect can be likened to Hooke's law of elasticity. Hooke's law declares that agitations up and down build up energy; the cause (for example, agitating a metal coat hanger back and forth) and the resultant effect (bend the hanger out of shape) expend energy in an exactly one-to-one proportion to the preceding energy built up.

In trading, the cause is created during the up and down buying and selling waves that occur during a trading range. The cause is measured and projected on the figure chart according to the Wyckoff Count Guide, which appears below (courtesy of the Wyckoff Stock Market Institute).

The Wyckoff Count Guide

The Wyckoff Count Guide shows the trader how to calculate the cause built up during a trading range. This helps the trader to make projections of future price targets. The process consists of the following elements:

- After having identified a *sign of strength* (SOS) on the vertical line chart, locate the last point at which support was met on a reaction—the *last point of support* (LPS). Locate this point on your figure chart also and count from right to left, taking your most conservative count first and moving further to the left as the move progresses.

- In moving to the left, turn to your vertical line chart and divide the area of accumulation into phases, adding one complete phase at a time. Never add only part of a phase to your count. Volume action will usually show where the phase began and ended.
- As the move progresses you will often see a lateral move forming at a higher level. Very often such a move will become a "stepping stone confirming count" of the original count. Thus, as such a level forms, you can often get a timing indication by watching the action of the stock as the potential count begins to confirm the original count. A resumption of the upward or downward trend could begin at such a point.
- For longer-term counts you should add your count to the exact low, or at a point about halfway between the low and the count line. You will thus be certain that the most conservative count is being used.
- Counts are only points of "stop, look, and listen" and should never be looked upon as exact points of stopping and turning. Use them as projected points where a turn could occur, and use the vertical line chart to show the action as these points are approached.
- In the case of a longer-term count, often the LPS comes at the original level of climax, and this level should be looked at first in studying the longer-term count. The climax itself indicates a reversal. The subsequent action forms the cause for the next effect. For the LPS to come at such a level of climax usually makes it a more valid count. Preliminary support and the LPS often occur at the same price level.
- A number three spring, or the secondary test of a number two spring, quite often constitutes the SOS and the LPS in the same action which is reached at the same point and at the same time. Usually, a spring will be followed by a more important SOS, and the reaction following that SOS is also a valid LPS.
- Frequently, long-term counts on three-point and five-point charts are confirmed by subsequent minor counts on the one-point chart as the move progresses. Watch for this confirmation very carefully as it often indicates when a move will resume.
- In case of three-point or five-point charts, the same count line should be used as for the one-point chart.

Analysts who wish to use the Wyckoff Count Guide must appreciate and comprehend certain philosophies and procedures unique to the Wyckoff figure chart. Three key elements of Wyckoff figure chart analyses are *function, procedure,* and *perspective.*

Function   Figure charts play a special supplementary and complementary role in the Wyckoff method. The key law of supply and demand relies on the vertical chart to diagnose the present position and future trend of the market. The figure chart is not used for determining the trend of the market per se, because the volume information provided by the vertical chart makes it a superior tool for determining the trend. Philosophically, Wyckoff analysts believe the vertical chart ought to be used for trend analysis; however, determining the potential extent of the move is the special province of the figure chart, sometimes referred to as the cause and effect chart.

Procedure   The building blocks of the figure chart are box size, intraday data, number of reversal points, and full-unit crossing. Most commonly the box size is one point. Hence, intraday price action must meet or exceed the full price levels to trigger a figure chart entry. Reversal points are normally one point or three points.

   For the one-point figure chart, a very special consideration to keep in mind under the Wyckoff figure chart procedure is the necessity of having at least two entries in any column. Many software programs change columns when price changes direction, even if only a single entry exists in a column. To compensate for this, the analyst must shift prices to create a column with at least two entries before price can move to the next column. Hence, a quick down, up, down of one point each would remain in a single column. For larger moves, the analyst has the option to either rely on the three-point reversal or to increase the box size.

Perspective   The analyst can visualize horizontal counts as fitting within a saucer-shaped bottom and a dome-looking top. The first count line should be conservative, nearest the lows, and be considered as the minimum possible. The next count line will usually be within the trading range, broader, and considered the likely objective. Finally, the pullback following the upside jump or valid breakout creates the widest count and the highest upside count, and is thus the least conservative measurement; this is the LPS that follows a more important SOS.

CHAPTER 6

The Wyckoff Method of Technical Analysis and Speculation

T he Wyckoff method—a practical, straightforward bar chart and point-and-figure chart pattern recognition method-has stood the test of time. Wyckoff's portrayal of primary market phases appears in Figure 6.1.

The Wyckoff method is a school of thought in technical market analysis that requires judgment. Although the Wyckoff method is not a mechanical system in itself, nevertheless high-reward, low-risk opportunities can

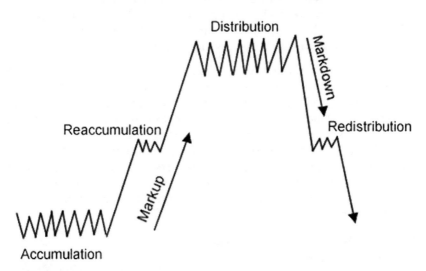

FIGURE 6.1 Wyckoff's Conception of Primary Market Phases
Source: Stock Market Institute, Inc.

be routinely and systematically identified by using three concepts of the Wyckoff method:

1. Three fundamental laws.
2. Nine classic buying tests and nine classic selling tests.
3. Wyckoff schematics of accumulation and distribution.

THE FOUNDATION: THREE FUNDAMENTAL LAWS

1. *The law of supply and demand* determines the price direction. When demand is greater than supply, prices will rise, and when supply is greater than demand, prices will fall. Using a bar chart, the trader-analyst can study the relationship between supply and demand by monitoring price and volume over time.

2. *The law of cause and effect* provides an insight into the extent of the coming price move up or down. In order to have an effect you must first have a cause; the effect will be in proportion to the cause. This law's operation can be seen as the force of accumulation or distribution within a trading range—and how this force works itself out in a subsequent trend or movement out of that trading range. Point-and-figure chart counts are used to measure a cause and to project the extent of its effect.

3. *The law of effort versus result* provides an early-warning indication of a forthcoming possible change in trend. Disharmonies and divergences between volume and price often signal a change in the direction of a price trend. The Wyckoff Optimism/Pessimism Index is an on-balance volume type of indicator helpful for identifying accumulation versus distribution, thereby gauging effort.

Taken together, these three Wyckoff laws shed light on the intentions of the smart money, the Composite Man. The law of cause and effect reveals the extent of preparation of the subsequent campaign to be conducted by the Composite Man, while the loss of supply indicates the Composite Man's intentions to carry out the campaign *now* to the upside or the downside. Anticipation of the direction of the movement out of the sideways area of preparation is often foreshadowed by the divergences or disharmonies that define the law of effort versus result. The power available to the trader that results from these three laws acting in concert is demonstrated in the next section.

Applying the Wyckoff Laws to the U.S. Stock Market

Figures 6.2 and 6.3 demonstrate how a trader can apply the three Wyckoff laws to isolate a high-reward, low-risk buying opportunity. The demon-

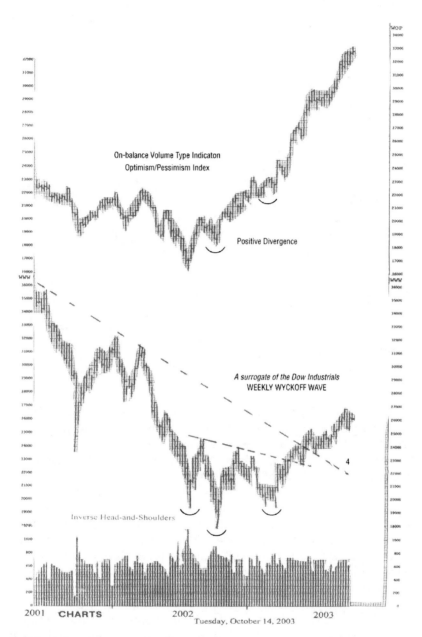

On-balance Volume Type Indicaton
Optimism/Pessimism Index

Positive Divergence

A surrogate of the Dow Industrials
WEEKLY WYCKOFF WAVE

Inverse Head-and-Shoulders

2001   CHARTS   2002   2003
Tuesday, October 14, 2003

FIGURE 6.2 Wyckoff Law of Effort versus Result and Law of Supply and Demand
Data Source: SMI.

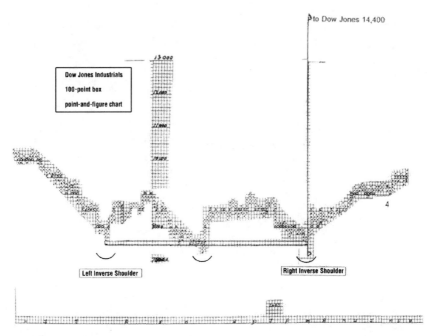

FIGURE 6.3   Law of Cause and Effect
Data Source: SMI.

stration in these figures relates the laws to U.S. stocks during 2002 and 2003. Figure 6.2, a bar chart, starts with the decline in price during 2001–2002. Thereafter, an inverse head-and-shoulders base, visible here as formed during 2002-2003, defines the extent of the new bull market that began over March-June 2003. The upward trend reversal out of that base of accumulation is defined by the law of supply and demand, as exhibited in the lower part of the chart. That upward reversal is presaged by the positive divergences from the price index, signaled by the Optimism/Pessimism (on-balance volume) Index. The expressions of positive divergence in late 2002 and early 2003 demonstrate the law of effort (volume) versus result (price) in operation. These divergences disclose an exhaustion in supply and a rising dominance of demand.

The bullish price trend during 2003 is confirmed by the steeply rising OBV index. Accumulation during the trading range thus continued upward as prices rose in 2003. Together, the law of supply and demand and the law of effort versus result made a persuasive case that a powerful bull market was getting under way during 2003. The trader at this important juncture could have bought a broad cross-section of the market and then switched into the monitoring mode until the price projection hit its target.

How far could this bull market rise? Wyckoff used the law of cause and effect and the point-and-figure chart to answer the question "how far?" Using the inverse head-and-shoulders formation as the base from which to take a measurement of the cause built during the accumulation phase, the point-and-figure chart (Figure 6.3) indicates 72 boxes between the right inverse shoulder and the left inverse shoulder. Each box has a value of 100 Dow points. Hence, the point-and-figure chart reveals a base of accumulation for a potential rise of 7,200 points. When added to the low of 7,200 the price projects upward to 14,400. Hence, the expectation would be for the Dow Industrials to continue to rise to 14,400 before the onset of distribution and the commencement of the next bear market.

In summary, use of the three laws of the Wyckoff method of technical analysis as the system for forecasting during 2003 leads to the conclusion that U.S. equities were in a bull market and had the potential to rise to Dow Jones 14,400.

NINE CLASSIC BUYING TESTS AND NINE CLASSIC SELLING TESTS

Whereas the three Wyckoff laws give a broader, big-picture approach to the Wyckoff method study of charts, the nine tests are a set of principles that are more narrow and specific in their applications. The Wyckoff tests logically follow as the succeeding step to the Wyckoff laws. For example, in Figures 6.2 and 6.3, point 4 indicates the juncture where the nine buying tests are passed. Table 6.1 defines each of these nine tests and how they are to be measured; Table 6.2 defines the nine selling tests.

The nine tests are important for defining when a trading range is finally coming to a conclusion and a new uptrend (markup) or downtrend (markdown) is commencing. In other words, the nine tests define the line of least resistance in the market. The charts of two Malaysian companies in Tables 6.3 and 6.4 illustrate the application of the nine buying tests and nine selling tests. These two examples from Malaysia exemplify the international applicability of the Wyckoff method of technical analysis.

The classic set of nine buying tests and nine selling tests was designed to diagnose significant reversals. The nine classic buying tests in Table 6.1

TABLE 6.1 Wyckoff Buying Tests: Nine Classic Tests for Accumulation*

Indication	Determined From
1. Downside price objective accomplished	Figure chart
2. Preliminary support, selling climax, secondary test	Vertical and figure
3. Activity bullish (volume increases on rallies and diminishes during reactions)	Vertical
4. Downward stride broken (that is, supply line penetrated)	Vertical or figure
5. Higher supports	Vertical or figure
6. Higher tops	Vertical or figure
7. Stock stronger than the market (that is, stock more responsive on rallies and more resistant to reactions than the market index)	Vertical chart
8. Base forming (horizontal price line)	Figure chart
9. Estimated upside profit potential is at least three times the loss if protective stop is hit	Figure chart for profit objective

*Applied to an average or a stock after a decline.

Adapted with modifications from Jack K. Huston, ed., *Charting the Market: The Wyckoff Method* (Seattle, WA: Technical Analysis, Inc., 1986), 87.

define the emergence of a new bull trend out of a base that forms after a significant price decline. The nine selling tests help define the onset of a bear trend out of a top formation following a significant advance (see Table 6.2). These nine classic tests of Wyckoff are logical, time-tested, and reliable. Each test represents a principle of the Wyckoff method.

As you approach this case of nine classic buying tests, you ought to keep in mind the following admonitions from Lefèvre's *Reminiscences of a Stock Operator*:

> *This experience has been the experience of so many traders so many times that I can give this rule: In a narrow market, when prices are not getting anywhere to speak of but move within a narrow range, there is no sense in trying to anticipate what the next big movement*

TABLE 6.2 Wyckoff Selling Tests: Nine Classic Tests for Distribution*

Indication	Determined From
1. Upside objective accomplished	Figure chart
2. Activity bearish (volume decreases on rallies and increases on reactions)	Vertical and figure
3. Preliminary supply, buying climax	Vertical and figure
4. Average or stock weaker than market (that is, more responsive on reactions and sluggish on rallies)	Vertical chart
5. Upward stride broken (that is, support line penetrated)	Vertical or figure
6. Lower tops	Vertical or figure
7. Lower supports	Vertical or figure
8. Crown forming (lateral movement)	Figure chart
9. Estimated upside profit potential is at least three times the indicated risk	Figure chart for profit objective, vertical chart for stop-order placement

* Applied to an average or a stock after an advance.

Adapted with modifications from Jack K. Huston, ed., *Charting the Market: The Wyckoff Method* (Seattle, WA: Technical Analysis, Inc., 1986), 87.

is going to be—up or down. The thing to do is to watch the market, read the tape to determine the limits of the get-nowhere prices, and make up your mind that you will not take an interest until the price breaks through the limit in either direction. A speculator must concern himself with making money out of the market and not with insisting that the tape must agree with him.

Therefore, the thing to determine is the speculative line of least resistance at the moment of trading; and what he should wait for is the moment when that line defines itself, because that is his signal to get busy.

The passing of all nine Wyckoff tests determines the speculative line of least resistance to the upside or downside.

Commerz: Example of the Nine Buying Tests

Figures 6.4 and 6.5 use data on Commerz Bank and Asia Pacific Land (AP Land), respectively, to demonstrate the application of the nine buying and selling tests. Point 3 on the Commerz and AP Land charts identifies the juncture where all nine Wyckoff buying tests and all nine Wyckoff selling tests are passed. The passing of all nine tests confirms that either an uptrending (or markup) phase or a downtrending (or markdown) phase has begun.

Tables 6.3 and 6.4 summarize the findings of the left-brained analytical checklist of Wyckoff principles for accumulation and for distribution. Table 6.3 reveals that all nine buying tests were passed; Table 6.4 reveals that all nine selling tests were passed. In each case, the passage of the checklist sets the stage for corroboration or disconfirmation by the right-brained pictorial observation of accumulation and distribution shown by the schematics.

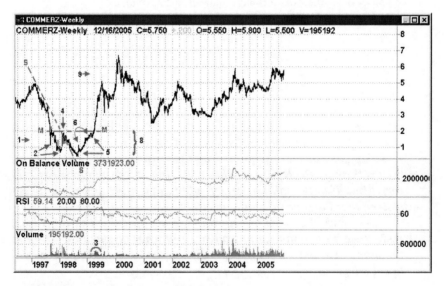

FIGURE 6.4 Commerz Bank, Weekly Chart: Wyckoff Accumulation Illustrated
Source: © TradeStation Technologies 1991–2007.

FIGURE 6.5 Distribution: Nine Selling Tests Passed by AP Land
Source: © TradeStation Technologies 1991–2007.

TABLE 6.3 Application of the Nine Wyckoff Buying Tests: Commerz Bank (Malaysia), 1997–1999

Wyckoff Buying Tests	Commentary
1. Downside price objective accomplished?	Yes. The distribution top formed during 1997 creates a point-and-figure (horizontal) chart count that gives the downside price projections that were met in the vicinity of the 1997–1998 market lows.
2. Preliminary support, selling climax, secondary test?	Yes. This sequence of price-and-volume actions signals that the downtrend from 1997 had stopped. Note the high volume on the early "big money" buying during mid- to late 1997. The sharp price rise on expanded volume during early 1998 indicates heavy demand overcoming weakening supply. This bullish action is confirmed by the subsequent secondary test from late 1998. Although prices fell below the levels of the previous selling climax low, volume was demonstrably less. Then, at the very end of 1998, prices rallied off the bottom on a relative increase in volume—a bullish sign!

(continues)

139

TABLE 6.3 *(Continued)*

Wyckoff Buying Tests	Commentary
3. Activity bullish (volume increases on rallies and decreases on reactions)?	Yes. Note expansions in volume during late 1998 and into 1999 as compared to the earlier lower level of volume while prices drifted lower in 1998.
4. Downward stride broken (that is, supply line penetrated)?	Yes. Downward sloping supply line SS was penetrated in early 1998 (note how the old supply S-S switched from acting as resistance to becoming support as price drifted lower during 1998).
5. Higher supports?	Yes. A series of ascending lows registers during late 1998 and early 1999.
6. Higher tops?	Yes. A series of advancing price peaks registers during late 1998 and early 1999.
7. Stock stronger than the market?	Yes, relative to the group that Commerz represents.
8. Base forming (horizontal price line)?	Yes. A complex inverse head-and-shoulders bullish reversal formation is discernable under the dashed horizontal price resistance line (MM).
9. Estimated upside profit potential is at least three times the possible loss?	Yes. If purchase was made on the pullback to the neckline of the stop is inverse head-and-shoulders pattern after the high-volume advance during second quarter 1999, then the price stop below support would be 1 and the price objective/risk ratio equal to 3/1.

TABLE 6.4 Application of the Nine Wyckoff Selling Tests: Ap Land Weekly, 1999–2000, Malaysian Market

Wyckoff Selling Tests	Commentary
1. Upside price objective accomplished?	Yes. The price objective generated during the previous accumulation was reached around the price highs of year 2000.
2. Activity bearish (volume decreases on rallies and increases on reactions)?	Yes. The dominance of sell-side volume over demand is evident during the third quarter of 1999 and the first quarter of the year 2000.
3. Preliminary supply, buying climax?	Yes. High-volume stopping of the uptrend (reversals in price) registers in 1999. The buying climax at the price peak is particularly pronounced.
4. Average or stock weaker than market (that is, more responsive on rallies and sluggish on rallies)?	Yes, weaker than the relevant group.
5. Upward stride broken (that is, support line penetrated)?	Yes. Demand line DD is definitively penetrated during the final quarter of 1999.
6. Lower tops?	Yes, a series of triple descending price peaks from the high to the top of the pullback rally in the third quarter of 2000.
7. Lower supports?	Yes. Lower supports register immediately after the buying climax and upon the breaking of horizontal support line MM.
8. Crown forming (lateral move)?	Yes. A large, classical pattern of distribution characterized by descending price peaks takes place over almost four quarters during 1999–2000 between 2.0 price and 1.2 price.
9. Estimated profit is at least three times the indicated risk for stop-order placement?	Yes. With a short sale at the pullback of 1.2 and a profit potential 1.1, and a stop-loss order placed at 1.5, the reward/risk ratio is a comfortable 3.67.

WYCKOFF SCHEMATICS OF ACCUMULATION AND DISTRIBUTION

Wyckoff empowers the trader-analyst with a balanced, whole-brained approach to technical analysis decision making. The Wyckoff schematics provide picture diagrams as a right-brained tool to complement the left-brained analytical checklists furnished by the Wyckoff three laws and nine tests.

This section explains and discusses applications of the three schematics used in the Wyckoff method of technical analysis. For each of the three schematics—one for accumulation and two for distribution—there is an idealized representation of the Wyckoff principle. With each schematic appear alphabetical and numerical annotations that define Wyckoff's annotations of key phases and junctures found during the evolution of accumulation or distribution. Many of these annotations reflect the work of Mr. Robert G. Evans, who carried on the teaching of the Wyckoff method after the death of Mr. Wyckoff in 1934. Mr. Evans was a creative teacher who was a master at explaining Wyckoff via analogies.

One objective of the Wyckoff method of technical analysis is to improve market timing when establishing a speculative position in anticipation of a coming move where a favorable reward/risk ratio exists to justify taking that position. Trading ranges (TRs) are places where the previous move has been halted and there is relative equilibrium between supply and demand. It is here within the TR that campaigns of accumulation or distribution develop in preparation for the coming bull or bear trend. It is this force of accumulation or distribution that can be said to build a cause that unfolds in the subsequent move. The building up of the necessary force takes time, and because during this period the price action is well-defined, TRs present favorable short-term trading opportunities with potentially very favorable reward/risk parameters. Nevertheless, great reward comes with participation in the trend that emerges from the TR.

To be successful, however, you must be able to anticipate and correctly judge the direction and magnitude of the move out of the TR. Fortunately, Wyckoff offers unique guidelines by which the trader-analyst can examine the phases within a TR.

Accumulation

Schematic 1 provides a visual representation of the four phases of Wyckoff market action typically found within a TR of accumulation

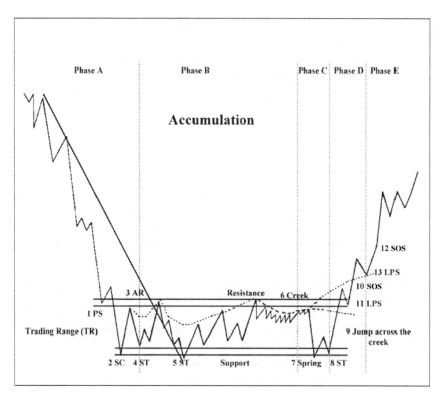

FIGURE 6.6 Schematic 1—Accumulation
Source: "Anatomy of a Trading Range," by Jim Forte, CMT, *MTA Journal*, Fall 1994.

(see Figure 6.6). While this basic Wyckoff model for accumulation is not a schematic for all the possible variations within the anatomy of a TR, it does provide a representation of the important Wyckoff principles that are often evident in an area of accumulation, and it also represents the identifiable phases used to guide our analysis through the TR toward our taking a speculative position.

Phases A through E are phases through which the trading range passes as conceptualized by the Wyckoff method and explained in the text. Lines A and B define support of the trading range, while lines C and D define resistance. The abbreviations used are as follows:

> PS—preliminary support, where substantial buying begins to provide pronounced support after a prolonged down-move. Volume and

spread widen and provide a signal that the down-move may be approaching its end.

SC—selling climax, the point at which widening spread and selling pressure usually climaxes and heavy or panicky selling by the public is being absorbed by larger professional interests at prices near a bottom.

AR—automatic rally, where selling pressure has been pretty much exhausted. A wave of buying can now easily push up prices, which is further fueled by short covering. The high of this rally will help define the top of the trading range.

ST—secondary test, revisiting the area of the selling climax to test the supply/demand balance at these price levels. If a bottom is to be confirmed, significant supply should not resurface, and volume and price spread should be significantly diminished as the market approaches support in the area of the SC.

The "creek," referring to the analogy described elsewhere in Chapter 6, is a wavy line of resistance drawn loosely across rally peaks within the trading range. There are, of course, minor lines of resistance and more significant ones that will have to be crossed before the market's journey can continue onward and upward.

"Jump"—continuing the creek analogy, the point at which price jumps through the resistance line; a good sign if done on increasing spread and volume.

SOS—sign of strength, an advance on increasing spread and volume.

LPS—last point of support, the ending point of a reaction or pullback at which support was met. Backing up to an LPS means a pullback to support that was formerly resistance, on diminished spread and volume after an SOS. This is a good place to initiate long positions or to add to profitable ones.

Springs or *shakeouts* usually occur late within the trading range and allow the market and its dominant players to make a definitive test of available supply before a markup campaign will unfold. If the amount of supply that surfaces on a break of support is very light (low volume), it will be an indication that the way is clear for a sustained advance. Heavy supply here will usually mean a renewed decline. Moderate volume here may mean more testing of support and a time to proceed with caution. The spring or shakeout also serves the purpose of providing dominant interests with additional supply from weak holders at low prices.

Note: A series of SOSs and LPSs provides good evidence that a bottom is in place and price markup has begun.

Phase A   In phase A, supply has been dominant and it appears that finally the exhaustion of supply is becoming evident. The approaching exhaustion of supply or selling is evidenced in preliminary support (PS) and the selling climax (SC) where a widening spread often climaxes and where heavy volume or panicky selling by the public is being absorbed by larger professional interests. Once these intense selling pressures have been expressed, an automatic rally (AR) follows the selling climax. A successful secondary test on the downside shows less selling than on the SC and with a narrowing of spread and decreased volume. A successful secondary test (ST) should stop around the same price level as the selling climax. The lows of the SC and the ST and the high of the AR set the boundaries of the TR. Horizontal lines may be drawn to help focus attention on market behavior.

It is possible that phase A will not include a dramatic expansion in spread and volume. However, it is better if it does, because the more dramatic selling will clear out more of the sellers and pave the way for a more pronounced and sustained markup.

Where a TR represents a reaccumulation (a TR within a continuing up-move), you will not have evidence of PS, SC, and ST as illustrated in phase A of Figure 6.6. Instead, phase A will look more like phase A of the basic Wyckoff distribution schematic (described in a later section). Nonetheless, phase A still represents the area where the stopping of the previous trend occurs. Trading range phases B through E generally unfold in the same manner as within an initial base area of accumulation.

Phase B   The function of phase B is to build a cause in preparation for the next effect. In phase B, supply and demand are for the most part in equilibrium and there is no decisive trend. Although clues to the future course of the market are usually more mixed and elusive, some useful generalizations can be made.

In the early stages of phase B, the price swings tend to be rather wide, and volume is usually greater and more erratic. As the TR unfolds, supply becomes weaker and demand stronger as professionals are absorbing supply. The closer you get to the end or to leaving the TR, the more volume tends to diminish. Support and resistance lines (shown as horizontal lines in Figure 6.6) usually contain the price action in phase B and will help define the testing process that is to come in phase C. The penetrations or lack of penetrations of the TR enable us to judge the quantity and quality of supply and demand.

Phase C   In phase C, the stock goes through testing. It is during this testing phase that the smart money operators ascertain whether the stock is ready to enter the markup phase. The stock may begin to come out of the TR on the upside with higher tops and bottoms or it may go through a downside *spring* or *shakeout* by first breaking previous supports before the upward climb begins. This latter test is preferred by traders because it does a better job of cleaning out the remaining supply of weak holders and creates a false impression as to the direction of the ultimate move. Phase C in Figure 6.6 shows an example of this latter alternative.

A spring is a price move below the support level of a trading range that quickly reverses and moves back into the range. It is an example of a *bear trap* because the drop below support appears to signal resumption of the downtrend. In reality, though, the drop marks the end of the downtrend, thus trapping the late sellers, or bears. The extent of supply, or the strength of the sellers, can be judged by the depth of the price move to new lows and the relative level of volume in that penetration.

Until this testing process, you cannot be sure the TR is accumulation and hence you must wait to take a position until there is sufficient evidence that markup is about to begin. If we have waited and followed the unfolding TR closely, we have arrived at the point where we can be quite confident of the probable upward move. With supply apparently exhausted and our danger point pinpointed, our likelihood of success is good and our reward/risk ratio favorable.

The shakeout at point 7 in Figure 6.6 represents our first prescribed place to initiate a long position. The secondary test at point 8 is an even better spot to buy, since a low volume pullback and a specific low-risk stop or danger point at point 7 gives us greater evidence and more confidence to act. A sign of strength (SOS)/ jump across the creek (point 9) shifts the trading range into phase D.

Phase D   If we are correct in our analysis and our timing, what should follow now is the consistent dominance of demand over supply as evidenced by a pattern of advances (SOSs) on widening price spreads and increasing volume, and reactions (LPSs) on smaller spreads and diminished volumes. If this pattern does not occur, then we are advised not to add to our position but to look to close out our original position and remain on the sidelines until we have more conclusive evidence that the markup is beginning. If the markup of your stock progresses as described to this point, then you'll have additional opportunities to add to your position.

Your aim here must be to initiate a position or add to your position as the stock or commodity is about to leave the TR. At this point, the force of accumulation has built a good potential as measured by the Wyckoff point-and-figure method.

Thus you have waited until this point to initiate or add to your position and by doing so you have enhanced the likelihood of success and maximized the use of your trading capital. In schematic 1, this opportunity comes at point 11 on the "pullback to support" after "jumping resistance" (in Wyckoff terms this is known as "backing up to the edge of the creek" after "jumping across the creek"). Another similar opportunity comes at point 13, a more important last point of support (LPS).

In phase D, the markup phase blossoms as professionals begin to move into the stock. It is here that our best opportunities to add to our position exist, just as the stock leaves the TR.

THE "JUMP ACROSS THE CREEK" ANALOGY

The term *jump* was first used by Robert G. Evans, who piloted the Wyckoff Associates educational enterprise for numerous years after the death of Richard D. Wyckoff. One of his more captivating analogies was the "jump across the creek" (JAC) story he used to explain how a market would break out of a trading range. In the story, the market is symbolized by a Boy Scout, and the trading range by a meandering creek, with its "upper resistance line" defined by the rally peaks within the range. After probing the edge of the creek and discovering that the flow of supply was starting to dry up, the Boy Scout would retreat in order to get a running start to "jump across the creek." The power of the movement by the Boy Scout would be measured by price spread and volume.

Defining the Jump
A jump is a relatively wider price-spread move made on comparatively higher volume that penetrates outer resistance. A backup is a test that immediately follows the jump—a relatively narrow price-spread reaction in comparatively lighter volume tests—and confirms the legitimacy of the preceding jump action.

The Wyckoff method instructs you to buy after a backup following an upward jump (a sign of strength) or to sell short after a backup following a downward jump (a sign of weakness). Also according to Wyckoff, you should not buy breakouts because that would leave you vulnerable to swift moves in the opposite direction if the breakout turns out to be false. Hence, at first glance, the Wyckoff method appears to be telling you to buy into weakness and sell into strength. Upon close examination, the rule is to buy the pullback test after a sign of strength.

Phase E   In phase E, the stock leaves the TR and demand is in control. Setbacks are unpronounced and short-lived. Having taken your positions, your job is to monitor the stock's progress as it works out its force of accumulation. At each of points 7, 8, 11, and 13 you may enter trading take positions on the long side and use point-and-figure counts from these points to calculate price projections that will help you to determine your reward/risk prior to establishing your speculative position. These projections will also be useful later in helping to target areas for closing or adjusting your position.

Remember that schematic 1 shows us just one idealized model or anatomy of a TR encompassing the accumulation process. There are many variations of this accumulation anatomy. The presence of a Wyckoff principle like a selling climax (SC) doesn't confirm that accumulation is occurring in the TR, but it does strengthen the case for it. However, it may be accumulation, redistribution, or nothing. The use of Wyckoff principles and phases identifies and defines some of the key considerations for evaluating most trading ranges and helps us determine whether it is supply or demand that is becoming dominant and when the stock appears ready to leave the trading range.

Distribution

Schematics 2 and 3, diagrammed in Figures 6.7 and 6.8, outline two variations of the Wyckoff model for distribution. While these models represent only two variations of the many possible variations in the patterns of a distribution TR, they do provide us with the important Wyckoff principles often evident in the area of distribution and the phases of a TR that can lead us toward taking a speculative position.

Much of the analysis of the principles and phases of a TR preceding distribution is the inverse of a TR of accumulation; only the roles of supply and demand are reversed.

Here, the force of "jumping the creek" (resistance) is replaced by the force of "falling through the ice" (support). It is useful to remember that distribution is generally accomplished in a shorter time period than accumulation.

The abbreviations used in Figures 6.7 and 6.8 are as follows:

PSY—preliminary supply, where substantial selling begins to provide pronounced resistance after an up-move. Volume and spread widen and provide a signal that the up-move may be approaching its end.

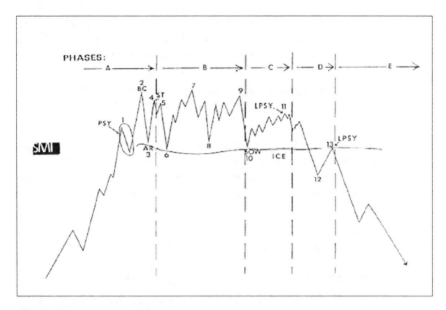

FIGURE 6.7 Schematic 2—Distribution
Source: SMI, with adaptations and modifications.

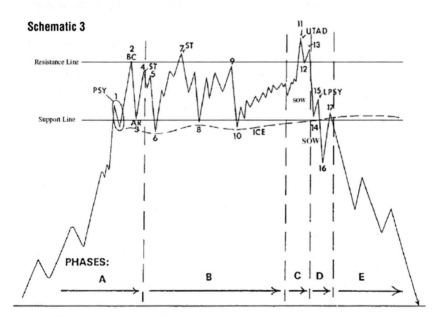

FIGURE 6.8 Schematic 3 with Upthrust after Distribution
Source: SMI, with adaptations and modifications.

BC—buying climax, the point at which widening spread and the force of buying reaches a climax, and heavy or urgent buying by the public is being filled by larger professional interests at prices near a top.

AR—automatic reaction. With buying pretty much exhausted and heavy supply continuing, an AR follows the BC. The low of this sell-off will help define the bottom of the TR.

ST—secondary test, revisiting the area of the buying climax to test the demand/supply balance at these price levels. If a top is to be confirmed, supply will outweigh demand and volume and spread should be diminished as the market approaches the resistance area of the BC.

SOW—sign of weakness, which will usually occur on increased spread and volume (point 10 in Figures 6.7 and 6.8, as compared to the preceding rally (to point 9). Supply is showing dominance. Our first "fall on the ice" holds and we get up try to forge ahead.

"Ice"—based on the analogy described elsewhere in Chapter 6, a wavy line of support drawn loosely under reaction lows of the TR. A break through the ice will likely be followed by attempts to get back above it. A failure to get back above firm support may mean a "drowning" for the market.

LPSY—last point of supply. After testing the ice (support) on a SOW, a feeble rally attempt on narrow spread shows us the difficulty the market is having in making a further rise. Volume may be light or heavy, showing weak demand or substantial supply. At LPSYs the last waves of distribution are being unloaded before markdown is to begin. LPSYs are good places to initiate a short position or to add to already profitable ones.

UTAD—upthrust after distribution. (See Figure 6.8, point 11.) Similar to the *spring* and terminal *shakeout* in the trading range of accumulation, a UTAD may occur in a TR of distribution. It is a more definitive test of new demand after a breakout above the resistance line of the TR, and *usually* occurs in the latter stages of the TR. If this breakout occurs on light volume with no follow-through, or on heavy volume with a breakdown back into the center of the trading range, then this is more evidence that the TR was distribution, not accumulation. This UTAD usually results in weak holders of short positions giving them up to more dominant interests, and also in more distribution to new, less-informed buyers before a significant decline ensues.

Phase A   In Phase A, demand has been dominant and the first significant evidence of demand becoming exhausted comes at point 1 at preliminary supply (PSY) and at point 2 at the buying climax (BC). It often occurs in wide price spread and at climactic volume. This is usually followed by an automatic reaction (AR) and then a secondary test (ST) of the BC, usually upon diminished volume. This is essentially the inverse of phase A in accumulation.

As with accumulation, phase A in distribution price may also end without climactic action; the only evidence of exhaustion of demand is diminishing spread and volume.

Where redistribution is concerned (a TR within a larger continuing down-move), you will see the stopping of a down-move with or without climactic action in phase A. However, in the remainder of the TR for redistribution, the guiding principles and analysis within phases B through E will be the same as within a TR of a distribution market top.

Phase B   The building of the cause takes place during phase B. The points to be made here about phase B are the same as those made for phase B within accumulation, except clues may begin to surface here of the supply/demand balance moving toward supply instead of demand.

Phase C   One of the ways phase C reveals itself after the standoff in phase B is by the *sign of weakness* (SOW), shown at point 10. The SOW is usually accompanied by significantly increased spread and volume to the downside that seem to break the standoff in phase B. The SOW may or may not "fall through the ice," but the subsequent rally back to point 11, a "last point of supply" (LPSY), is usually unconvincing for the bullish case and likely to be accompanied by less spread and/or volume.

Point 11 gives you your last opportunity to exit any remaining longs and your first inviting opportunity to take a short position. An even better place would be on the rally that tests point 11, because it may give more evidence (diminished spread and volume) and/or a more tightly defined danger point.

An upthrust is the opposite of a spring. It is a price move above the resistance level of a trading range that quickly reverses itself and moves back into the trading range. An upthrust is a *bull trap*—it appears to signal a start of an uptrend but in reality marks the end of the up-move. The magnitude of the upthrust can be determined by the extent of the price move to new highs and the relative level of volume in that movement.

As seen in schematic 3, phase C may also reveal itself by a pronounced move upward, breaking through the highs of the TR. This is shown at point 11 as an *upthrust after distribution* (UTAD). Like the terminal shakeout discussed earlier in the accumulation schematic, this gives a false impression of the direction of the market and allows further distribution at high prices to new buyers. It also results in weak holders of short positions surrendering their positions to stronger players just before the down-move begins. Should the move to new high ground be on increasing volume and relative narrowing spread, and price returns to the average level of closes of the TR, this would indicate lack of solid demand and confirm that the breakout to the upside did not indicate a TR of accumulation, but rather a formation of distribution.

Successful understanding and analysis of a TR enables traders to identify special trading opportunities with potentially very favorable reward/risk parameters. When analyzing a TR, we are first seeking to uncover what the law of supply and demand is revealing to us. However, when individual movements, rallies, or reactions are not revealing with respect to supply and demand, it is important to remember the law of effort versus result. By comparing rallies and reactions within the TR to each other in terms of price spread, volume, and time, additional clues may be discovered as to the stock's strength, position, and probable future course.

It will also be useful to employ the law of cause and effect. Within the dynamics of a TR, the force of accumulation or distribution gives us the cause and the potential opportunity for substantial trading profits. The TR will also give us the ability, with the use of point-and-figure charts, to project the extent of the eventual move out of the TR and will help us determine if those trading opportunities favorably meet or exceed our reward/risk parameters.

Phase D   Phase D arrives and reveals itself after the tests in phase C show us the last gasps or the last hurrah of demand. In phase D, the evidence of supply becoming dominant increases either with a break through the ice or with a further SOW into the TR after an upthrust. In Figure 6.7, at point 13, after a break through the ice, a rally attempt is thwarted at the ice's surface (now resistance). The rally meets a last wave of supply before markdown ensues.

In phase D, you are also given more evidence of the probable direction of the market and the opportunity to take your first or additional short positions. Your best opportunities are at points 13, 15, and 17 in Figures 6.7 and 6.8. These rallies represent LPSYs before a markdown cycle

THE ICE STORY

In Robert Evans' ice story analogy, we imagine the market in the person of a Boy Scout walking over a frozen river in the midst of winter. If support (the ice) is strong, the river covered with ice has no difficulty in supporting the weight of the Boy Scout. That support is seen as a wiggly dashed line connecting the lows, the supports, in a TR.

A failure by the Boy Scout to reach the upper resistance level of the TR would be a warning of potential weakness. Weakness of the ice would be signaled by the Boy Scout breaking support, or falling through the ice.

The Boy Scout has two chances to get back above the ice (that is, creating a bullish "spring" situation). On the first upward rally the Boy Scout may fail to regain a footing above the ice. If so, he will sink lower into the river in order to gather strength to try and rally once more and crack the ice. If on this second attempt the Boy Scout again fails to penetrate above the ice, he would most likely sink downward and drown. (That is, a bear market/markdown phase would occur.)

begins. Your legging in of the set of positions taken within phases C and D as just described represents a calculated approach to protect capital and maximize profit. It is important that additional short positions be added or pyramided only if your initial positions are in profit.

Phase E   Phase E depicts the unfolding of the downtrend; the stock or commodity leaves the TR and supply is in control. Rallies are usually feeble. Having taken your positions, your job here is to monitor the stock's progress as it works out its force of distribution. This is the markdown phase of the cycle. You should be out of your long positions by this phase of the cycle and aggressive traders should be carrying short sale positions.

Wyckoff Schematics Applied to Charts of Nokia

Weekly charts of Nokia display the overall cyclic progress of Nokia from markup to distribution, decline, accumulation, and finally to the commencement of a markup phase. The weekly charts furnish a big-picture backdrop for the detailed applications of the schematics for distribution and then accumulation. The "jump across the creek" and "ice" analogies (see boxes) are used to help explain the important junctures of distribution and accumulation illustrated on the daily charts of Nokia.

Nokia's bull market advance was stopped during the year 2000 around the 500 level by the entry into the market of a dominant force of supply. This force of supply first appeared around March 2000, where it created a sharp sell-off down to the vicinity of 350 on the Nokia chart, as shown in Figure 6.9. The demand that came to market to halt this sell-off marked the point at which the "ice story" commenced. We can see that support occurring at points 1, 2, 3, and 4 in Figure 6.10. The rallies from these support levels were becoming increasingly feeble as witnessed by the progressive diminution in volume coupled with the halting of the price advances at a resistance level near 540. Then from point 4 there was a rally that failed to reach the horizontal resistance line. Here the volume shrank appreciably. Moreover, the price level stopped in July near the same 500 level as did the earlier preliminary supply (PSY) in March–April. Hence, this juncture is annotated as a last point of supply for the possible completion of a line of important distribution.

The failure to reach the upper resistance level was a warning of potential weakness. Indeed, a sign of weakness ensued on the next sell-off. It is here that we witness support breaking around the 425 level in August 2000. Note the extremely wide price spread and the enormous increase in volume as Nokia plunged through the meandering support line drawn across the previous lows.

The significance of the price breaks below the support levels of this TR in Nokia is confirmed by the subsequent tests. In the ice analogy the Boy Scout has two chances to get back above the ice (that is, creating a bullish "spring" situation). As can be seen in the second Nokia chart (Figure 6.10), there were two such rallies. The first attempt stopped at LPSY 2 while the second attempt was halted at LPSY 3 at about the same level as PSY and LPSY 1. It can also be seen that the ice, which had provided support, now reversed its role and began acting as resistance against the attempt to move higher. These latter LPSYs 2 and 3 also expand the possible extent of the distribution (supply) pattern, thus generating the potential for a greater descent in price. Nokia ultimately declined to under 100 in year 2004 (see Figure 6.11).

Nokia's decline was stopped by the selling climax (SC), automatic rally (AR), and secondary test (ST) during July and August 2004. This sequence of stopping actions helped to form a small base of accumulation that in turn helped to propel Nokia upward to the resistance level around 110. There followed a prolonged period of backing and filling on the chart. Bearish forces remained in control, as seen by the line of floating supply around the 110 levels in Figure 6.11. Another, lesser branch of the creek

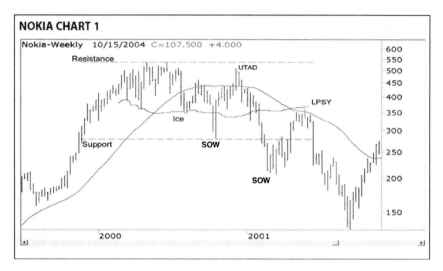

FIGURE 6.9 Nokia Chart 1—Weekly, 2000 and 2001
Source: © TradeStation Technologies 1991–2007.

FIGURE 6.10 Nokia Chart 2—Daily, 2000 to Early 2001
Source: © TradeStation Technologies 1991–2007.

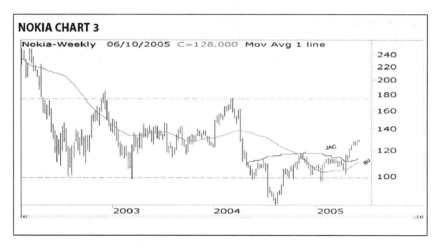

FIGURE 6.11 Nokia Chart 3—Weekly, 2002–2005
Source: © TradeStation Technologies 1991–2007.

was formulated, however, by the dominance of supply over demand during the intermediate down channel that occurred during late 2004 when Nokia's stock price declined from about 115 down to under 100 in early 2005. (See Figure 6.12.)

The Boy Scout was cognizant of these developments, as he would have been following along the edge of the creek around the 110 level so as to best judge the relative powers of supply and demand. Earlier he would have been following the minor creek as it flowed downward under the weight of supply from 115 to below 100. Then, near the end of 2004 and in early 2005, the Boy Scout would have sensed that the floating supply was drying up. He would have noticed the narrowing price range, the diminishing volume, and the absence of material price progress on the downside. At this point he would have said to himself, "Now if I back way up to make a good run for it, I bet I can jump across the creek." In the process of backing up, he would have caused the price to drop below minor support. In this process the remaining bears (floating supply) would have been flushed out of the market, as evidenced by the downward gap in price that exhausted the supply. A Wyckoff "spring" thus occurred.

Note the wide price spread of about 10 points as Nokia climbs from around 98 to 108. More significantly, note the dramatic expansion in volume that accompanies that 10 point upward move in price. The large vol-

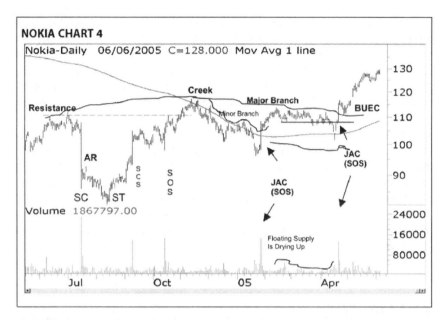

FIGURE 6.12 Nokia Chart 4—Daily, Late 2004 to Early 2005
Source: Michael Östlund & Company. © TradeStation Technologies 1991–2007.

ume day is where the "jump" occurred. Thus we also know this is where the edge of the meandering (minor) creek is. In other words, this successful JAC was also a sign of strength (SOS). A long position could have been initiated during the pullback test following the jump, at around 104, with a protective stop-loss order entered below the support level, around 95. In practice, such a long is not typically entered by a student of the Wyckoff method, because it is evident the major branch of the creek still lies ahead.

After jumping the lower and lesser branch of the creek, the Boy Scout continues upward to the vicinity around 115 where earlier he had found the flow of supply too fast and too deep to jump across. Here again, in early 2005, around the 115 price level, the creek creates a squiggly line of resistance, along the peak prices of the recovery rally, or slightly above the 110 price level of Nokia. However, this time things are different. The Boy Scout observes that the volume is shrinking and price level narrowing. He is witness to a drying up of the floating supply creating the edge of the major creek/major resistance level just above 110.

As in the instance of his earlier preparation to jump across the minor creek, the Boy Scout again creates a "spring" as he backs up to the 100 level. A relative increase in upward price spread is coupled with a notable expansion in the level of volume mark where the Boy Scout has jumped the major creek. But, by the time the propulsion of the jump dissipates, the Boy Scout would be temporarily tired out by his exertion in jumping across the creek. Hence you would logically anticipate that he would rest and consolidate his strength. He does so by backing up to the edge of the creek (BUEC). At this point we observe further confirmation that supply has been exhausted and demand is in control. The pullback comes on a relatively smaller price spread and shrinkage of volume, thus showing that supply cannot regain control. Consequently, it is now safe for the trader or the investor to enter a long position in the vicinity of 110 to 115 and to place a sell stop-order just below the 100 level.

CONCLUSION

Chapter 6 plays a vital role in spelling out for the trader-analyst the three conceptual cornerstones of the Wyckoff method: the Wyckoff laws, the Wyckoff tests, and the Wyckoff schematics. The Wyckoff method is built upon these three conceptual building blocks. It is through the application of these laws, tests, and schematics that the trader-analyst builds his skills and judgment. Moreover, these three components are uniquely powerful tools for analysis and action: The application of the three fundamental Wyckoff laws and the nine classic Wyckoff tests systematically incorporates the left-brain, analytical hemisphere, while the Wyckoff schematics for accumulations and distribution engage the right-brain, visual hemisphere. This chapter has shown that the Wyckoff method offers the trader the wherewithal to analytically support what he is seeing or what he thinks he is seeing with the hard evidence of Wyckoff principles that he can add up under the three Wyckoff laws and the nine Wyckoff tests.

In this chapter the trader-analyst was taken step by step on an excursion through phases A through E of accumulation and distribution trading ranges shown on the schematics. These were then applied to the charts of Commerz Bank and AP Land from Asia and the charts of Nokia from Europe. Furthermore, the bar and point-and-figure charts for the DJIA revealed a bull market with an upside price projection on the Dow of 14,400. Additional details and insights for taking a position as these trading ranges came to a conclusion and for the line of least resistance were provided by the nine tests operating in sympathy with the schematics and with the further compelling conclusions flowing from the use of two analogies, "Jumping across the Creek" and "The Ice Story." The laws, tests, and schematics of Chapter 6 set the stage for a more thorough application of the Wyckoff method in Chapter 7 and the harnessing of mental state control discussed in Part Three of this book.

CHAPTER 7

Anatomy
of a Trade

T he Wyckoff laws, tests, and schematics introduced in Chapter 6 set
the stage for a more thorough application in this chapter. Here, I dis-
cuss the analysis of a trading range and then the analysis of a trade
within a trending market, employing terms and principles developed by
Richard Wyckoff. The purpose of this chapter is to provide the trader with
comprehensive, concrete illustrations of the Wyckoff method of technical
analysis and the Wyckoff art of speculation. In addition, I introduce nine
new buying tests for the trader to apply when she encounters a consolidation or reaccumulation trading range.

It has been my experience while learning and then later when teaching trader-technicians the Wyckoff method that repetition is important.
Repetition of the Wyckoff laws, tests, and schematics under varying circumstances helps to ingrain a deep knowledge, comfort, and competence
with the Wyckoff method. The repeated application of these laws, principles, and schematics to a variety of concrete cases helps to cultivate in the
trader-technician a level of mastery with the Wyckoff method that I like to
call "unconscious competence"—an almost automatic, instinctive use of
the Wyckoff method. Hence, by design, the concepts and principles found
in Chapter 6 are repeated here in Chapter 7.

The Wyckoff method of technical market analysis necessitates judgment. The analyst-trader acquires judgment through experience and well-
guided illustrations of basic principles. Although the Wyckoff method is
not a mechanical system per se, high-reward, low-risk entry points can be
routinely and systematically judged with the aid of a checklist of nine
tests. Each test in the list represents a Wyckoff principle.

In this chapter I use a case study of a stock to demonstrate the nine

161

classic buying tests of the Wyckoff method at work and to describe a trader's actions from the opening to the closing of a trade. Although the case name is disguised as the San Francisco Company (SF), it does represent an actual company in the energy sector and an actual trade executed by a Wyckoff expert. For the sake of economy, the illustrations feature the bull side of the market, but they can be inverted to illustrate the bear side of the market.

As outlined in Chapter 6, the set of nine classic buying tests (and nine selling tests) was designed to diagnose significant reversal formations. The nine buying tests define the emergence of a new bull trend (see Table 7.1); a new bull trend emerges out of a trading range base that forms after a significant price decline. (The nine selling tests help define the onset of a bear trend out of a top formation following a significant advance.) Wyckoff's nine classic tests are logical, time-tested, and reliable. However, the original set of nine tests was not designed to include all of the very crucial consolidation periods that occur during both bull and bear markets.

TABLE 7.1 Wyckoff Buying Tests: Nine Classic Tests for Accumulation*

Indication	Determined From
1. Downside price objective accomplished	Figure chart
2. Preliminary support, selling climax, secondary test	Vertical and figure
3. Activity bullish (volume increases on rallies and decreases on reactions)	Vertical
4. Downward stride broken (i.e., supply line penetrated)	Vertical or figure
5. Higher supports (daily low)	Vertical or figure
6. Higher tops (daily high prices rising)	Vertical or figure
7. Stock stronger than the market (i.e., stock more responsive on rallies and more resistant to reactions than the market index)	Vertical chart
8. Base forming (horizontal price line)	Figure chart
9. Estimated upside profit potential is at least three times the loss if protective stop is hit	Figure chart for profit objective

*Applied to an average or a stock after a decline.

Adapted with modifications from Jack K. Huston, ed., *Charting the Market: The Wyckoff Method* (Seattle, WA: Technical Analysis, Inc., 1986), 87.

TABLE 7.2 New Wyckoff Buying Tests Modified for Reaccumulation

Nine Reaccumulation Tests
Resistance line broken (horizontal line across the top of the trading range)
Activity bullish (e.g., volume expanding on rallies, shrinking on declines)
Higher lows (price)
Higher highs (price)
Favorable relative strength (equal to or stronger than the market)
Correction completed in price and/or time (e.g., one-half retracement, support line reached)
Consolidation pattern formed (e.g., triangular formation)
Stepping-stone confirming count
3:1 reward-to-risk ratio

Followers of the Wyckoff method refer to consolidations as reaccumulation or redistribution. There is, however, a void in the Wyckoff method with respect to tests to define the trends that emerge out of consolidation formations. This chapter attempts to fill this void by introducing a new set of nine buying tests for reaccumulation (see Table 7.2). The following SF case study is used to illustrate this new set of nine buying tests for reaccumulation.

As previously mentioned, this case study reflects an actual trade made by an expert in the Wyckoff method. This expert used the stock options listed on SF as his trading vehicle. We use both a vertical line, or bar, chart (Figure 7.1) and a point-and-figure chart (Figure 7.2) of SF to illustrate both sets of buying tests for accumulation and reaccumulation.

When approaching this case of nine classic buying tests, the reader ought to keep in mind the following admonitions from *Reminiscences of a Stock Operator*:

> *The average ticker hound—or, as they used to call him, tapeworm—goes wrong, I suspect, as much from overspecialization as from anything else. It means a highly expensive inelasticity. After all, the game of speculation isn't all mathematics or set rules, however rigid the main laws may be. Even in my tape reading something enters that is more than mere arithmetic. There is what I call the behavior of a stock, actions that enable you to judge whether or not it is going to proceed in accordance with the precedents that your observation has noted. If a stock doesn't act right*

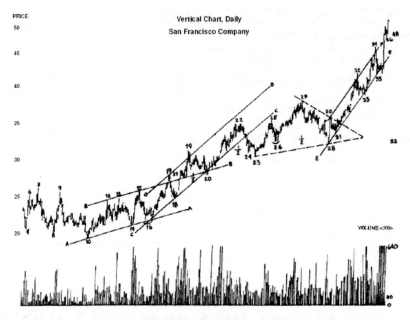

FIGURE 7.1   Bar Chart for the San Francisco Company
Source: SMI, with adaptations and modifications.

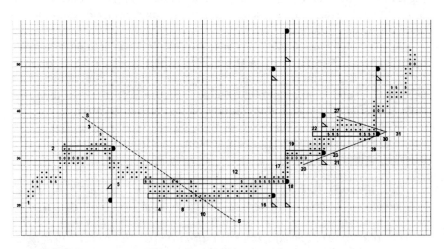

FIGURE 7.2   Point-and-Figure Chart for the San Francisco Company
Source: SMI, with adaptations and modifications.

don't touch it; because, being unable to tell precisely what is wrong, you cannot tell which way it is going. No diagnosis, no prognosis. No prognosis, no profit. This experience has been the experience of so many traders so many times that I can give this rule: In a narrow market, when prices are not getting anywhere to speak of but move within a narrow range, there is no sense in try-ing to anticipate what the next big movement is going to be—up or down. The thing to do is to watch the market, read the tape to de-termine the limits of the get-nowhere prices, and make up your mind that you will not take an interest until the price breaks through the limit in either direction. A speculator must concern himself with making money out of the market and not with insist-ing that the tape must agree with him.

Therefore, the thing to determine is the speculative line of least resistance *[emphasis added] at the moment of trading; and what he should wait for is the moment when that line defines itself, because that is his signal to get busy.*

The Nine Classic Buying Tests of the Wyckoff Method

In essence, the passage of all of the nine classic buying tests of the Wyck-off method defines the *line of least resistance*.

The case study we are using follows a Wyckoff-oriented trader as he identifies and capitalizes on trading opportunities in SF. While the general market index is not shown here, the SF Company exhibited good relative strength compared to the general market index. The nine classic buying tests, listed in Table 7.1, are passed at the conclusion of the base-building period and the trader elects to buy call options on SF and to enter stop-loss orders just below prior supports in the trading range. Later, as peri-ods of consolidation come to a halt, the trader rolls his options forward to a later month and to a higher strike price. At the end of the SF case, the option trader is in a position to wrap up his campaign, take his profit, and go home.

Test One   The first Wyckoff buying test to be passed was downside price. Objective accomplished. This test was passed at point 4 on Figure 7.2, which is the $21 level for SF. The preceding top in SF around point 3 built the cause for the decline, and at $21 the maximum effect of that cause was realized.

Test Two   The second Wyckoff buying test was passed at point 8 on the bar chart, which was a secondary test that occurred on relatively light volume and narrowing downside price movement compared to the selling climax at point 4. At point 4 the relative increase in volume and the price closing at the high of the day signaled to our trader that a provisional selling climax might be at hand. At point 4, demand was entering the market to absorb the supply of stock being offered in the vicinity of the downside price objective (buying test one). At this juncture the trader should have covered any outstanding short sales on SF at the open of the next day.

The successful secondary test at point 8 revealed that supply was being exhausted for the moment and so the downtrend was stopped, at least temporarily. It was now the job of the trader to sit patiently on the sidelines until an accumulation base had been formed.

Tests Three and Four Buying test three requires judging the volume on the rising and falling price waves in the trading range. A visual inspection reveals that by point 16 on the SF chart, volume was expanding on the rallies and shrinking on the declines. By the time point 16 was reached on the vertical chart, SF would have passed the test: activity bullish. Turning once again to the figure chart discloses that in the vicinity of point 10 the downward sloping supply line (dashed line SS) was broken. Thus around point 10, buying test four was passed. These four foregoing tests, although necessary, were not sufficient evidence of accumulation, so the trader had to remain patient until all of the buying tests clearly revealed that a base had been formed and that the evidence had accumulated to prove that the line of least resistance was decidedly upward.

Tests Five and Six The next two Wyckoff tests are crucial to the definition of an upward line of least resistance. Buying test five is higher lows (higher supports) and test six is higher highs (higher tops). The vertical line or bar chart of SF showed higher price lows along the gradient of points 14, 16, and 18. In a parallel fashion, a series of rising price peaks appeared at points 12, 13, 15, and 17. At points 17 and 18, the trader-analyst could clearly declare that the higher highs and higher lows had been reached, and, therefore, Wyckoff buying tests five and six had been passed.

Test Eight Points 15 and 16, and then again 17 and 18 on the charts, may also be viewed as "jumps and backups," hence legitimate junctures at which to enter a long position. At point 16 on the charts, and even more definitely at point 18, the trader in the SF case concluded that a base had been formed, a cause had been built, and a favorable reward-to-risk ratio was present. The count taken along the $22 line of the figure chart from point 16 back to beyond point 4 generated a cause of 27 points for upside projections of $47 to $49, when that count was added to the low of the trading range at $20 and to the count line itself at $22.

Moreover, the count along the $25 level at point 18 sanctioned price projections as high as $57. As a result of these analyses, the trader was justified in concluding that the eighth test had been passed. (See Appendix B at the end of Chapter 5 for a guide to making price projections using a figure chart.)

Tests Seven and Nine Entering a long position in SF at $25 (point 18) and setting a protective stop-loss order just below support at $19 would create a risk exposure of $6. The figure chart count along the 25 line equaled 31 points of upside potential. Thus, the estimated profit potential exceeded the indicated risk by over three times, so buying test nine was also passed. A comparison of the SF chart to its relevant market index (not shown) would have revealed that SF was comparatively stronger than the market. Consequently, SF was favored as a candidate with superior upside prospects (buying test seven was passed).

By the time SF had reached point 18, all of the nine classic buying tests had been passed. At point 18, the line of least resistance had defined itself as upward trending and the trader could have entered call option positions with favorable reward-to-risk parameters. At this stage the trader purchased SF call options that were at the money.

Nine New Buying Tests for Reaccumulation

In a quest for unity and economy, numerous principles of the Wyckoff method were distilled into nine classic buying tests and nine selling tests. As explained earlier, the nine buying tests were originally designed to define trends coming out of major areas of accumulation that followed significant price declines. In addition to these major reversal formations at bottoms and tops, there are also many important continuation patterns known by students of Wyckoff as reaccumulation and redistribution. However, these important consolidation patterns lack an appropriate set of nine tests to define the resumption of the upward trend or downward trend. Reaccumulation and redistribution areas simply lack a set of buying or selling tests that are equivalent to the classic nine tests for major accumulation or major distribution.

Unfortunately, the original set of Wyckoff tests that were used to define departures from bottoms or tops cannot be transferred easily nor applied *in toto* to zones of reaccumulation or redistribution. Some tests, such as the second one, "preliminary support, selling climax, and secondary test," simply do not apply. The selling climax is good for signaling the onset of a bottom after a bear market decline, but reaccumulation zones start after a price advance, and thus most often commence with a buying climax. A straightforward modification of this climax rule to fit reaccumulations is made even more ambiguous by the fact that distribution after a bull market advance may likewise start with preliminary supply and a buying climax.

Similar limitations apply to other tests found in the original list of nine. For instance, neither test one, "downside (upside) price objective accomplished," nor test four, "downward (upward) stride broken," is necessarily relevant for analyzing reaccumulation (redistribution). In their place, I substitute other Wyckoff rules that tell us more clearly that a correction has been completed in time and price. These substitute measures are, for example, the interception by price of the upward-sloping demand line and/or the reaching of the one-half retracement level.

In place of "downside price objective accomplished," the relevant buying test for reaccumulation becomes the breaking of the horizontal resistance line along the top of the trading range. That horizontal resistance line confines the sideways trend channel in much the same way as the downtrend slanting supply lines confine a bearish trend channel. Moreover, when a wedge or triangular formation appears, Wyckoff literature advises the trader to enter upon the significant price-and-volume breaking of the resistance (support) line.

The "stepping-stone confirming count" (new test eight) measures the amount of potential generated during a reaccumulation trading range. This confirming count deserves special consideration as a reaccumulation test because it possesses an important Wyckoff timing principle. Thus the trader should be alert to the possible resumption of the upward trend when the figure chart has generated enough reaccumulation potential, or "count," to confirm the target from the original base.

In the case of SF, this means the trader should be poised for a resumption of the upward trend when the count generated during a consolidation grows large enough to meet the price objectives that equal the objectives generated during the original accumulation base. If along the $35 level, for instance, the up and down price waves during a period of sideways consolidation reach a point where the figure chart count measures 14 points, thereby projecting to $49, then the trader should become highly alert for the possible resumption of the upward trend. Remember that the original base count along the $22 level (point 16) projected to a maximum of $49. If a consolidation projects to the same objectives, then we say that it *confirms* the original count taken along the base.

Failed Tests To illustrate the new list of modified Wyckoff tests for reaccumulation, let us return to the case study of the SF Company. After the base had been completed, the Wyckoff-oriented trader entered a long option position at point 18 on the SF charts. The SF stock then moved up sharply from point 18 to point 19, where it encountered enough supply to halt its advance, and so SF entered a period of hesitation and sideways movement starting at 19. This period of hesitation commenced with a buying climax around point 19, which would also have alerted the trader of the possible onset of reaccumulation before resumption of the upward trend or even possibly distribution leading to a reversal of trend. The trader, who was actually operating in SF at the time of this case study, recounted his upside figure chart objective to $49 and chose to wait out this interruption in the trend.

At point 20 the trader observed a "spring" situation, so presumably he could have ventured a long position around the $29 level. At this juncture he could have consulted the checklist of reaccumulation tests and concluded that reaccumulation buy tests two and three had been passed. At point 20 the volume had dried up considerably and the downside price progress was minimal, which taken together revealed a lack of supply being pressed upon the market. Moreover, the interception of the rising support line CC indicated that a sufficient correction in time and price had taken place (test six).

However, it was not until the surpassing of the resistance at $31 on the move to point 22, on wide upside price movement and expanded volume, that SF satisfied several other reaccumulation tests, such as test one, "resistance line broken" and test four, "higher high (price)." Then at point 23, a pullback to a "higher low" was executed (test three) and a count of the figure chart along the 31 level would have projected upward to a range of $37 to $39. However, this count was insufficient to confirm the earlier price target projections of $47 to $49 taken along the $22 level. Hence, reaccumulation test eight was not passed. Moreover, a trade taken at 31 also would have fallen short of the 3:1 reward-to-risk minimum because a stop would need to have been placed 3 points away at 28, and the reaccumulation count was only 8 points. Thus, test nine also failed. Presumably, a pattern analyst could have labeled the consolidation from points 19 to 20 a *pennant* (test seven).

Reaccumulation Tests Passed   With two tests already failed, our trader chose to pass up adding to his position at the point 23 juncture on the charts. Shortly thereafter the SF stock shot up from point 23 to point 27 and underwent a more prolonged correction. This complex correction would have been a challenge to the pattern recognition skills of most Wyckoff analysts. Nonetheless, the Wyckoff expert who was operating in the stock identified it as a large wedge or apex, which fulfilled reaccumulation test seven. He took a count across the $35 level back to the zone around point 22. That count indicated a reaccumulation that was sizable enough to reach the $47 to $49 target that was first established at point 16, and in the process it flashed a "stepping-stone confirming count" (reaccumulation buy signal number seven).

As price broke out of this wedge formation, it burst through the (downward sloping) resistance line connecting points 27 and 30, triggering a passage of reaccumulation test one. On balance, the volume tended to expand during the rallies and shrink during the declines while the SF stock was in the triangular trading range (passage of reaccumulation test two). Price registered a series of higher lows from point 23 to point 28 to point 31 (passed reaccumulation test three). This series of higher lows by SF contrasted sharply with the series of lower lows that was occurring in the general market index at that time (passage of reaccumulation test five). Moreover, at points 28 and 31, price met support near the one-half retracement level of the move from point 20 to point 27 (the "$^1/_2$" mark on Figure 7.1), thus fulfilling reaccumulation test six. At either point 28 or point 31, the trader would have had a better than 3:1 reward-to-risk ratio (14 count versus 3 to 4 points of risk) for the passage of reaccumulation test nine.

The trader under the foregoing reaccumulation circumstances should, and did, roll his options contract forward to a later expiration and higher strike price. He simultaneously increased the size of his line. The passage of all nine reaccumulation tests had created a compelling enough case for him to roll his option contracts forward at the $35 strike and to add to his position.

Conclusion

When SF reached the $49 level, the trader exited his SF options position. He judged that the relatively high volume occurring in the price-objective zone around $49 was sufficient reason to exit. Making the case for exiting even more enticing, the general market index had started to weaken and diverge from the higher price set by SF around $49.

There were targets outstanding at $51 to $57, but this Wyckoff-oriented trader elected to take his profits at $49 because that was the maximum effect of the cause built during the reaccumulation stepping-stone count along the $35 line (point 22 to point 31). He reckoned that he would have to weather another sideways to down correction/consolidation as further preparation for the final advance. He further reckoned that the risk did not justify waiting to capture the final eight points available beyond $49. Of course, as we can see retrospectively, he exited prematurely because SF promptly advanced to $54. (Upon further reflection, this Wyckoff trader said that he would do the same thing again because "bulls make money, bears make money, and pigs get slaughtered.")

The case study of the San Francisco Company demonstrated how, with the help the Wyckoff nine classic buying tests, an options trader could have entered favorable reward-to-risk long positions just as the line of least resistance became defined with the passage of the nine classic tests for accumulation and as the stock was leaving the base formation. This case study also demonstrated how an options trader could have later employed the new set of nine reaccumulation tests both to roll his contracts forward and to add to his position. The fulfillment of the "stepping-stone confirming count" nature of this reaccumulation consolidation gave the trader added reason to hold on to his positions until his longer-term base targets were being reached at $49. Furthermore, the stepping-stone confirming count provided an additional compelling reason for him to exit his long options on the burst of strength as SF reached the $49 level.

The Wyckoff nine classic buying tests and the set of nine new tests for reaccumulation enabled the trader in the SF Company to execute a fine campaign and realize a sizeable increase in his equity. Together with good judgment and experience, the tools outlined in this chapter will help you in your quest to control risk, ride winners, and take home maximum profits.

APPENDIX A: EXIT STRATEGIES

As with most other technical analysis approaches to Wall Street, the Wyckoff method devotes the majority of its attention to the ways that one can identify relatively low-risk, high-reward entry points. On the other hand, the Wyckoff literature mentions exit strategies only incidentally. Indeed, when Wyckoff exits are brought up, most attention is devoted to provide for loss-minimizing exit strategies rather than to exit strategies for profit maximization. In an effort to bring more attention to Wyckoff *exits* for profit, this section marshals together the incidental remarks of Wyckoff on exit strategies and extends them into a more useful framework. The result of my research and thinking reveals that Wyckoff strategies for exits can be usefully classified as simply as one, two, three.

The three Wyckoff-oriented exit strategies, ranked according to their degree of desirability, are as follows:

1. Take profits, eliminate positions, and exit the market upon climatic action in the price objective zone.
2. Exit the market when there is repeated evidence that the current trend will not continue, and indeed may reverse.
3. Exit the market automatically upon the hitting of a trailing stop (loss) order.

Why isn't strategy 1 turned into an automatic exit strategy by entering a sell or buy order somewhere in the price target zone, say in the middle of the zone? The answer is that exit strategy 1 also requires climactic volume action that halts a price movement.

Exit strategy 2 requires that you monitor a market, a group, or a stock for price and volume clues that warn you of trend exhaustion. Diagnosis of the health of a trend requires you to apply all of your Wyckoff savvy in order to reach judicious conclusions. Be aware that the discretionary nature of this exit strategy can challenge your mental and emotional capacity to take action.

The "stop-out strategy," or exit strategy 3, is the backup, default, passive approach. And for those who lack the skills and knowledge to exit on strategies 1 or 2, the stop order approach of exit strategy 3 is the ultimate fallback way to exit a market. Moreover, placement of trailing stops below (above) prior important turning points is essential to the Wyckoff method of risk control.

You are urged to practice all three exit strategies until they became second nature to you.

PART THREE

Mental State Management

CHAPTER 8

Trader Psychology and Mental Disciplines

ichard D. Wyckoff observed many years ago that the mastery of a sound technical analysis methodology was only one half of the game of speculation in the securities and commodities markets. The other half of the game was the control of one's own emotions and the mastery of certain mental qualities or mental discipline. Wyckoff argued that "rigid self-control is half the battle. . . . You must operate with no emotions whatsoever . . . until you can learn to trade and invest without hope or fear you will not meet with all the success you should."

Wyckoff went on to cite the injunctions of a famed nineteenth-century cotton speculator, Dickson G. Watts, who said that "the qualities essential to the equipment of a speculator are judgment, self-reliance, courage, prudence and pliability. To these could be added another quality, patience." Wyckoff concluded: "If you do not possess courage, self-reliance, patience, prudence and pliability, cultivate those qualities. . . . You must train yourself . . . make a searching analysis of your own mental process."[1]

Although this need for mental discipline in traders was recognized over 100 years ago, the serious study of trader psychology and concepts and techniques for understanding and enhancing the trader's mental discipline did not become popular until the late twentieth century. In his June 1994 article "Mind Games" in *Futures* magazine, David Nusbaum wrote: "Many traders are turning to psychological 'coaches,' eager to find an edge on the unknown they can control—their own behavior." He went on to report that:

This trend—of course—started in California. The study of the psychology of trading began in 1988 for the Zim's group, an informal

collection of money managers, retail and institutional brokers and
independent traders named for a small hamburger chain in San
Francisco where they first held meetings.

  Psychology was the focus, says Zim's member Hank Pruden,
also editor of the Market Technicians Association Journal, *because*
following a mechanistic program is all right for beginners, "but not
if you wish to be a world champion. . . . There are other elements in-
volved, including the ability to trust your intuition to perceive
things differently." In other words, using your head.[2]

Nusbaum's article profiled several popular "trader's coaches" and
their techniques. Notable among them were Mark Douglas, author of *The*
Disciplined Trader: Developing Winning Attitudes (Upper Saddle River,
NJ: Prentice Hall Press, 1990); Charles Faulkner of Mental Edge Trading
Associates, Chicago; and Dr. Van K. Tharp of the Van Tharp Institute in
Raleigh, North Carolina, who at the time of publication had written five
books on trading psychology.

Starting in 1988, I collaborated with Tharp on a study of trader psychology and mental discipline. Our collaboration culminated in the creation of "The Ten Tasks of Top Trading," which led to an article that was
ultimately published in the *MTA (Market Technicians Association) Jour-*
nal, Winter 1992–1993.

I was inspired to create the *"Seven* Tasks of Top Trading" after reading
John Sweeny's article entitled "Van K. Tharp, Ph.D.: Trader's Psychologist"
in the April 1987 issue of *Technical Analysis of Stocks & Commodities*
(TASC) magazine. In the article, Tharp was quoted as saying that, based
on his training, experience, and six years of research and testing, he was
convinced that "Everything is psychological in terms of investing. So it's
really understanding those psychological variables that are most important for winning and losing. . . . For example, each system typically has a
number of discrete trading steps that one must follow and each step is associated with some distinct psychological state. If you follow the steps
but you don't have the right psychological state associated with it, you're
going to be in trouble."[3]

That interview in *TASC* prompted me to start thinking about the possible task steps and corresponding mental states. I came up with a model
composed of seven different tasks and the mental state appropriate for
each task. Table 8.1 is the original model that I created to share with
Tharp and the members of the Zim's group.

I called the model "Know How by Hobbes." *Know How: Guided Pro-*
grams for Inventing Your Own Best Future (San Rafael, CA: FuturePace,
Inc., 1986), by Leslie Cameron-Bander, David Gordon, and Michael
Lebeau, is a Neuro-linguistic Programming book, and Hobbes is the

TABLE 8.1 Seven Tasks of Top Trading

Steps	Mental State
1. Out (of the market, no trades on)	Indifferent, calm, detached, contented, appreciative
2. Analysis (of market opportunity using charts and indicators)	Curious, alert, objective, systematic, thorough, dispassionate
3. Action I ("stalking the market" like a cat stalks its prey)	Patient, vigilant, controlled, cautious
4. Action II (making the decision, giving the order, taking the trade)	Prompt, courageous, aggressive, abandoned
5. Abort (exit, quit the market, break even, or take a loss)	Anxious, fearful, confused, protective, urgent, disappointed, accepting
6. Monitor (let profits run, ride with the trend)	Patient, calm, detached, resolved, tenacious, vigilant, pliable
7. Take profits (initiate an exit strategy)	Motivated, satisfied, encouraged

comic-strip tiger of "Calvin and Hobbes." Both Tharp and Tony Robbins (*Unlimited Power*, New York: Free Press, 1997) stress the importance of using physical posture to evoke a desired mental state; my original model included corresponding cartoons of Hobbes with appropriate facial expressions and physical postures for each task/mental state. The idea is that external facial expressions associated with a mental state can trigger that mental state internally and lead to internal self-talk and feelings.

As we will see in Chapter 9, the "Abort" task in Table 8.1 reflects a powerful and efficient mental strategy: visual, auditory, and kinesthetic (see it as a bad trade, tell yourself it is a bad trade, and get the feeling of fear to take action). You will come to appreciate how your ability to access the emotion of "fear" in the circumstance of a "bad trade" is *good* because fear helps to protect you! Notice also the importance of reframing. You, the trader, need to place the frame "bad" around your deteriorating trade; otherwise you may lull yourself into believing that it remains a "good" trade, causing you to hope, procrastinate, give it another chance, and maybe even pull your stop-loss order.

I created the initial model for myself and soon I shared it with the Zim's group mentioned in Nusbaum's article and with Tharp. Soon thereafter Tharp and I started working together in 1988 to perfect the model and, after several months of discussion, reworking, and checking out "Know How by Hobbes" with outstanding professional traders, the final and complete model became the Ten Tasks of Top Trading.

When he saw the final model, market wizard Ed Seykota told Tharp that, in his opinion, the Ten Tasks of Top Trading was an important contribution to the discipline of trading. We soon discovered that many other traders found that these ten tasks made it much easier for them to attain the mental discipline they needed in order to follow through on their trades.

As an educator, I felt strongly that the Ten Tasks should be published and made available for other traders to use. Tharp agreed with me, and as I mentioned earlier, "The Ten Tasks of Top Trading" appeared in the Winter 1992–1993 issue of the *MTA Journal.* I strongly believe that the Ten Tasks will be invaluable in helping you appreciate and achieve necessary mental state control for your own top trading. With the *MTA Journal* editor's permission, I have reproduced the original article here for your convenience.

THE TEN TASKS OF TOP TRADING

by Van K. Tharp, Ph.D. and Henry O. Pruden, Ph.D.

Our purpose . . . is to model or duplicate successful trading. . . . The first and most important aspect of modeling is task decomposition to determine the different tasks involved in the behavior you want to model. Unfortunately, most traders, even the best ones, don't know what those tasks are. When you ask them, you get responses like:

- "I don't really know. I trade when it feels right. It's mostly gut feel."
- "Well, I get up in the morning, and I do other things until the markets close, and then I turn on my computer and the data comes in via the modem, the computer cranks out an analysis, the orders go out to the brokerage network, and then I do other things. That's effectively what I do, broken down into tasks."
- "The formula for what I do is look for X, Y, and Z. When I see that pattern and the market hits my entry point, I get in."

These responses only begin to detail the tasks that are involved in trading. . . . *This model is the starting block for understanding successful trading.*

The Ten Tasks

The ten stages in the model are illustrated [in Figure 8.1]. These ten tasks fit the metaphor of a hunter, a predator, or a warrior. For example, in his book, *The Art of War,* Sun Tzu points out that *battles are won before they start.* Think about the implications of that statement. In the case of trad-

FIGURE 8.1   The Ten Tasks of Top Trading

ing, it means that your mental state and preparation virtually determine whether you will win or lose in a given trade before you even open the position. Perhaps that statement is a little strong, but I believe that your mental state and preparation determine whether you will win on the average. The statement also points out the importance of the first stage of successful trading, a task called *self-analysis*.

1. Daily Self-Analysis   Successful trading is 40% risk control and 60% self-control. In turn, the risk control portion is one half money management and one half market analysis. Thus, market analysis is only about 20% of successful trading. Yet most traders emphasize market analysis while avoiding self-control and de-emphasizing risk control. To become successful, traders need to invert their priorities.

Trading involves human performance, and that performance can be objectively measured in terms of profits and losses. You can't hide from your performance record. Your performance is profitable, breakeven, or losing. Since *you* are the most important factor in *your* performance, doesn't it make sense to spend time analyzing yourself? The best traders do it subconsciously. You will probably be one step ahead of them if you make a conscious effort to begin each day with self-analysis.

Stressors, or anything that detracts from your performance such as a cold or illness, are going to impact upon your trading. What if your normal performance is breakeven and you have a cold which reduces your performance by 10%? Suddenly, you're going to start losing money. Even if your typical performance is profitable, if some stressor reduces it by 10%, then you might find yourself at breakeven or losing money. As a result, you are better off staying away from trading until you eliminate the stress from your life. If you don't spend some time analyzing yourself prior to trading, then you are likely to trade out of habit. And if you do trade under these circumstances, then you'll wonder why you suddenly start losing.

Numerous people find that their best trades are the hardest trades to take. You generally go against the crowd in the best trades. As a result, when most people believe you are wrong with enough conviction to be in the market, and you're around a lot of them, it's very hard to go against them. As a result, people who trade in a crowd perceive their good trades to be "hard trades." Let's assume that for you the hard trades are the big winners. How do you know if a trade is hard, or whether you are simply not in the mood to trade? You don't. Self-analysis allows you to distinguish between the "hard" trade and those times when you make the trade seem hard.

You might do self-analysis in several ways. The easiest method is to develop a rating scale going from 1 to 8, with 1 being poor and 8 being great. A sample rating scale is illustrated [in Figure 8.2].

At the beginning of each day, spend about 30 seconds meditating. Go inside yourself and determine how you are feeling that particular day. Rate yourself on the scale, with 1 being your worst, 8 being your best, and

How I Feel Today

1   2   3   4   5   6   7   8
Poor   **Great**

FIGURE 8.2 Sample Rating Scale

4 to 5 being average. For a month or so, compare your trading performance with your morning ratings. You will find that trading may not be worthwhile unless your rating is above a particular level. When you discover what that rating level is, make a rule not to trade unless your self-rating is above it.

An even more effective way to conduct self-analysis is by means of a parts analysis. In essence, I find the belief that we are composed of parts, most of which are in your unconscious mind, to be useful. You might think of your parts as your various roles in life, although they are probably more extensive than that. Each part is formed to carry out some positive intention. For example, you might establish a part to protect you or to increase your security, to help you make money, to have fun, to bring love into your life, to bring excitement into your life, etc. Since most of these parts are unconscious, you are not aware of them. In fact, you probably don't pay attention to any of them. As a result, each part simply finds behaviors to fulfill its intention. Those behaviors are not necessarily in your overall best interest, since the behaviors of one part often will conflict with the behaviors of another. For example, if a part wants your attention, it will produce some signal to get that attention. If you ignore the signal that it gives you, it will produce a more dramatic signal. This process continues until it finally gets your attention. Unfortunately, many traders do not respond to these signals until they become very dramatic such as extreme anxiety or a major loss.

People can learn to determine what parts are active and how to communicate with those parts easily. What happens is that once parts know that you are willing to pay attention to them, they do not have to produce dramatic signals to get your attention. Self-analysis, using the parts model, amounts to a short dialogue with your parts in the morning. It might simply amount to asking yourself, "Does anybody (i.e., any of your parts) need anything?" while you pay attention to any signals you get. Be sensitive to a range of internal cues. Your parts might communicate by means of a voice, a visual image, or a feeling of some type. Be open to such signals throughout the day.

When you do this process every morning, it only takes 15 seconds to a minute to complete. Furthermore, the parts dialogue method of self-analysis has an advantage over the self-rating method in that if you have a problem, you can deal with it immediately by finding an appropriate way to meet the needs of the part in distress. In contrast, if you just give yourself a poor rating without knowing the source of the problem, then all you can do is not trade.

Self-analysis, when practiced regularly, can make an immense difference in your trading. If you do it, we think you will be amazed at the improvement in your trading results.

2. Daily Mental Rehearsal   One of the most important activities to improving almost any form of human performance is mental rehearsal. Trading is no exception. Remember how important mental rehearsal is for top shooters. The top shooter in the world rehearsed every single shot that might be necessary in a shooting match. The second best shooter believed that rehearsal was important, but he did not rehearse the entire match. Most shooters, in contrast, do not even practice mental rehearsal. Similarly, most traders fail to practice mental rehearsal. How about you?

Top athletes—from professionals to Olympians—mentally rehearse their performance prior to acting. For example, Billy Casper, one of the best golfers on the PGA Senior Tour, almost never three-putts a green. Casper claims that he learned to putt in almost total darkness and that experience taught him to really concentrate on the internal image of the putt he is attempting to make. Extreme concentration on his internal mental image is what makes him one of the world's best putters.

The rehearsal task allows you to pre-plan how you will carry out any of the trading tasks so that the actual task is automatic. It allows you to anticipate problems and develop appropriate solutions to them. And most importantly, mental rehearsal helps you avoid mistakes. Nevertheless, there are appropriate and non-appropriate ways to do the rehearsal.

One of my clients uses a planning log for his next trading day. One entry he showed me went something like this:

> *Tomorrow will be hell. I will be tempted to trade—probably from both sides of the market and probably several times. In addition, the market is due for a big swing tomorrow and they will try to grab my stops. It'll be a real test of my mental state control.*

His plan anticipates problems, but from the wrong framework. He is actually programming himself for a day of "hell." Typically, you get what you program yourself to get. Instead, he could have said the following:

> *Tomorrow will have some interesting challenges. The market may come close to my stops. That is part of the game of trading. I will stick to my rules and practice mental state control throughout the day.*

In this second form of mental rehearsal, he is anticipating the same events. However, the events are *challenges*, not "hell." More importantly, he is rehearsing carrying out his plan and following his rules, despite potential challenges. As a result, his rehearsal will be very effective.

A client in my Super-Trader Program performs his mental rehearsal by listening to a 60-minute tape each day. He has made tapes covering most of the important tasks in this model. Each tape includes a description of the task and the appropriate mental state, as well as music and poetry to help him achieve the correct mental framework for the task.

3. Developing a Low-Risk Idea The predator must know the location of his prey, the water holes used by his prey, and the habits of his prey. Once he knows that information, the predator can relax until the prey appears. The next stage in the model, as a result, involves *developing a low-risk idea*.

I initially called this task "market analysis." However, one of the best traders in the world told me that for most traders their market analysis amounts to building a straw house. They collect data about the markets; they look at different patterns of charts and specific market indicators; and they even make predictions about the future direction of the market and then focus on trying to help those predictions come true. However, they don't consider the probabilities of winning and losing or the amount that might be won or lost. In other words, what most traders do in terms of market analysis has nothing to do with making low-risk trades. Hunters like to build straw houses, but that activity has nothing to do with catching prey. It amounts to spending time and energy on what you think is important, while you avoid the really important issues. Building a straw house has more to do with giving you a false sense of security. Your straw house might indicate where you live and dictate the boundaries of your territory. In that sense, having a straw house is important.

A fundamental principle of modeling is that those elements which are important to a skill will be present in everyone who performs that skill at a top level. In contrast, elements which are present in one person at the top of a skilled area, but not in another, are probably idiosyncrasies. Since successful traders analyze the market in different ways, the type of analysis one does is not that important as long as it helps to minimize the risk taken. In addition, since there are countless examples of successful traders training other people in their methodology yet not being able to transfer their success, the methodology per se must not be a critical aspect of that success. What top traders *all* do, on the other hand, is develop a low-risk idea. If your market analysis focuses on developing a low-risk idea, then you are performing a useful task in terms of making money as a trader.

Most traders analyze the market in order to predict prices. Predicting prices has little to do with successful trading. What is important is determining when the risk is overwhelmingly in your favor and then controlling that risk (i.e., through the next five tasks in the model). You have already learned that the development of a written game plan for generating low-risk ideas is a critical task in preparing to become a top trader.

There are several subtasks to *developing a low-risk idea*. The first subtask involves *gathering data* (i.e., recording the high, low, opening, and closing prices; the volume; the advance/decline ratio in the stock market; sentiment indicators; etc.). It involves transferring information into your charts, your computer, or your tables. Other subtasks involve *creative brainstorming* and *determining the risk behind those ideas*.

Most traders gather data and jump to a conclusion at the same time. For example, if you have a bearish bias, then most of your trades will tend to be on the short side—even in a major bull market. When you interpret data you begin to form an opinion which will strongly influence any subsequent operations that you do. Be objective and dispassionate while you are doing the analysis. Complete the entire data gathering phase of market analysis before you brainstorm. Once you have generated a number of ideas, determine the risk behind each idea. Don't jump to conclusions until the entire sequence is complete.

Avoid the opinions of others while you are developing your low-risk idea. The thoughts of others can easily result in your jumping to a conclusion prior to completing your own analysis. In addition, other people are usually wrong, so you do not want to accept the crowd sentiment. The only exception to this rule is if you know someone who accurately signals market turns by his euphoria about the market continuing a move. If you know such a person, then consider using that person's reaction as one of your sentiment indicators.

Document the development of your ideas. This documentation will provide you with valuable information in some of the later tasks that you will need to do, such as your daily debriefing and your periodic review.

Once you have a low-risk idea about how to trade, you must take that idea to the market. Thus, the next task in the model is "stalking" your idea in the market.

4. Stalking Imagine the following scenario: You have developed an idea that you think has little risk and you want to open a position. You have two choices. You could just jump into the market or you could attempt to find the best possible price by becoming a day-trader. The essence of "stalking" is to find the best possible price for entry. Thus, stalking is another form of risk control.

Think about the predator after its prey. Have you ever watched a young cat chase a bird? It sees the bird and then runs after it. The young cat gives the bird a lot of warning, so it has little chance of catching the bird unless the bird flies right into it. Contrast the young cat with the mature cat. The mature animal stalks the bird. It waits until the bird gets close enough so that the kill is almost certain. At that moment it pounces. The mature cat will expend little energy unless it knows that there is a good chance of success.

Top traders love the hunting metaphor to describe what they do. One of them, for example, claims he is like a cheetah. The cheetah can outrun any animal, but it still stalks its prey. It won't attack until it is right on top of its prey. In addition, the cheetah usually waits for a weak or lame animal to get close. Another top trader told me that he trades like a lion. He watches the herd for weeks until something *other* than his presence causes the herd to panic. When the herd panics, he then chases a weak or lame animal that appears most confused. The difference between an average hunter and a really skilled animal like the swift cheetah or the cunning lion is that the skilled hunter waits until the odds are overwhelmingly in his favor.

Stalking means making sure the odds are even more in your favor by paying attention to the smallest time frame possible for you. This means that you must narrow your focus to find the best possible entry price in the day (e.g., by selling an intraday rally or buying on an intraday decline). Steidlmayer's Market Profile® was designed for this purpose, but other technical signals will give you the same information.

Stalking is difficult for most people because it requires a mental state that is totally different from the mental state required in the next task, the action phase of training. The mental state for stalking your idea involves a broad focus, a slowly moving time frame, and a strong intensity. These qualities are a distinct contrast to the mental characteristics that most people have when they have developed a low-risk idea about the market. Most traders, after analyzing the market, are energized and ready to act. By doing so, they don't miss an opportunity, but they also increase their risk because they are rehearsing action rather than responding to actual market conditions.

When you are stalking, you need to get into the flow of the market. Become sensitive to a range of cues! The market is sending you numerous signals if you pay attention to them. Learn how to read and interpret those cues. One of my clients, a long time frame trader who only puts on occasional trades, begins the stalking task by paper trading a position in the opposite direction of the one he is planning. This helps him develop "finger-tip" feeling for the market. At the same time, he knows that the best time to get out of his paper trade is also the best time to open his planned position.

5. Action   The action stage only takes an instant. But to perform it correctly, you must be aggressive, bold, and courageous. You just do it. The trader must have quickness, accuracy, and a narrow focus of attention— concentrating on getting the trade off accurately and quickly. He must be quick or he will miss the opportunity. And he must be accurate, or he might find himself with something other than his prey.

The action phase of trading must be strong and intense. A weak response will not get the job done, because it lacks the necessary commitment. Imagine what would happen if a lion or tiger fails to go all-out when it attacks its prey. The answer is obvious. It would go hungry.

Action involves commitment to entering a market position. If the trader has completed the first three tasks, then he knows the consequences of this commitment. He knows he is ready. He knows the maximum loss he is willing to tolerate and the potential profit. He knows that the risk is overwhelmingly in his favor, and as a result, the commitment is easy to make.

When action is appropriate, reflection, second guessing, and delays are inappropriate. You should have reflected on the consequences of your trade in the tasks prior to the action stage. When a trader thinks about consequences at the time of action, he cannot act with abandonment. The action stage is a time for prompt, courageous action.

Similarly, the action stage needs to be very accurate. Both you and your prey are moving rapidly. If you are not extremely accurate, then you are likely to miss. You may even get hurt. Accuracy should not be a problem, however, if it is carefully practiced and rehearsed in advance. For example, write down your order ahead of time. Read it to your broker in a clear firm voice. Have your broker read it back to you after you finish and at the time of confirmation.

The contrast between the requirements for the stalking task and the "action" task is so dramatic that many traders cannot make the abrupt shift. They are either energized and prepared to act or they are cautious and wary of any action. As a result, they either take the trade immediately and increase the risk of the situation, or they concentrate on getting the best possible trade and end up getting nothing.

6. Monitoring   Once a trader has a position in the market, he must monitor that position. In a sense, the hunting metaphor breaks down for monitoring. Imagine a tiger attacking a buffalo. Monitoring would occur at the split second the tiger lands on the back of the buffalo. He must instantaneously decide to either make the kill or to abort because the buffalo is bigger and stronger than he is. Fortunately, traders have a longer time frame to make the same decision about the market.

The nature of the monitoring task depends upon the trader's time frame for keeping his position. For a top day-trader, the stages of stalking, monitoring, taking profits, and aborting are somewhat circular. Day-traders may take several positions each day and may do all these tasks together. The constant need to shift mental states between tasks is one reason that so many people lose money day-trading.

A top position trader, in contrast, will wait for exceptional opportunities and then allow them to unfold. As a result, the monitoring process is more relaxed for the position trader. Nevertheless, complacency can destroy even the longest term trader.

Monitoring may consist of two subtasks, especially for the longer-time-frame trader. The first subtask, *detailed monitoring*, is similar to stalking. It involves paying detailed attention to the pulse of the market while getting ready to take action by adding to your position, by aborting, or by taking profits. On the other hand, when the market is moving comfortably in your favor on a long-term time frame, the trader can step back from the market into more of an "overview" position. Thus, the second subtask might be called *overview monitoring*.

Detailed Monitoring   Detailed monitoring begins as soon as one opens a position, then the market should move in your favor soon after you open it. If it does not, then you probably do not belong in that position. As a result, a trader needs to pay close attention to the fine details of the market. He should be alert, vigilant, and suspicious.

I frequently recommend that my longer-time-frame clients rate their position three times a day for the first three days according to "how easy it feels." A typical scale might look like the one illustrated [in Figure 8.3].

Use a scale similar to this one at the beginning, middle, and end of each of the first three trading days. If the position does not feel "easy" by the end of the three-day period, then it probably is a bad trade for you to be holding. On the other hand, if it is easy to hold, then you can probably switch to overview monitoring. If you trade around other traders and are influenced by their opinions, then a good trade might feel "hard" because you are holding it against the crowd. If this is the case, then reverse the rules given above.

Switch back to detailed monitoring only when action of some sort might soon be necessary or for a periodic check of your position. You might, depending on your time frame for the trade, switch back to detailed monitoring once each day or once every three days.

Overview Monitoring   During overview monitoring, the trader broadens his focus and steps back from the market. He is looking at the forest

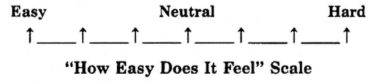

"How Easy Does It Feel" Scale

FIGURE 8.3   "How Easy Does It Feel" Scale

instead of the detail of the trees. When a trader is in the overview phase of monitoring, he is more detached and objective. He is more patient and calm. His focus is much broader and his time frame is slower.

The worst mistake that one can make during the monitoring phase is to rationalize and distort data according to expectations. The purpose of monitoring the market is to pay attention to market signals. The trader who interprets signals according to his expectations is not performing this task adequately.

During overview monitoring, the trader is simply surveying the conditions. He is comparing market events as they unfold with his plan and his knowledge of what various market events mean. If everything is going according to his plan, then monitoring can remain a detached and relaxed process. Some traders give away big profits simply taking a dollar profit. On the other hand, if events do *not* unfold according to plan, then the trader needs to focus on the details of the trade (i.e., switch to detailed monitoring).

The monitoring stage is a form of risk control. If a trade is good, then it should be easy to hold because it is moving in one's favor. When the market moves in support of your position, the trader can change his stop level to decrease his risk or even lock in a profit. On the other hand, if nothing happens, if the market behaves unexpectedly, or if the trader is uncertain, then he should get out or, at minimum, reduce his exposure to a loss by reducing the size of his position.

7. Abort   The two stages which occur after monitoring are action-like stages much like the task of opening the position. These stages are "abort" or "take profits." One could argue that these stages involve "searching for the right opportunity to act" and "acting." On the other hand, since many traders search for the right opportunity during the detailed monitoring phase, we simply call these "action" stages.

Developing a low-risk idea and marketing your idea allow you to plan risk control. *Planning your risk is not nearly as important* as executing your trades in a manner in which you can *actually control your risk*. In executing trades, the golden rule of trading, "Cut your losses short and let your profits run," comes into play. Controlling risk involves aborting and taking profits under the appropriate conditions.

Most successful traders have one or more of the following three beliefs about aborting a position:

Belief 1   If the market is going against you, then that is the most critical time to get out. You can't afford to lose big. Some traders enter a position with a stop and get out when the stop is hit. However, other traders expect the market to go in their favor as soon as they open the position. If it does not, then they get out. The issue of when to get out depends upon the maximum amount of loss you are willing to tolerate. However, if your best trades immediately go in your direction, then when you open a position and the market starts going against you, don't wait for your stop to be hit. If it's going against you, then it's not the trade for you. Get out! Limit your risk.

Belief 2   When the original reason for a trade no longer exists, get out of the market. And when you are uncertain, get out.

One of my clients, for example, had a problem with uncertainty. He said "I don't know what to do when uncertainty comes up. You haven't described uncertainty in your books and I don't know how to handle it."

I responded, "What percentage of your trades make money?"

"About 40 percent," he said.

Then I asked, "When you're uncertain, what percentage of those trades make money?" He couldn't remember ever making money when he was uncertain, so I said, "If you're uncertain, just get out." Rather than trying to control your uncertainty, treat it as a valuable signal about what you should do. [reported by Tharp]

Belief 3   When time is against you, you probably should be in a better position, so get out. Many of the people reading this are speculators, as opposed to floor traders or commercial traders. *Your primary advantage to trading is that at any particular time you don't have to be in the market.* Use that advantage! Enter and stay in a position only when it is fully advantageous for you to do so.

Aborting involves a quick, accurate, and very focused mental state. Once you determine, through the monitoring process, that it is appropriate to get out of the market, then you must immediately shift mental states to abort properly. If the predator decides that the prey he's selected is inappropriate (i.e., it's too big and strong for him), then he retreats quickly. A quick retreat allows him to survive to hunt again another day.

A quarterback can sense if the play is going to work out as soon as he gets the ball. If he senses that he is in a "busted" play, then he needs to do whatever is necessary to keep from losing ground. He may throw the ball out of bounds just to make sure that he doesn't lose yardage. What's important for him is to have the best possible position when the next opportunity comes. He doesn't want to lose ground.

If you have trouble aborting a position, then look at "pro" and "con" scenarios together. Allow the evidence against your position to unfold and then allow the evidence for your position to unfold and compare the two pictures together in your mind. If the evidence is against your position, them simply call it a *bad trade* and get out.

8. Take Profits   Many traders claim that their game plan emphasizes trade entry but not trade exit. As a result, they argue that they do not make enough profit on each trade. If you have not thought about trade exit prior to opening a position, then you have a problem with your game plan because you have not adequately calculated the risk involved in the position. If you've calculated risk properly, then you should know two elements ahead of time: (1) your chances of being right on that trade and (2) the size of your potential profit versus your potential loss. If you don't have that information (at least generally), then you still need to work on your game plan.

A properly designed low-risk game plan will give you optimum profits within your comfort level for trading. Thus, the task of maximizing your profits should simply be one of following your plan. For example, if you have a plan that gives you a 50% return each year and you maintain that record year after year, compounding your profits, then you will be one of the best traders in the world. Some of my clients have designed plans that give them three-digit rates of returns each year. As a result, all it takes for any of them to become one of the best is to avoid self-sabotage by becoming too greedy or too fearful. If you concentrate on anything other than maintaining consistency, then I believe your concentration is misplaced.

Top traders have four primary beliefs about taking profits. Taking profits is equivalent to the predator's skill. When the predator acts, he must be quick and decisive. Thus, the first belief is that if market conditions change so that your reason for your trade no longer applies, then take your profits. Avoid being greedy. Just react to the signals provided by the market.

A second belief about taking profits is to do so when the market reaches your objective. Be patient and allow the market to move toward the target. If you set your targets at extreme levels, then you probably don't give up much by taking your profits at those levels. In most cases, market conditions will probably change before your target is reached, so you can get out simply by acting when those occur. If the market hits your target, however, I recommend that you take profits by continuing to move your stop closer to the market price as the target is reached. Wait for the market to take you out. If the market keeps moving rapidly in favor of your position, then you have no reason to take profits.

A third belief about taking profits is that one should do so if market volatility changes dramatically, thus altering the risk parameters of the trade. Volatility typically increases when a market becomes popular and mass hysteria exists. Although a lot of profit potential may exist in that market, the risk is much greater than the potential profit. As a result, increasing volatility after you're in the market might be a good reason to take profits.

Bear market moves are often climactic, and that climactic portion of the move may go past your target area. However, if you wait for the climactic portion of the move to end, you might get whipsawed in the opposite direction as soon as the move ends. As a result, the fourth belief is that when such a move occurs, you should take profits immediately.

9. Daily Debriefing The ninth task in the model is a *daily debriefing*. Most good traders do it, either formally or informally. I think a daily debriefing is essential for consistent, top performance. It provides an important transition period between trading and being out of the market.

The idea behind the daily debriefing is to determine whether or not you made a mistake during the day. A mistake, however, has nothing to do with losses. *A trading mistake means not following one's trading rules and one's plan of action.* In fact, traders should *pay special attention to mistakes made while making money.* Just because a predator chases its prey through an area filled with quicksand or tar without setting stuck, doesn't mean that it is safe to do so again. The La Brea Tar Pits in Los Angeles contain the bones of many more predators than prey because numerous predators made the mistake of going after the other animals caught in the tar.

Look at your written trading rules and the written notes you made when you were developing your low-risk idea. What can you do if you made a mistake by not following your rules?

- First, avoid self-recrimination—telling yourself that you "should have" done this or you "could have" done that. Instead, resolve not to repeat that mistake again.
- Second, replay the trade in your mind. Prior to making that mistake, you reached a choice point. At that choice point, you had a number of options available to you.
- Third, mentally go back in time to that choice point and review your options.
- Fourth, for each possible option, determine what the outcome would be if you had taken it. Be sure that you give yourself at least three good choices and mentally rehearse them. Some generals are known for fighting the strategies of the last war. Those who do usually lose the battle. Always give yourself as many choices as possible, so that you don't get stuck with limited options or a forced choice.

- Fifth, once you've found at least three options with favorable outcomes, mentally rehearse carrying them out in the future when you encounter similar situations. Once you've practiced them in your mind, you will find that selecting one of them is easy when you encounter a similar situation in the future.

When you do follow your rules, pat yourself on the back at the end of your debriefing. If you followed your rules and lost money, then pat yourself on the back twice. You may have lost money this time, but in the long run following your rules will make you money. Mistakes, on the other hand, will not result in long-term, consistent profits.

Once you have analyzed your day's trading, summarize it in writing. Write down your mistakes and your new choices for that situation. This written information will be very important when you begin the next task of doing a periodic review of yourself and your game plan for trading.

The daily debriefing shouldn't take more than 5 or 10 minutes; therefore, do one every day. It is one of the most important tasks of the ten-part model. Get through it. Then put the trading day behind you, because tomorrow is a new trading day.

10. Periodic Review   The tenth task in the model is a periodic review of what you're doing. Markets change and you change. As a result, you need to be sure that your rules are still appropriate for both you and the markets. In addition, once you develop a sound business plan, I don't recommend that you change your rules on the spur of the moment or without a thorough review. The day you do your periodic review is the time for rule changes. It's also a time to be away from the market. You cannot objectively review *yourself* and *your rules* while you are actively involved in the markets.

How often you need a periodic review depends upon your time frame for trading. If you make several trades (or more) each day, then you need to review your rules every three to four weeks. If you trade three or four times each week, then a periodic review is necessary every three to four months. If you trade several times each month, then a semiannual review is appropriate. Finally, if you trade less than once a month, then an annual review is probably sufficient.

When you do your periodic review, you need to first go through your written debriefing statements. Once that information is fresh in your mind, go through your entire business plan step by step. You need to review your trading diary and determine your strengths and weaknesses. Give yourself a whole day to do a periodic review. It is an important part of maintaining consistency.

THE TASK OF BEING OUT OF THE MARKET

I have saved the most important part of the model until last—taking care of yourself when you are out of the market.

The Top Traders Who *Last* Lead Well-Balanced Lives

To understand the importance of how you live your life when you are out of the market, consider the parts model discussed earlier in the daily mental rehearsal section. You've created a number of parts with various needs. All of your parts have good intentions. *If you do not take care of your needs when you are away from the market, then your parts will act to fulfill those needs while you are in the market.* If you don't play or add excitement to your out-of-the-market life, for example, and part of you desires those aspects of life, then you're going to get those needs met while you're in the market. Getting those needs met while you are in the market will not make you money in the long run. I guarantee it. As a result, you must deal with the needs of your parts while you're out of the market.

You might argue that being out of the market is not a trading task. Yet it is the most important task for trading success. If you ignore important aspects of your life when you are out of the market, you will have trouble ignoring those aspects while you are in the market.

Many people want to be in the market to avoid personal issues. You cannot escape personal problems by trading in the market. What happens, unfortunately, is that the market magnifies those problems. A compulsive gambler is probably the best example of how failure to deal with personal issues can result in market disasters.

One of my clients called me, saying that he couldn't follow my suggestions. He couldn't bring himself to trade most of the time. When he did trade, he did the opposite of what he really wanted to do. He also told me that the material didn't seem to help him in solving his personal problems. During our conversation he also told me that he only had $5,000 with which to trade commodities and he had been trading for over nine years with no nest egg and never more than $5,000 in his trading account.

I recommended that he immediately suspend trading and seek help in solving his personal problems, which I believed to be serious. *Traders with serious personal problems cannot trade successfully because they will bring those personal problems to the market.* I also recommended that once he had solved those problems he should continue to stay away from the market until he had enough capital to trade with—in his case, about $50,000. Once he had solved his personal problems and raised enough money to trade effectively, he had a chance of becoming a good trader. Although my advice would have saved him thousands of dollars and would have given him the opportunity to become a successful trader, I doubt if he took me seriously.

Consistent, top traders keep their lives in balance, and that makes trading fun. In addition, they also seem to realize their overall purpose in life. Predators are helpful to the whole system. They weed out the weak members of their prey and in doing so strengthen the herd. As a result, they serve a very useful purpose. Similarly, strong traders serve as predators for weaker traders and weed them out of the market. As a result, they strengthen the markets by their presence. As long as you keep that perspective in mind, then you can continue to have success. Traders who have a lot of initial success tend to lose that perspective. They suddenly believe they are bigger than the markets. As a result, the market teaches them humility by wiping out most, if not all, of their capital.

Many traders will make a lot of money at some time in their trading lives and then give it back because they don't keep the overall ecology of the system in mind. They use the markets to prove something to themselves that has nothing to do with trading. What happens to them? They ignore their overall purpose. They increase their trading dramatically or, if they are big enough, they try to corner the market (as the Hunts tried to do with silver) and fail miserably. As a result, they lose everything and are forced out of the market.

Being out of the market means *being out* of the market. It's important to exercise, take a vacation, and even take a break during the day. And when you do those things, do not take the market with you. When you start worrying about trades that you might have missed and a thousand other possibilities, you are like a puppet on a string and the market is pulling your strings. If you take the market with you, then those parts of you that wanted the vacation or the break will disrupt your performance during those times in which you need to give your full attention to the market. Remember:

You don't have to catch every move!
There is always another opportunity![4]

APPLYING THE TEN TASKS TO THE SAN FRANCISCO COMPANY

Chapter 7 concluded with the anatomy of a trade using the case study of the San Francisco Company to demonstrate the decisions made by an advanced Wyckoff-oriented trader. Now, you can apply the Ten Tasks of Top

Trading to that same case study. You can match the key junctures encountered with the appropriate mental state from the Ten Tasks.

Charts of the San Francisco Company are reproduced in Figures 8.4 and 8.5 for your convenience. As in the original San Francisco Company case, there are juncture points numbered 1 through 34 on the chart. But in these charts, several of those junctures are circled. These junctures in circles are the ones where you select the right mental state from the Ten Tasks.

Exercise

Before proceeding to the commentaries on the Ten Tasks applied to SF Company, I urge you to try to match the appropriate task and mental state with each of the circled junctures on the SF Company chart. In addition, if you also wish to attempt to access the appropriate mental state within yourself via visualization, self-talk, and feelings, you are encouraged to do so. Such a rehearsal is a good way for you to start instilling the Ten Tasks in yourself. I suggest that you label each of the Ten Tasks i through x with Roman numerals, then place the appropriate Roman numeral next to the corresponding task or challenge posed at each juncture on the chart.

When you have completed this exercise, please turn to end of the chapter and consult the chart with the correct or ideal answers. Compare your answers with the ideal and, where you discover that you have made an error, change it to the correct/idealized response and replay the correct

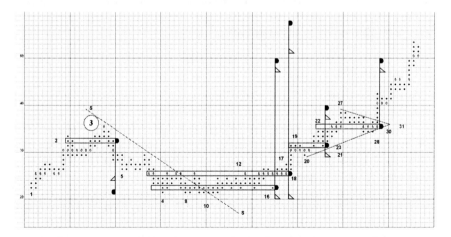

FIGURE 8.4 San Francisco Company Point-and-Figure Chart for Mental State Assignment
Source: SMI, with adaptations and modifications.

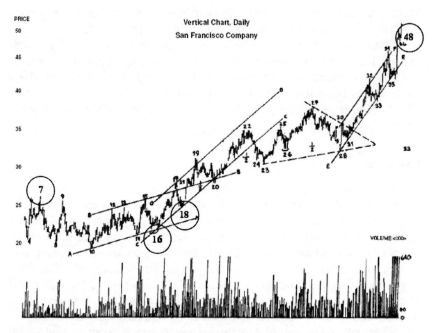

FIGURE 8.5   Bar Chart, San Francisco Company
Source: SMI, with adaptations and modifications.

version in your mind until you are confident that you have firmly grasped it. You may make ample use of the following commentaries to help you complete the replay of this exercise.

Commentaries

Chart Juncture 3   From chart juncture 2 to 3, the first four tasks of the Ten Tasks of Top Trading can be applied.

Upside price objectives may be exhausted at point 3 and volume may be nonconfirming of the new price high at $35/share (bar chart not shown). Presuming that is case, the trader switches from being a passive onlooker to an engaged stalker. He is vigilant and poised to act, but remains confident, cautious, and patient, yet prepared. Doing the task of stalking can help the trader minimize the risk of whipsaws; moreover, the *stalking* stage will precondition the trader to take action.

At the $32 price level, following the plunge back into the trading range from the $35 high, the trader moves out of the mental state of *stalking* and into the active, aggressive, fully committed, no-second-guessing mental state of *action*! The trader takes a short position around $32 with a stop loss at $36 or just above $35. The point-and-figure chart count along the $32 level of 11 points is barely sufficient to meet the 3:1 reward risk requirement of Wyckoff money management principles.

Once the entry position is complete, the trader is advised to step back, to dissociate from the trade, and to enter the patient *monitoring* state of mind, while remaining resolved and tenacious in pursuit of the downside price objectives flagged between $24 and $21 per share.

Chart Juncture 4   The relative increase in volume as price probed the $20 range only to close on the high of the day at $22 alerts the trader that a new task is at hand: *exiting* the market, or *taking profits*. This calls for a dramatic change of mental state: from passive, detached, longer time frame, and patient *monitoring* to active, involved, immediate time frame, and urgent closing of the position. The trader is thus mentally prepared to take in profits near the close of the selling climax day itself or early the following day.

The sequel to *taking profits* is recapping the trade, the *debriefing* stage. This is a more elaborate reflecting back on the efficiency and effectiveness of the trade and the trader than what takes place during the daily debriefings that occur at the end of each day during the *monitoring* phase. The trader would do well to keep a journal and record the details of the previous trade/campaign, with special note of profit versus loss and careful details regarding the trader's mental poise or lack thereof during the trading campaign.

Chart Juncture 7   Detachment from the market is difficult to accomplish but very essential for long-term performance and survival in the stressful occupation of trading. Remember that after a successful trading campaign, Larry Livingston, the hero in Edwin Lefèvre's book, *Reminiscences of a Stock Operator*, would go an extended vacation, usually a fishing trip. This would get him out of New York City and away from the market to a place where he could be indifferent to the market and appreciate some of the fruits of his labor in calm and contented conditions.

Chart Juncture 16   The upside move from juncture 14 to juncture 16 alerts the trader to the fact that the Composite Man may be testing the market. A trading range has developed from juncture 7 to juncture 15, and the Composite Man does his testing at the boundaries of a trading range.

Around chart juncture 16 the trader could put his thinking/technical analyst cap on. He could wake up in a curious, questioning state of mind. Then, with the aid of the Wyckoff nine buying tests, the trader could objectively, systematically, thoroughly, and dispassionately seek to *develop a low-risk idea.* (Note: To make doubly certain that you are appraising chart evidence with an objective and dispassionate state of mind, it is a good tactic to reverse the chart and make a bull market look bearish or vice versa. To learn the procedure for conducting this inversion, please consult the section titled "Chart Reading in the R-Mode," located in Chapter 9.) Once Wyckoff's nine tests seem to be nearing completion, the trader could confidently transition once again into the *stalking* frame of mind around chart junctures 16, and 17, and 18.

Chart Juncture 18   With the passing of all nine Wyckoff buying tests at point 18, the trader is obligated to take action and buy SF Company. The backup to the breakout point in the vicinity of juncture 18, coupled with the several days of quiet price and volume action around the $25 per share level, make buying *action* comparatively easy to do. Prompt and aggressive buying is definitely called for as the price gaps upward immediately after juncture 18, and the mental state defined in the task, *action*, prepares the trader for a swift and decisive purchase.

Chart Junctures 18 to 27   As the "old Turkey" character would state in *Reminiscences of a Stock Operator*, it was the "sitting" that made the money for him, the "sitting tight." But *Reminiscences* also points out that the twin talents of "being right" and "sitting tight" are a rare combination and seldom found together in a Wall Street trader.

The need to sit tight underscores the importance of the upside target zone around $49 functioning as the trader's anchor point, his benchmark, his reference point. Indeed, the visualization of that price objective, which is made easier by the flagged price targets on the point-and-figure chart of the SF Company, help to make the $49 level a compelling future! Note how this compelling future ties into the task of *mental rehearsal*. (As discussed in the next chapter, the price history recorded on a chart can become a debilitating deadweight that is difficult to overcome.) Chart junctures 27, 28, 30, and 31 are excellent opportunities for the application of the tasks/mental states you identified at the start of this exercise as vii, iii, iv, and v, respectively. But I shall leave that chore in your hands.

Chart Juncture 48   Wyckoff exit strategy 1 can be seen at work here as the volume of SF Company becomes extremely large when the stock approaches the price target zone of $49. Also, the dramatic price run-up from $43 to $49 on the bar chart sensitizes the trader to the approaching need for *profit taking.* The trader should start to gear up for initiating this exit from the San Francisco Company in the face of accelerating price volatility, and thus he should rehearse the exit strategy during his *daily debriefing* and *daily mental rehearsal.* These two tasks will help him en-

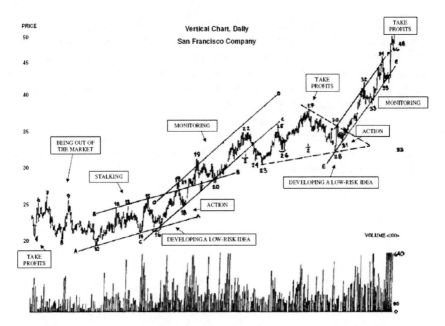

FIGURE 8.6 San Francisco Company Bar Chart with Accompanying Mental States
Source: SMI, with adaptations and modifications.

ter the correct mental framework for *taking profits*. The debriefing that follows after closing out the trade should bring satisfaction. Please look back at the SF Company case study and reread the trader's self-talk as he prepared himself mentally to accept *taking profits* around the $49 level of the SF Company.

I want you to carefully and completely replay this exit scenario in the SF Company, including canceling your trailing stop-loss orders, recapping the trade, and recording in your journal. In preparing to complete the task of *debriefing*, please resolve to access the appropriate mental states. Then, after a day or so, follow this up with a *periodical review*. To assist you in conducting this review, I urge you to consult the sections entitled "A Sealed Room" and "Only One Client," located in Chapter 10.

SUMMARY

This chapter focused on the importance of mental state management to prepare and follow through on trades. In The Ten Tasks of Top Trading you saw how to attain and keep the appropriate mental state for the various trading situations you will encounter. In addition, the Ten Tasks broke the job of trading down into 10 discrete tasks of trading, each of which calls for the trader to use courage, patience, fear, and so on, as called for by the task. Finally, you had the opportunity to assign mental states to a case study and learn first-hand how a trader employs mental states for opening, monitoring, and closing options positions.

It is vital that you, as a trader, have the capacity to access and maintain the proper mental states. The next chapter investigates the various approaches available to help you access and maintain mental state control and to otherwise empower your trading.

CHAPTER 9

The
Composite Man

I n this chapter you become the center of attention! The spotlight shifts
to the middle of the three-in-one model introduced in Chapter 1, where
the centerpiece of *The Three Skills of Top Trading* is you, represented
by the profile of the man located within the triangle that links together the
three skills (see Figure 9.1).

Now you will have the unique opportunity to tie together, to integrate,
and to instill these skills in yourself. This chapter presents six methods for
you to use to modify your mental state, giving you the capacity to gain and
keep winning habits.

METHODS FOR MENTAL DISCIPLINE

The following six methods will help you gain control of your mental state
and increase your success in following through on your trades.

1. Re-presenting the outside world to yourself.
2. Changing your physical self.
3. Calling upon your own resources.
4. Fantasizing.
5. Analyzing and integrating parts of yourself.
6. Modeling yourself after others.

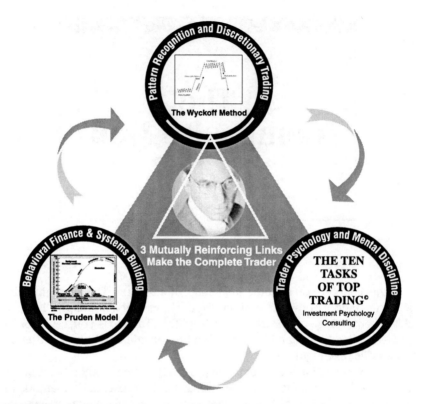

FIGURE 9.1   The Connecting Link for the Three Skills: You

RE-PRESENTING THE OUTSIDE WORLD TO YOURSELF

We perceive the outside world through the senses of our nervous system: seeing, hearing, feeling, and smelling. We seldom use the last sense in market analysis and trading except metaphorically, as in "the market stinks" or "it has bad breath." Otherwise, our decisions about what actions we should take in the market typically start with the visual, such as reading a daily price and volume chart. Our hearing or auditory sense is lodged in our brain's left hemisphere and our feelings in the right one. Problems come about when what we convince ourselves we see on the charts is what we tell ourselves we *should* find because we have filled our heads with verbal miscues. In other words, we see what we want to hear.

In my own trading experience, I know that I had a bearish bias. Hence, I was always on the lookout for a top and for a short-selling opportunity. On the other hand, I found it difficult to go long, and when I did go long, it was hard for me to stay in my long position. To overcome this bearish habit, I needed to reframe my observations and re-present the world to myself; therefore, I ended up creating "Chart Reading in the R-Mode."

I advise you to get into the habit of reframing or re-presenting your chart observations to yourself. You can master this by using the techniques in the next subsection, "Chart Reading in the R-Mode." By quieting the noisy and nosey left hemisphere of your brain, you gain a higher degree of mental state control.

Very importantly, "Chart Reading in the R-Mode" will help you to overcome cognitive biases. You already know that you need to control your emotions; cognitive biases and distortions are important, too. I urge you to read *Judgment in Managerial Decision Making* by Max Bazerman (New York: John Wiley & Sons, 2005) for a full discussion of cognitive errors made by business decision makers and ways to overcome these errors. Meanwhile, following the techniques found in "Chart Reading in the R-Mode" will give you a big boost toward mastering the cognitive part of mental state control.

Chart Reading in the R-Mode

> *"Turn off" your dominant L-mode of verbal categorizing and "turn on" the R-mode processing part of your brain, so that you can see the way an artist sees.*
>
> —*Dr. Betty Edwards*

"The eyes have it!" proclaims Bennett W. Goodspeed in his delightful little book, *The Tao Jones Averages* (New York: Penguin, 1984). Such a proclamation ought not to surprise technical traders since ours is such a visual world, a world of reading charts with our eyes. So why bother with the obvious fact that we spend our lives reading charts?

It is worth the bother because you and I get into trouble by seeing what we believe rather than believing what we see, while going about our trading affairs. The trader is vulnerable to falling into this trap of seeing what we believe because most traders have been schooled to rely too heavily upon the left hemisphere of the brain, with its sequential, verbal, logical, rational reasoning. We may state that one picture is worth a thousand words, but somehow the thousand words get in the way and we end up distorting the picture.

You must guard against reading something into a chart pattern that isn't really there. Be careful that you don't harbor a bearish bias built upon the belief that the market has risen too far and for too long, such that you feel it is entitled to a correction. With that mind-set, every time you see the first sideways pattern on your market chart, it becomes a reversal pattern in your mind. Later, it turns out to be a continuation pattern.

Or perhaps you heard the tightly reasoned argument of a well-respected technician who claimed that a sharp decline had cleared the air. Afterward, the more you looked at the consolidation pattern before your eyes, the more you perceived the outline of a bullish reversal pattern. Only later when the downtrend had clearly resumed did you admit that it was merely a bear market rally after all.

Be alert that you don't succumb to the most deadly trap of all, when some of your tried-and-true indicators are no longer reliable, but you don't yet know it. Thus your indicators, whether momentum, sentiment, or whatever, say the market is too overbought or oversold. So when you cast your gaze upon your charts you filter out from your visual field any graphic data conflicting with your verbal label "overbought" or "oversold."

Here is how Goodspeed sums up the issue: "To avoid playing a loser's game, it is essential to use the 'right' brain to see reality in time to avoid tragedy." Our logical left hemisphere of the brain is simply not adept at dealing with incomplete or partial information; indeed, the left hemisphere interferes by sticking new data into already established categories, and if the data do not fit, then the left mode, our dominant mode, tends to ignore them. Moreover, our left hemisphere, educated as it is in our Western culture, tends not to challenge assumptions.

R-Mode   A remedy for the mental malady of not seeing accurately what is before our eyes requires that when we *first* analyze our charts we turn off the logical left hemisphere of the brain and turn on the wholistic, artistic right hemisphere, otherwise known as the R-mode. This injunction was essentially the thesis of Dr. Betty Edwards' unusual book dealing with visual education, *Drawing on the Right Side of the Brain* (Tarcher, 1979). As technicians and chart readers, we need to reframe our thought processes into what Dr. Edwards calls the R-mode:

> In contrast to L-mode, the right half of the brain (for most individuals) functions in a non-verbal manner, specializing in visual, spatial, perceptual information. Its style of processing is nonlinear and nonsequential, relying instead on simultaneous processing of incoming information—looking at the whole thing, all at once. It tends to seek relationships between parts and searches for ways that parts fit together to form wholes. Its preferences are for perceiving information, searching for patterns or relationships that satisfy requirements for visual fit, and seeking spatial order and coherence. It seems undaunted by ambiguity, complexity, or

paradox, perhaps because it lacks the "reducing glass" of L-mode, which opts for general rules and resists acknowledging ambiguity and paradox. Because of its quickness, complexity, and non-verbal nature, R-mode thinking is almost by definition difficult to put into words.

The essential trick, according to Professor Edwards, is to shut off the L-mode so as to allow the R-mode to become saturated with the visual information before your eyes. In other words, it asks you to gain an alternative state of consciousness so as to view more accurately what is before your eyes.

Here is how she suggests you might subjectively experience an R-mode state of consciousness:

Let's review the characteristics of the R-mode one more time. First, there is a seeming suspension of time. You are not aware of time in the sense of marking time. Second, you pay no attention to spoken words. You may hear the sounds of speech, but you do not decode the sounds into meaningful words. If someone speaks to you, it seems as though it would take a great effort to cross back, think again in words, and answer. Furthermore, whatever you are doing seems immensely interesting. You are attentive and concentrated and feel "at one" with the thing you are concentrating on. You feel energized but calm, active without anxiety. You feel self-confident and capable of doing the task at hand. Your thinking is not in word but in images and, particularly while drawing, your thinking is "locked on" to the object you are perceiving. The state is very pleasurable. On leaving it, you do not feel tired, but refreshed.

Our job now is to bring this state into clearer focus and under greater conscious control, in order to take advantage of the right hemisphere's superior ability to process visual information and to increase your ability to make the cognitive shift to R-Mode at will.

Stages in Reaching Chart Reading in the R-Mode   What I now propose to present is a process to follow, a set of techniques for you to incorporate in an effort to bring the R-mode into a clearer focus and under your control so that your chart reading can benefit from the R-mode's superior ability to process visual information. The first stage calls for preparing your chart information in a form that will facilitate reading it in the R-mode. The second step adapts several procedures from the art of drawing to the art of chart reading in the R-mode. The third and final stage calls for crossing back over to the L-mode in order to incorporate your visual insights with your verbal and quantitative procedures.

I. Preparatory Stage: TEC MAN© or 3-D Charts   TEC MAN stands for Technical Analysis Machine and/or Technical Manipulation. TEC MAN is a system I developed to represent technical data so as to incorporate more of one's senses (sight, touch, sound, and smell) in interpreting market data. My findings using this three-dimensional model were published in the summer of 1990 in the *MTA Journal* as part of my article, "Chart Reading in the R-Mode."

Market behavior is traditionally represented in a two-dimensional plane, whether in chart books or on computer screens. The three variables that are typically presented are price, time, and volume. The first innovative step of TEC MAN is to represent price, time, and volume in *three dimensions* rather than two. (See Figure 9.2.) Volume is presented as the third, vertical dimension on a two-dimensional grid of price and time. Human vision is stereoscopic—we see the natural world in three dimensions. Moreover, a three-dimensional representation allows more degree of freedom to manipulate the variable in our brain, to use what Edward de Bono calls *lateral thinking*.

The second innovative step is the sense of touch afforded by the three-dimensional structure of TEC MAN. Something called *haptic touch* or feel creates a visual impression as well. Richard M. Restak, M.D. spoke of this in his book *The Brain* (New York: Bantam Books, 1984): "The brain is able to utilize different sensations to build up a coherent reality. It does this by combining inputs from various senses, oftentimes correcting for visual distortion by touch and manipulation."[1]

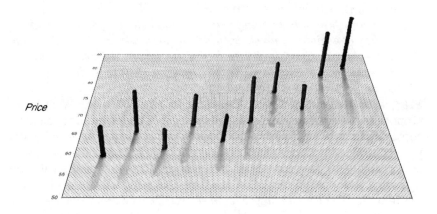

Price

Time, weekly

FIGURE 9.2   TEC MAN, Charting in Three Dimensions

The third innovative step of TEC MAN has already led to the first revision in TEC MAN. Sentiment data was initially represented by coloring the vertical volume columns blue for bullish and red for bearish. The degree of bullishness versus bearishness perceived in an array of sentiment indicators would determine how much blue and/or how much red color would appear on a given volume peg for a given day. As it turned out, this practice led to confusion and cross-purposes because; rather than reinforcing the analyst's conviction in following a strong trend, the appearance of more and more "contrary" color (for example, more blue in a falling market) sent contrary signals. Indeed, overemphasis on sentiment could encourage shorting into an uptrend or buying into a downtrend. The revised TEC MAN version simplified the representation of sentiment by limiting the indicators to the end of day closing and the colors to one per column, with any down day on closing basis painted red and any up day colored blue.

II. Procedures for Chart-Reading in the R-Mode   For the first procedure you can use a simple device that works just as easily on a two-dimensional chart as one rendered in 3-D. Simply turn your chart upside down and stare at it. What do you really see? Look at the funny subcomponents, then fuzz your eyes a little and look at the chart as a whole. Refrain from concluding what it is and thus labeling it. But if you find yourself drawn toward an inevitable "flash" conclusion, then force yourself to go to beyond the first and most obvious answer to at least a second and third alternative answer, and label these in your mind as well. Then leave it for a while, and sleep on your images while the unconscious mind has time to mull over this input. Voila! The answer you get might not accord with your original supposition. Chances are the answer will be accurate, even if you are forced to reinterpret your indicators.

The second procedure is one we have all done at various times; this procedure works well with a two-dimensional chart. Again, turn your chart upside down, but this time turn it around and press it against a lighted window or glass so that you are viewing it from the other side of the page. This procedure effectively turns a bear market into a bull market. (See Figure 9.3.)

The real dividend, though, is what it does beyond that. Suddenly you will discover yourself taking in more and different data than you did before. Often you will see some movement earlier in the trend which you had blocked out, or some support or resistance level heretofore overlooked. Earlier you thought you knew it was a bear (bull) market and so the L-mode economized your mental efforts by shutting off a lot of seemingly extraneous information. By turning things around, and breaking up prejudgment, you allow the R-mode to see more of what is really there.

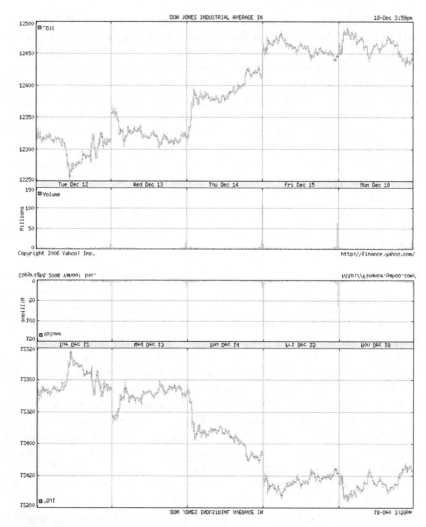

FIGURE 9.3   Procedure 2, Window Effect
Source: Copyright 2006 Yahoo! Inc.

The result might be to reinforce your original opinion; the result might also be to revise your opinion!

Third, when you go beyond these simple techniques, you will be aided significantly by a three-dimensional chart (see Figure 9.2). There is the "ground floor" view. You place your eye down at the surface level to observe the profile produced by the varying heights of volume action. From this perspective it is difficult for your mind to ignore the waxing or waning of buying power or selling strength. It is particularly useful to scan the last few weeks, then to visually scan the horizon back over several months.

Another approach using 3-D charts I call "the four cardinal directions." For this procedure I have discovered that using a mirror to look back on the data, which is to have the data reflected back to you from the other side, unlocks a large number of new patterns and combinations. In fact, there are usually so many and they are so confusing that they tend to boggle your mind, which of course is precisely what you want to have happen for turning off the L-mode and turning on the R-mode! A variation of this technique in action would be to place your chart against the wall so that you are forced to read it vertically from down to up, or vice versa. Furthermore, if you wish, you could place your 3-D charts on the floor, then stand on your desk to gaze down at them as if you were a bird above a forest. And for you night owls, you could slip back into your office after hours with a flashlight in order to contemplate the shadows cast by your 3-D charts.

Fourth, further manipulative methods are suggested in Dr. Edwards' *Drawing on the Right Side of the Brain.* For instance, you can focus on the negative or black spaces between your chart recordings; or you can widen or narrow the frame around your chart; or you may even spy your chart through a rolled-up piece of paper or a view finder. All in all you will discover having her book around as a ready reference will assist you in becoming a more creative chartist.

III. The Cross-Over Stage   Ideally, you will soak up all of your chart visualizations and then retire from the scene for a period of time to permit incubation. I have personally discovered that sleeping on it for an overnight incubation yields good results. More frequently, however, I have found myself "crossing over" to check out an R-mode insight with some L-mode technique. At these times my favorite L-mode method has been the Elliot Wave principle.

The Elliott Wave principle has an appeal to me as the starting L-mode technique for what I believe is a very sound reason: *dynamic symmetry.* As the poet Keats once wrote, "Beauty is truth, truth beauty," and so it is with Elliott because it rests upon that 3:5 "divine proportion" that the human eye finds so attractive. Thus when the R-mode comes up with a pattern that creates, that stimulates, an "aha!" response, you will often find that the pattern fits with several Elliot principles very nicely.

Once you've grasped the essence of your wholistic chart pattern with the R-mode, you can proceed with confidence through analytical checklists of technical indicators. Expect to find yourself looping back and forth several times between the R-mode and the L-mode.

You finally exit from this three-stage procedure when you are in possession of what Dr. Edwards calls an "aha!" sensation. This might occur at first sight, or it may come to you hours, days or sometimes even weeks later. The "aha!" effect may come to you in words like "It's a top!" or a picture in your mind that shows a clean and clear uptrend, or some combination of auditory, visual, and kinesthetic sensations. To help you master this creative process consult such fine texts as James Adams' *Conceptual Blockbusting* (Perseus Books Group, 2001), Edward deBono's *Lateral Thinking: Creativity Step by Step* (Harper Paperbacks, 1973), and Betty Edwards' *Drawing on the Artist Within* (Fireside, 1987).

Summary and Implications

In *The Tao Jones Averages*, Bennett Goodspeed brought to our attention the need to use our whole brain, both the dominant left hemisphere with its logical and verbal talents and the less dominant, more visually astute, right hemisphere. With the proper use of our right hemisphere we are empowered to see our charts more accurately with more consistency.

Dr. Betty Edwards, in *Drawing on the Right Side of the Brain*, furnishes us with the insight, the rationale, and the techniques for making better use of our visually more intelligent right-brain hemisphere or R-mode. The insight is that by tricking our L-mode into confusion or disinterest, we allow our R-mode to come forth, enabling us to see our charts more thoroughly and accurately. Dr. Edwards' rationale is based on the findings of scientific research on the "spilt brain" or two hemispheres phenomenon plus her own extensive experience with helping and observing her own art students make seemingly dramatic and speedy improvement in their drawing ability. By inference, you technicians ought to be able to reach a parallel degree of progress in your ability to read charts accurately.

To acquire the techniques for enhancing your chart reading acumen, I recommend that you proceed through a three-stage process. In the first stage you prepare your chart data. Ideally, you are in a position to decipher the most information from a chart when it is placed into three dimensions, similar to the TEC MAN©. The second stage calls again upon Dr. Edwards' *Drawing on the Right Side of the Brain* for techniques on how to interpret visually in the R-mode. Then in the third stage you are free to cross over once more to your analytical tool kit in order to integrate your R-mode with your L-mode.

To secure your commitment to reading your charts in the R-mode, I want to emphasize that *seeing* is the lynch pin in a good decision-making strategy. Based on his extensive research with traders, market psychologist Dr. Van K. Tharp concludes that the decision strategies of successful traders start with visual information. Thus, you will want a fresh view, uncontaminated with words, to gain an accurate reading of your charts before proceeding on to your more formal technical analysis. By following this course of action you can truly make a single picture worth more than a thousand words.

CHANGING YOUR PHYSICAL SELF

An inescapable, strong body-mind connection exists in all of us. If you are slump-shouldered and slack-jawed with downcast eyes, it will be difficult to get yourself into the mental state of confidence and aggression that you will need to put on a trade. But if you change your posture, firm up your facial muscles, and lift your eyes, the desired mental state for executing a trade will come more easily.

Managing your body posture or facial expressions is a quick, simple, reliable way for you to gain control over your mental states; no doubt, you already can visualize how you would look if you were to become fearful, patient, impatient, alert, relaxed, aggressive, and so on. As a memory aid and pictorial trigger, you ought to create a series of icons for yourself.

Let me share an example of a series of icons that worked well for me. In Chapter 8, I told you the "Hobbes" story about how I came to create the Ten Tasks of Top Trading with the help of the comic strip "Calvin and Hobbes." The cartoonist had done a remarkable job of placing the tiger, Hobbes, in bodily stances and giving him facial expressions that pictorially telegraphed his internal mental states. I used Hobbes as a way to communicate the essence of the Ten Tasks of Top Trading.

You are most likely familiar with "Calvin and Hobbes" and therefore I am confident that you will be able to create your own mental images of Hobbes and his mental states as I proceed through a recap of the Ten Tasks of Top Trading (Table 9.1). Remember that I was using Hobbes to demonstrate the power of body stance to capture and convey effective mental state control.

In sum, to carry out each of the Ten Tasks of Top Trading, you need to take on the right physical posture for the correct frame of mind. You will execute your tasks with ease. Mistakes and losses often result from a mismatch between task and mental state. For example, don't remain calm when it is time to abort a trade and don't be fearful when it is time to enter a trade.

TABLE 9.1 Ten Tasks of Top Trading

Trading Task	Depiction of Mental State
1. Being out of the market	Hobbes is stretched out, asleep, with a calm, contented look on his face. He is detached, indifferent to the market.
2. Self-analyzing	Hobbes is awake, alert, and curious as he looks himself over in a mirror.
3. Developing low-risk Idea	Hobbes, with one eye open and one eye closed, is withdrawn in a discerning posture; this allows him to be curious, objective, systematic, thorough, and dispassionate.
4. Stalking	Hobbes is in a slinking posture with tail waving, ears pinned back, and in a crouching stance ready to pounce. This is associated with vigilance and confidence but also with caution.
5. Taking action	Hobbes is airborne in attack with claws opened and forelegs straight out in a grasping posture. This reflects the mental states of aggression, abandon, courage, promptness, and determination.
6. Monitoring	Hobbes is reclining on his haunches and patiently twiddling his thumbs as the world passes by. Thus his mental state reflects calm detachment.
7. Aborting	Hobbes turns tail and flees a dangerous situation. His mental state is dominated by fear and urgency.
8. Taking profits	Hobbes again is actively reaching out with both paws to grab the meat off the table. He is alert, focused, aggressive, and impatient.
9. Conducting a daily debriefing	Hobbes is seated with his palm up in a receiving posture with an expression of questioning on his face. This look reflects the mental states of curiosity, introspection, and appreciation.
10. Performing a periodic review	Hobbes is stretched out on the floor and and poring over his charts. His appearance suggests that he is curious and creative while analyzing and synthesizing.

CALLING UPON YOUR OWN RESOURCES

Even after careful preparation and extensive practice, traders can find themselves in situations where the resources they need and normally have are suddenly unavailable. Later in this section I present a sequence of steps that you can take yourself through to ensure that you will be able to avoid feeling overwhelmed in that way again. The sequence is called the "resource strategy."

The resource strategy provides a method for usefully coping with situations where you get stuck in emotions such as anxiety, anger, embarrassment, or misplaced fear and you are unable to respond appropriately and resourcefully. The strategy allows you to detach from those destructive feelings, to step outside those unproductive states, as if you were an observer watching a movie. In an observer's position, you can be more objective about the situation and more resourceful about choosing appropriate responses. Once you possess appropriate responses to choose from, you can step back into the situation with any one of those new responses, feeling more in control and experiencing more useful emotions such as feeling capable, confident, or even curious.

The Experience of Association and Dissociation

The significance and effect of the strategy is based on the difference between being *associated* and *dissociated* with respect to the situation that is giving you trouble. To be associated is to be inside yourself, seeing, hearing, and feeling the situation as it transpires. To be dissociated is to have your senses separated from, and outside of, yourself; you are *observing* yourself from the outside as you interact in the situation.

Make a picture of yourself on a rollercoaster as if you are watching a movie of yourself. See yourself in the front seat going up that first big hill and watch the car climb slowly up the hill. Watch as the car tips over the hump and you see yourself speeding down the track, your hair blowing, and hear the screams that you can see coming from your mouth.

Now, as the rollercoaster car dips up from the bottom of the run and starts up again, enter your own body so that you can *feel* yourself sitting in that seat. You look up and see the greasy chain pulling you toward the top, hear the clanking of that chain, and feel the car pulling you higher and higher toward that peak. As you reach the peak, you can see all the way down, and as the car suddenly dips down the hill, the wind hits you in the face, you feel your stomach rise as your body drops, and you hear your own screams as you race toward the bottom.

Obviously, there is a big difference between the two experiences. That difference is crucial. When you are watching yourself, as on a movie screen, you see yourself in the picture; you are in a dissociated state. As such, you are not directly experiencing the feelings, sounds, and sights that are an integral part of the situation. This is the opposite of what we were doing when we did anchoring; then the outcome was to associate into the experience, to reexperience all of the sensory stimuli that were present in the earlier situation as if we were there again.

The resource strategy is based on dissociation. It is designed to detach you from all the sensory stimuli that are operating within the overwhelming situation—the stimuli that hook you—so that you have the time and space to think clearly and access the resources that will help you deal with the situation. In this way, your response can become a matter of choice rather than a knee-jerk reaction.

The Resource Strategy Steps

The following eight steps are a guide to implementing the resource strategy.

1. *Establish the context* that prevents you from responding appropriately (for example, being caught in a losing trade). *Identify the trigger* (words, tone, analogue, and so on) for the nonproductive state (regret, anger, bad self-talk). *Identify a specific example of a situation* (perhaps the last bad trade).

2. *Associate into the situation* at the point when you first realize you are having the undesired response (for example, see the stock tick downward on your computer screen).

3. *Dissociate from the situation* (literally step back from the screen).

4. *Identify the most appropriate response(s)* for the "other you over there" (for example, reframe the trade from "good" to "bad"; become fearful of it becoming worse).

5. *Reassociate back into the situation, taking with you the new responses.*

6. *Future-pace* (see yourself in the future exiting bad positions).

7. *Test* using a different but similar situation to the one previously tested.

8. *Identify the most appropriate response(s).*

At step 8 you could assume the role of the Composite Operator, and/or you may ask such questions as:

- Now that I am over here, what would the Composite Operator do?
- What would the Composite Operator do in a situation similar to this one?
- What choices are available to the Composite Operator? Which choice would he prefer?

If you find yourself slipping back into the negative response state, then you need to take yourself through the strategy step-by-step until it becomes an automatic response to the situation. If, when you test, you find yourself going through the stages of the strategy, you will know that you are ready to face that sort of situation in the real world once again.

This strategy bears repeating enough times so that it becomes an automatic part of your repertoire of responses. It offers much more than just greater flexibility of response. The breathing space and objective perspective of the resource strategy provide you with an opportunity to perform at your best!

FANTASIZING

Engaging in the creation of fantasy persons, places, instruments, and so on can deepen your personal treasure chest of resources. The creation of a fictional "happiness room" and your own "sealed room," discussed in chapter 10, are examples of resourceful fantasies. You can add a mascot or icon to safeguard you in trading. Warfare, as a metaphor for your trading life, is popular among traders, but it can be dangerous. A different metaphor such as planting, growth, and harvest, or the market as your dancing partner, might be better for you.

One particularly appealing fantasy exercise comes out of the use of organizational *fictions* created to assist the decision maker in a world of risk and uncertainty. Robert Dubin examined how fictions enable decision makers to cope more adequately with the unknown. Creating fictions facilitates the taking of action. With reference to fictions within formal organizations, Dubin wrote:

A fiction is defined as "the act of feigning or imagining that which does not exist or is not true." Organization fictions are those fictions that are necessary in order that action within the formal organization may proceed.

*Furthermore, these systems are dynamic. They undergo modifi-
cation by virtue of changes in the organization of which they are an
integral part. In their very nature, these systems of behavior standards can never be wholly prescribed. Yet each individual member
of the organization has to be able to operate as if his behavior were
truly oriented to a body of fixed standards. Where voids exist in the
standards, as they inevitably must in a dynamic formal organization, there is a strain toward creating guides for behavior that will
fill the voids. These creations are the organization fictions.*[2]

You may empower yourself through the creation of a market super-
trader based on a fictional character composed of the best traits of other
traders you know or have heard about. Imagine how that trader would
handle a trade that is bothering you. Imagine what that trader would see,
hear, and feel about the situation. Which state of mind should that trader
be in to deal with the trading situation aggravating you? Once you have
answers to those questions, replay the role of that fictional trader solving
your problem.

ANALYZING AND INTEGRATING PARTS OF YOURSELF

At some time or another most traders complain of suffering from "self-
sabotage" or of being beset by "internal conflicts." These are real issues
and you should have the know-how to deal with them. A divide-and-
conquer approach is an effective way to quell self-sabotages and to sub-
due your internal conflicts.

First, divide yourself into parts. This division might be along the lines
of the functions or roles that you play. In any case, it is an empowering fiction for you to assume that you are composed of parts. One useful model
contains three parts: analyst, trader, and accountant.

Next, assume that each of these roles or characters acts with the best
of intentions. The analyst wants you to be right in your market calls, the
trader wants you to be actively involved, and the accountant wants to see
large equity growth and small drawdowns. Things get out of kilter when
one of these roles becomes too dominant, or when there is a conflict between two of the parts. You may catch yourself arguing with yourself
about overtrading but not making enough profit on any one trade because
you become fearful about the risk exposure involved in carrying an open
position for a longer period of time. Every part has good intentions but
their internal conflicts can become stressful to you and undercut your
trading performance.

Now negotiate! You may literally set up a board of directors, made up of these three parts, within yourself. Ask each of these three (or more) parts of yourself for its permission to be included in the internal dialogue among your parts. The feedback you receive may be a voice or a feeling or a flash visualization. If the reply is hesitation or a no, then a direct negotiation with that part may be necessary before you call a meeting of the board. Ultimately you will wish for problems to be defined, trade-offs made, priorities set, and an agreement for each part to perform its function in support of an overall internal team effort.

Make this communication with and among your internal parts a daily routine. Consult your parts in the morning or before an important trade. Be sensitive to negative voices, feelings, or internally generated pictures. These negative clues are probably warnings. Again, at the end of the day consult your parts during debriefing. Keep notes in your trader's logbook or journal of anything you believe to be of significance revealed to you by your parts' analysis.

Be sure to perform a periodic review of your trading. Refer to your logbook for patterns that correspond negatively or positively with your trading performance. Use these patterns to help you revise your trading plan. If and when possible, use it to help you upgrade your trading to a higher level of professionalism.

MODELING YOURSELF AFTER OTHERS

The three skills this book discusses are separate parts of the composite or complete trader. (Figure 1.1 from the first chapter is reproduced at the beginning of this chapter for your convenience—see Figure 9.1.) Each of the three skills can be absorbed independently into the character of a trader through study and practice; however, they are designed to build on each other in an ever-enriching, mutually reinforcing cycle to create the complete trader. Here in Part Three, the circle of skill building and pattern recognition is completed with the addition of mental discipline. The circle is ultimately united by you, the trader-analyst. You can tie the three skills together when you take a big step and adopt or play the role of the Composite Man. Please note the man located in the center of the diagram in Figure 9.1.

Now you will learn how to play the role of the Composite Man. To gain and to keep a winning edge in the new high-concept, high-touch era of the twenty-first century, the trader-analyst must leapfrog the competition and jump into the seven-league boots of the Composite Man. Viewing your charts from the vantage point of the Composite Man will automatically give you a timing advantage. The Composite Man is always in sync with the market because in a very real sense he *is* the market. As you will discover, the Composite Man plays a variety of different roles.

The Merchandiser Role of the Composite Man

The role that I wish to explore in depth is that of the Composite Man as merchandiser. The merchandiser accumulates a line of stock, or inventory; next he leads the markup in price, then distributes his line of inventory at the top and continues liquidating inventory during the markdown phase of the merchandising cycle. To accomplish this four-phase merchandising cycle, the Composite Man also adopts the role of a manipulator who uses the ticker tape, tips, gossip, and the news to attract a public following of either buyers or sellers to join him in moving security prices upward or downward.

To carry out his manipulation, the Composite Man must act like a master trader at all times, a realist with respect to the real and latent powers of supply versus demand. Passages in *Reminiscences of a Stock Operator* illustrate the Composite Man at work in his role of merchandiser as well as in the supporting roles of manipulator and trader.

The market is composed of a cast of other characters who provide the wider context in which the game of the Composite Man is staged. In Part One, Chapter 3, we categorized investors according to the time they entered the market. The categories, or characters, ranged from innovator, to early adopter, to early and late-middle majority, and finally, at the end of the adoption cycle, to the laggards. In the innovator category you can observe the smart money, the strong hands, the better-informed, most able traders. Here among the most astute and financially able we imagine the Composite Man, planning and preparing his campaigns. In the second category, the early adopters, we see the floor traders of a bygone era or the astute trader of the current day. Together, the innovator and the early adopter categories are made up of players who possess the know-how and emotional discipline to place them in the winners' circle, campaign after market campaign.

The middle majority is dominated by the institutional giants. They, too, are arranged in a spectrum from early to late. During long bull markets they have portfolios with a mixture of early low-cost purchases to late high-cost acquisitions.

Finally, at the bottom end of the food chain, the recurring loser end of the market cycle, we find the laggard, the odd-lotter. This is the Johnny-come-lately who is attracted to a market trend in its final stages. The laggard investor is pulled into the market by the repeated demonstration of rising prices and by the hoopla of good news and favorable fundamental events. At this last, speculative stage of a market trend when the laggards enter the market, we find the Composite Man switching, on balance, from buying to selling. Hence, the market reverses direction, with distributional sales blanketing individual issues and the market as a whole.

Interactions of Winners and Losers

Figure 9.4 pulls together the Life Cycle Model of Crowd Behavior developed in Part One with the concept of the Composite Man developed in Part Two. This framework shows interactions between the Composite Man and the public over time, for both a bull and a bear cycle.

The game of the market is played out over a bull/bear cycle. To play this game, you are to assume the mantle of the Composite Man. You are to visualize yourself buying low (from the laggards, who panic at the bottom

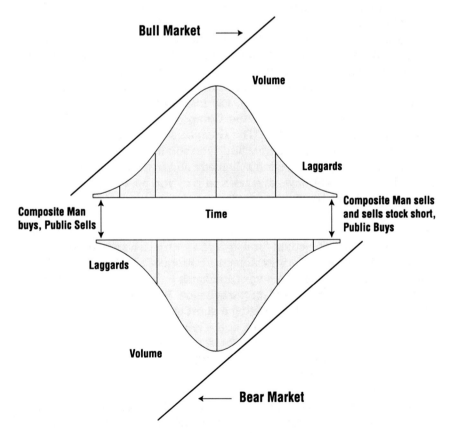

FIGURE 9.4 Interactions of Composite Man and Public

of the market) at the start of the upper life cycle and then see yourself selling to the laggards (as the "smart money"/Composite Man) at the extreme right of the life cycle model in Figure 9.4. The latter scenario occurs when the late-coming bullish public eagerly buys from you.

This all looks like a simple trick to pull off—and fun and profitable. And for those trader-analysts who have mastered the game and know-how to avoid the distractions thrown at them by the market, playing this game with success becomes second nature. You can make full use of *The Three Skills of Top Trading* to successfully maneuver yourself over the market cycle.

Part 1 Use the Life Cycle Model from Part One to set up low-risk buying opportunities and low-risk short-selling opportunities. The lower left quadrant of the Life Cycle Model defines the ideal mixture of price, volume, time, and sentiment parameters that set up a low-risk buying opportunity. It is up to the individual trader-analyst to select an appropriate mix of indicators that suits her time frame, that meets her needs for reliability, and with which she is comfortable.

The Life Cycle Model of Crowd Behavior can be seen as underpinning the Wyckoff cycle of accumulation, markup, distribution, and markdown. In fact, the S-shaped curve of the Life Cycle Model fits neatly under the S-shaped curve of the accumulation markup and distribution of Wyckoff. You should assume that the indicators used in the Life Cycle Model are further evidence of the Composite Man at work. Since the Wyckoff method asserts that "The Composite Man carefully plans, executes, and concludes his campaigns,"[3] you should turn with confidence to the visual given by the Wyckoff schematic and to the analytical checklists given by the Wyckoff laws and tests to give you perspective and insight when you set up a trade.

Part 2 Rely on the Wyckoff method as your guide to trigger your trades. The Wyckoff method furnishes you with a rich array of triggers. On the buy side, you have springs along the bottom of a trading range of accumulation, and jumps and backups (breakouts and pullbacks) along the top of a trading range. Similarly, on the sell side, Wyckoff furnishes you with the up-thrust principle for entering a short sale near the top of a trading range of distribution. Then again, at the lower range of a distribution pattern, you have the breakdown and its test and the passage of the nine selling tests as another Wyckoff short-selling juncture.

The Composite Man relies on his own judgment when deciding to buy or sell. He becomes so skilled, so unconsciously competent, that he executes his trades without apparent calculation. You can strive to become as unconsciously competent as the Composite Man, but for now, you can rely on the Wyckoff complex of laws, tests, and schematics to anchor your decisions, with the confidence that these tools mirror the actions of the Composite Man.

Trading and investment decisions using the whole mind are a hallmark of the Composite Man. He satisfies the left hemisphere of his brain with a checklist of indicators that add up to a bullish story. He then turns to his right hemisphere to see all the market parameters acting together. The two sides of the Composite Man, working together, create a compelling case for taking action.

But the Composite Man in the twenty-first century is on his guard against being bamboozled by the verbal, dominant hemisphere of his brain—even he might talk himself or be talked into seeing something in his charts that is not really there. For an antidote to seeing what you want to believe rather than believing what you see, the Composite Man inverts his charts and relies on a bag of corrective tricks similar to those found in the section titled "Chart Reading in the R-Mode" earlier in this chapter. These techniques can help you when you are conducting the task of identifying a low-risk idea in the Ten Tasks of Top Trading.

Now return to Figure 9.4 and imagine going through base building with the Composite Man. Remember that he is constantly comparing the waves of buying and selling in order to judge whether the bulls or the bears are gaining the upper hand. A strong trail of evidence emerges when price reveals a pattern of rising bottoms or descending tops within a horizontal trading range. The emergence of such patterns within a trading range provides compelling evidence that the Composite Man's intervention in either accumulation or distribution is becoming successful.

Part 3 Follow through your trades with the Ten Tasks of Top Trading. To follow through on your positions, you must employ trader discipline in order to withstand the many temptations to abort the trade prematurely. Those persons who do not easily adopt the Composite Man's skills and attitudes must abide by a regime of strict mental discipline. The Wyckoff-oriented trader's regime would consist of the Ten Tasks of Top Trading.

At this stage of the game it would be to your advantage to both add to and easily access your reservoir of resources. The resource strategy exercise outlined earlier is designed to help you build your capacity to play the role of Composite Man, just when you might need him most—when you're caught in the midst of a trade!

Once you have your position established in the buying zone and the stock or the market leaves the base, you can rest your oars alongside those of the Composite Man. You can be confident in the knowledge that the market's advance will continue as new groups bring buying power to the market and propel upward the price of the limited quantity of stock available. This insight, based on my experience and supported by the Life

Cycle Model and the Wyckoff model, makes it easier for you to relax and go with the flow of the market. Here you can rest upon the mental task of monitoring, taken from the Ten Tasks of Top Trading.

Concluding Your Campaign   Exit strategies and money management are too often overlooked or underplayed in the training of technical traders. But, effective exits mean "pay day" for the Composite Man. Please refer back to the description of the three types of Wyckoff exit strategies in Chapter 7 and recall the Wyckoff philosophy of *active* and *responsible* money management. Such management includes exit strategy 1, the reaching of a price target, and exit strategy 2, abandoning a weakening position. Here again, necessity creates a compelling case for you and for the Composite Man to reframe your open trade from being a "good" trade to being a "bad" trade. Reframing from "good" to "bad" will do wonders for your motivation to abort your trade and get out of the market!

Concluding one campaign leads naturally to grooming the market or the stock for the next campaign. Through the eyes of the Composite Man we see the need to read the mood and makeup of the public participants in the market. If the signs of market behavior reveal the maturity stage, then we again see the Composite Man engaging in the manipulations that exhaust the remnants of demand.

Figure 9.4 shows the Composite Man distributing his line of long stock to the laggards who are hungry to take it off his hands. But he does the bulk of his selling on the way down, during the markdown phase, because the now-bullish late-comers measure the bargains they perceive by how many points the stock has declined from its recent peak price. At this stage the surface news and gossip is so bullish that the trader must be on his guard against being diverted from seeing the true picture of the market the way that the Wyckoff Composite Man would see it—bearish.

Playing the Role of the Composite Man

You can learn to play the role of the Composite Man and thereby gain a trading edge for yourself by first understanding and then practicing the Wyckoff Method. The Wyckoff repertoire of three laws, nine tests, and schematics was designed to help you follow in the footsteps of the Composite Man. Role-playing can both further and enhance your skill and judgment; one of the best ways to learn via role-playing is to immerse yourself fully in a simulation of trading. I have developed the Action Sequence method of active learning for that very purpose.

As an educator, a trader, and an analyst, I encourage you to use the Action Sequence method to train yourself to acquire winning habits by applying the Wyckoff method and by following in the footsteps of the Composite Man. You can gain a good feel for the Action Sequence method by going through the practical exercise in the Appendix to this chapter.

APPENDIX A: THE ACTION SEQUENCE METHOD

For over a quarter of a century, I have taught technical analysis to traders and analysts at the university level. I am proud to have won multiple "best teacher" and "best scholar" awards based on my ability to teach motivated beginners in finance and to challenge experienced professional investors and traders. The feedback from investment professionals during that time brought about continuous improvements in the application of behavioral finance and technical analysis principles and procedures. I found my greatest educational challenge to be helping people progress from the definition level of instruction to the application of theory.

Over the years, I have used my own experiences, coupled with secondary research, to develop an innovative, workable educational system, the Action Sequence method, for building the skills and knowledge of intermediate learners of technical analysis. While the Action Sequence may be very roughly thought of as paper trading, the method includes extensive feedback and replays the original sequence, incorporating lessons learned from the previous experience. The replay portion of the model is critical; in this way, the student-trader is being trained to react appropriately to future market circumstances.

Analytical Framework

The Action Sequence in technical market analysis is a modification of the case study method of instruction. At the Harvard School of Business, students actively learn from experience using the case method. There are several strong parallels between the Action Sequence and the case method:

- Analysis of practical problems drawn from real-life situations.
- Students putting themselves in the positions of managers.
- A decision-making orientation.
- Learning by doing or an experiential approach.
- Developing the student's understanding, judgment, and communication leading to effective action.
- Building dependable self-reliance within the student.

In addition, the Action Sequence emphasizes the application of time-tested Wyckoff principles of market behavior to concrete case histories of market action. The student gains knowledge as well as skill and judgment through the practical application of the substantive material of the Wyckoff method of stock market analysis.

Perhaps the essential value of this dynamic education technique lies in its ability to excite interest in the trader-analyst. The trader will become an active participant in the educational process instead of remaining a passive recipient. Often, our participation in education that is exciting, challenging, and relevant disturbs our sense of adequacy and causes us to seek self-improvement. If the educational experience provides opportunity for the trader to encounter groping, self-discovery, and the uncovering of blind spots, real change in behavior can result where it counts—back on the trading desk.

An exercise with an action sheet and feedback follows; I encourage you to practice trading using the Action Sequence method.

Action Sheet and Feedback Exercise

In this exercise, you will conduct a technical analysis of the daily vertical line chart of a stock and enter or exit trading positions. The period covered is December of the first year until November of the next year. During this period, you will find intermediate swings for covering and going long near the bottoms and selling out and making short sales near the peaks. Use protective stops on all trades. Pyramiding with a trend is sometimes advisable.

Use all appropriate Wyckoff principles and techniques at your command. This is an "open book" exercise; as you go through the Action Sequence, feel free to consult other sections of *The Three Skills* or any notes you've taken.

With this exercise, you will find an "Action Form," accompanied by a chart with a slice of the year's data. You are to reconstruct the chart price and volume in your own hand on tracing paper, then interpret the present position and probable future trend of the stock, gauging the relationships between supply and demand. Next, judge the underlying motive of the Composite Man and take definite action: buying, selling, or remaining neutral.

Following each action sheet, you will find a "Feedback" section. Feedback is composed of two parts. The first part consists of the feedback from the market itself. This "what really happened" type of feedback is the most powerful feedback of all. The second part of feedback is the commentary from some person skilled in interpreting the Wyckoff method, the Life Cycle Model of Crowd Behavior, and The Ten Tasks of Top Trading. In the case of the stock chart sequence used in this exercise, I will play the role of the commentator offering expert opinion.

You can replay the previous action if you are not in sync with the market. Following the feedback and replay, go on to the next action sheet in the series and so on until the sequence is complete. At the conclusion of the Action Sequence series, take note of which Wyckoff principles were particularly useful to you so they will be in your arsenal the next time you are given an opportunity to trade.

In the future, when you are on you own, I encourage you to apply the same sort of logic contained in this Action Sequence exercise to your own trading. You will discover this approach especially helpful during instances when you are back-testing or paper-trading a stock, commodity, future, or any other instrument you wish to add to your inventory. In addition, the logic and procedures demonstrated in this exercise can assist you greatly in conducting the debriefing and periodic review tasks of the Ten Tasks of Top Trading.

Since the Action Sequence is wrapped up with a learn-by-doing educational philosophy, it is imperative that you become fully engaged in the exercise by carefully and completely filling out each and every one of the components you see on the Action Sequence form. Please do not just skip over some items or skip writing down your thoughts. Doing the thinking and the writing helps immeasurably in building skills and forming the correct habits for a judgmental method. Studying the feedback from the market and from the commentaries is essential to building your skills, your knowledge, and your judgment.

Action Sequence 1 Interpreting supply and demand: Using Figure 9.5, complete this action sequence in its entirety before moving on to the next action sequence; do not look ahead!

1. Redraw the chart on transparency paper in your own hand so as to get a feel for the price and volume action. (Verbalize to yourself, in Wyckoff terms and principles, your observations.)
2. Interpret the relationship between supply and demand. What is the present position and probable future trend of the market?

   _____

   _____

   _____

3. What is the motive of the Composite Operator?

   _____

   _____

   _____

4. Select one of the following. Fill in the blanks.

    a. Buy or go long at _____ with a stop at _____.

    b. Sell or go short at _____ with a stop at _____.

    c. Close out an existing position at _____.

    d. Move the stop on an existing position to _____.

    e. Do nothing; await further developments.

5. Which of the Ten Tasks of Top Trading would you want to adopt to gain the proper mental state for the implementation of the type of task you believe is involved in this action sequence? (For example, *stalking*.)

_____ is the proper task for the mental state management needed in this action sequence.

ACTION SEQUENCE #1

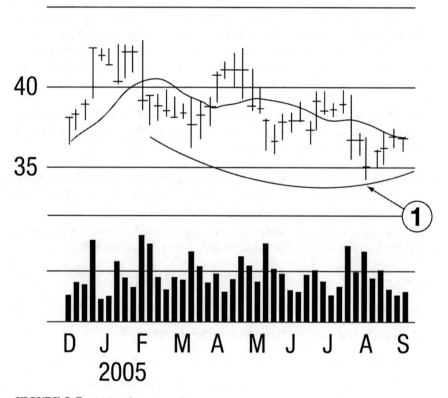

FIGURE 9.5 Action Sequence 1

Feedback on Action Sequence 1   The market itself gives the essential feedback lesson. If you look ahead to the chart for action sequence 2 (Figure 9.6), you will see that from point 1 to point 2, the market rose sharply on expanding volume. This was a bullish action. Moreover, price traced out a pattern of higher lows and higher highs within the trend channel connecting points 1 and 2. That, too, was bullish action. But this feedback and commentary have the benefit of 20/20 hindsight.

The foresight analysis called for in action sequence 1 was not so easily done. Yet, by carefully examining the price and volume from December 2004 to August 2005, the trader-analyst could discern clues that the downward to sideways price action was probably accumulation and not distribution. The large volume entering the market at the market low points of March and May–June 2005 also points to accumulation. Those

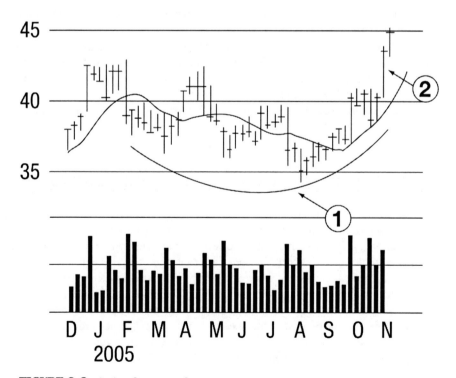

ACTION SEQUENCE #2

FIGURE 9.6   Action Sequence 2

turning points showed that the Composite Man and the forces of demand were willing to absorb the offerings that were pressed upon the market.

Point 1 was used by the Composite Man to test the market's readiness to advance. It shows a penetration below prior support that the Composite Man created in an effort to attract a following of public sellers. The comparatively heavy volume during the last weeks of July and the first week of August 2005 revealed a substantial effort and following by the bears. But the continuation of this bearish decline failed to materialize and in fact was reversed by the rally in late August.

Everything now depended on the power of the next decline. The very shallow downside price action into mid-September coupled with a diminishment in volume indicated that the bears were exhausted and/or losing control and that the bulls were gaining the upper hand. The Wyckoff principle of a *spring* appeared to be at work, with an action below support levels in the trading range, and then its successful test on smaller price spread and lower volume. A trader could have elected to buy his first one-third of his capital position in the vicinity of the price lows of mid-September 2005.

A protective sell stop-order must be entered by the trader a few points below the price low at point 1.

A trader would have needed to exercise patience throughout the weeks of January to August 2005 as the market groomed itself in a trading range for either a markup or a downtrend. Then, as the market sprang upward from the low at point 1, the trader would have been wise to go through the mental tasks of building a low-risk idea, stalking the trade, and then taking action.

Side Note to Traders

The astute trader-analyst who is going through exercise 1 will observe that a periodic rhythm of hovering around a 10- to 13-week cycle low-to-low appears from December 2004 onward. There were trading opportunities both long and short for the trader of this security during those swings. You can apply the same sort of principles being demonstrated in this action sequence to profit from them. Of course, you would need to be using daily-basis charts for that shorter time frame as opposed to the weekly-basis charts used in this exercise, but the principles are much the same. What you learn in this action sequence will equip you to trade the shorter time frames, as well.

Action Sequence 2 Interpreting supply and demand: Using Figure 9.6, complete this action sequence in its entirety before moving on to the next action sequence, do not look ahead!

1. Redraw the chart on transparency paper in your own hand so as to get a feel for the price and volume action. (Verbalize to yourself, in Wyckoff terms and principles, your observations.)

2. Interpret the relationship between supply and demand. What is the present position and probable future trend of the market?

   _____

   _____

   _____

3. What is the motive of the Composite Operator?

   _____

   _____

   _____

4. Select one of the following. Fill in the blanks.
   a. Buy or go long at _____ with a stop at _____.
   b. Sell or go short at _____ with a stop at _____.
   c. Close out an existing position at _____.
   d. Move the stop on an existing position to _____.
   e. Do nothing; await further developments.

5. Which of the Ten Tasks of Top Trading would you want to adopt to gain the proper mental state for the implementation of the type of task you believe is involved in this action sequence? (For example, *stalking*.)

   _____ is the proper task for the mental state management needed in this action sequence.

Feedback on Action Sequence 2 What are the present position and probable future trend of the market and the Wyckoff principles involved? As you can see on the chart of action sequence 2, the market under study has surmounted all resistance points seen on the chart and has entered a markup phase. There was a sign of strength on the week with wide price spread and heavy volume in late September and early October that confirmed the buying action a trader would have taken in action sequence 1. On the pullback test or any day thereafter, the trader could enter a second buy. It appears the intention of the Composite Man is to absorb all of the overhead supply of stock offered and create excitement with the rapid price advances above all previous highs in an effort to attract a public following.

A Wyckoff type trading range of reaccumulation has been completed with a base extending from October back to February–March. Stop-loss orders on both the first and second purchase should now be raised to just under the supporting price preceding point. The trader is advised to relax into the mental state of *monitoring* and let his profits run!

Action Sequence 3   Interpreting supply and demand: Using Figure 9.7, complete this action sequence in its entirety before moving on to the next action sequence, do not look ahead!

1. Redraw the chart on transparency paper in your own hand so as to get a feel for the price and volume action. (Verbalize to yourself, in Wyckoff terms and principles, your observations.)

ACTION SEQUENCE #3

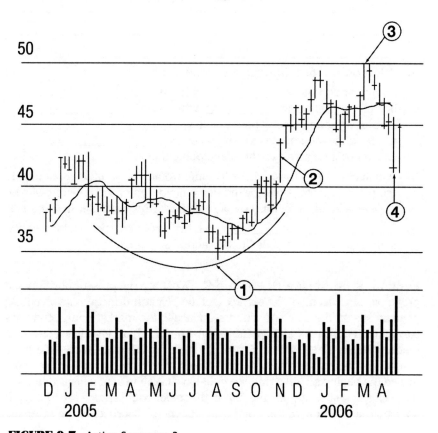

FIGURE 9.7   Action Sequence 3

2. Interpret the relationship between supply and demand. What is the present position and probable future trend of the market?

_____

_____

_____

3. What is the motive of the Composite Operator?

_____

_____

_____

4. Select one of the following. Fill in the blanks.
   a. Buy or go long at _____ with a stop at _____.
   b. Sell or go short at _____ with a stop at _____.
   c. Close out an existing position at _____.
   d. Move the stop on an existing position to _____.
   e. Do nothing; await further developments.
5. Which of the Ten Tasks of Top Trading would you want to adopt to gain the proper mental state for the implementation of the type of task you believe is involved in this action sequence? (For example, *stalking*.)

   _____ is the proper task for the mental state management needed in this action sequence.

Feedback on Action Sequence 3   The chart reveals a reversal of fortune. The promising rally that commenced at point 2 continued from $42 up to about $49. There was a small consolidation around $45, which the trader could use as a benchmark for new stop-loss orders on both of his previous positions. Thus, he can raise his stops to $43 to lock in profits while allowing the trend to unfold. The sharp sell-off into late January 2005 would have stopped out the traders. At that point he could have counted his profits and retired to the sidelines to enjoy the task of *being out of the market*.

Sometimes you might be able to exit around the $46 to $48 level. You had extensive clues because of the diminishing volume on the rally and the shortening upward price thrusts. Your action could then be triggered by a penetration of the steep trend-line that could be drawn along the lows of the channel that started two weeks before point 2 and continued sharply upward to late December or early January. There was no other Wyckoff principle to act upon, other than exit strategy 2.

A much more promising short-selling opportunity came at point 3. Here, the Composite Man may have been unloading his long positions because the small net price advance over the previous high coupled with lower total volume at point 3 indicated that the bullish following was becoming exhausted. Furthermore, a cause for a decline would have been forming from point 3 back to the previous high, around $48. Therefore, as soon as the stock fell back to about $48 on still comparatively high volume, you, the trader, could take the short sale position with a stop placed just above the $50 level.

On balance, this would have been a nice intermediate trade. The high-volume selling climax just after point 4 shows the Composite Man covering his short sales and going long. Not only was there the high-volume clue but the stock had corrected 50 percent of its advance from the $34 low to $50. Furthermore, at $42, the old resistance along the highs of the previous trading was now acting as support.

It is at junctures like point 4 that the trader comes to appreciate the importance of *action* in the Ten Tasks of Top Trading to provide her with the necessary intestinal fortitude to buy somewhere between $42 and $45 and set a protective stop-loss order around $40.

Once the position was on, the trader should use the *monitoring* phase to step back from the market and to prevent fear from talking him out of his trade. The larger trend is still upward and there is a substantial base of reaccumulation behind the trade. For further backup, the trader could consult the checklist of indicators found in the Life Cycle Model of Crowd Behavior tool kit.

Action Sequence 4   Interpreting supply and demand: Using Figure 9.8, complete this action sequence in its entirety before moving on to the next action sequence; do not look ahead!

1. Redraw the chart on transparency paper in your own hand so as to get a feel for the price and volume action. (Verbalize to yourself, in Wyckoff terms and principles, your observations.)

2. Interpret the relationship between supply and demand. What is the present position and probable future trend of the market?

   _____

   _____

   _____

3. What is the motive of the Composite Operator?

   _____

   _____

   _____

4. Select one of the following. Fill in the blanks.
   a. Buy or go long at _____ with a stop at _____.
   b. Sell or go short at _____ with a stop at _____.
   c. Close out an existing position at _____.
   d. Move the stop on an existing position to _____.
   e. Do nothing; await further developments.

5. Which of the Ten Tasks of Top Trading would you want to adopt to gain the proper mental state for the implementation of the type of task you believe is involved in this action sequence? (For example, *stalking*.)

   _____ is the proper task for the mental state management needed in this action sequence.

ACTION SEQUENCE #4

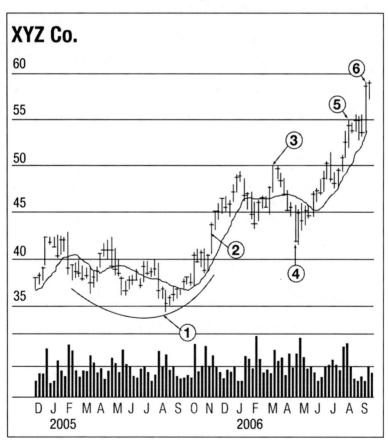

FIGURE 9.8 Action Sequence 4

Feedback on Action Sequence 4   Although it was not revealed to you in Action Sequence 3, there was a second buying opportunity around the $45 level. You can see from an inspection of the chart that a classic Wyckoff pattern was set up around $45 following the selling climax rally from $42 to just above $50 on comparatively heavy volume. The Wyckoff rhythm of action, then test, is evident. Following the selling climax action on heavy volume and wide price spread, there were successful secondary tests on narrowing price spread and diminished volume on the pullbacks to just under $50. Note also that the weekly lows in this vicinity continued to rise, another sign that the Composite Man was absorbing the offerings and thus lending support to the market. Such instances of support are comforting to the public and so set the stage for a public following to throng in the path laid down by the Composite Man.

The trader should make his second purchase somewhere around $50. The stop ought to be placed at just under point 4. During this process, the trader could call upon the Ten Tasks to help him follow through on his trades. Most helpful would be analyzing for a *low-risk idea, stalking, action,* and *monitoring* together with *daily debriefing, daily self-analysis,* and *rehearsing the trade.*

The XYZ chart in Action Sequence 4 shows the ample reward gained by the trader for using his head and controlling his heart. The rally to around $58 per share again shows telltale signs of possible exhaustion of the public following and the engineering of a climactic parabolic dash from $54 to $58 (point 6).

But that parabolic rise was on diminishing volume relative to point 6 and it hints of a squeezing of premature short-sellers who may have entered when XYZ hesitated around $55 per share. In sum, this is clearly an overbought market and a good time for the trader to slip out of the passive *monitoring* frame of mind and into an aggressive *take profits* mode. Also, remember to cancel your protective trailing stop-loss orders!

As a wrap-up to this trading campaign, you ought to rehearse the *periodic review* task by going back over this action sequence. This will help fix in your mind and body clear thinking and strong feeling about playing this trade. Should you have made any mistakes along the way, this would be the time to replay them the Composite Man way to profits.

CHAPTER 10

Putting It All Together: Ten Principles for a Trader to Live By

This chapter introduces or recapitulates the ten principles for a trader to live by. The discussion of the first nine principles is integrated and illustrated by the tenth principle using a case study of an ace foreign exchange trader, Weylin Canada, 2004 graduate of the Golden Gate University graduate certificate program in technical market analysis. The case study, Canada of Esoteric Investments, San Francisco, California,

The Ten Principles

1. Be your own boss: Create a "sealed room" for yourself and commit yourself to "only one client."
2. Leapfrog your competitors: Gain the winning edge by acquiring high-concept and high-touch talents for the twenty-first century.
3. Learn the Wyckoff method of technical analysis and master the Wyckoff art of speculation.
4. Become the complete trader: Play the role of the Composite Man.
5. Always be disciplined: Follow through your trades with the Ten Tasks of Top Trading.
6. Build your trading systems on the solid, scientific foundations of behavioral finance.
7. Use decision support systems to help set up your market timing.
8. Test your trading system and train yourself to use it via the action sequence method for active learning.
9. Adopt a planning and control process.
10. Integrate the Three Skills of Top Trading and make them an inseparable part of yourself.

235

provides a concrete demonstration of the Three Skills of Top Trading that includes charts and a recounting of actual trades by Canada.

PRINCIPLE 1: BE YOUR OWN BOSS

This first principle lays the groundwork for your success as a trader. Discipline is necessary to make trading profitable, and discipline is what it takes to follow the advice given in this principle.

A "Sealed Room"

This is where a trader does his best work. To understand the origins of this concept we must travel to the Boston area and go back in time to the early 1950s so as to observe John Magee seated in his famous "sealed room," designed to cut him off from all outside information so that he could reach decisions about market timing and direction based solely on his chart analysis. John Brooks, author of *The Seven Fat Years: Chronicles of Wall Street* (New York: Doubleday, 1961), found Magee there. From the pen of Brooks the fact, the fable, and the myth of the "sealed room" became heralded as the symbol of the pure technician at work in a purely technical world. This is how Brooks told the story of his first meeting with John Magee:

> *Hanging on the wall nearby was a bulletin board, on which were posted several notices, written in symbols too esoteric for me, and a motto, not so esoteric, that read, "MY MIND IS MADE UP, DON'T CONFUSE ME WITH THE FACTS. . . ."*
>
> *Magee gave me an owlish glance and pointed to the motto on the bulletin board. "So, you see, in a sense there's as much truth as humor in that," he said. "Of course, the sign is just a gag and is intended as a rebuke to know-it-alls, but to the technician the last part of it has a special significance and in a peculiar way means what it says—'Don't confuse me with the facts.' Facts, as used here, are the daily outpouring of newspaper stories and radio news bulletins dealing with announcements of mergers, reports of earnings, decisions in tax cases—all that sort of thing—to say nothing of a great variety of opinions and predictions and just plain scuttlebutt. Even if you could separate the hard core of fact from the chaff of scuttlebutt, you would find that much of it is irrelevant information that is either trivial or, more often, has already been noted, evaluated, and acted on, and thus has been reflected by the market, days,*

weeks, or even months before it reaches you. "Discounted in advance," as Wall Street says. It is simply so much confusing dross to the technician, who therefore does his best to avoid it.

"Let me give you an example," said Magee. "Before I came to work here, I was on my own, making my charts and operating in the market out of an office at 360 Worthington Street, a few blocks from here, where I had nothing but a table, a chair, a telephone, a ticker and an air-conditioning machine. I sealed up the windows with boards and putty, so there would be no outside sights and sounds to distract me. I had no fundamental information at my disposal whatever, which left me free to make up my mind solely on the basis of my charts." Magee continued, "I've still got a lease on the Worthington Street Office—keep a lot of my private files there. I've always hung onto it as a place where I can go every now and then and think—a kind of safety valve, you might say. . . ."[1]

Like Wyckoff, like Richard Schabacker, and like Humphrey Neill before him, Magee ran a pennant up the flagpole emblazoned "The Tape Tells All!" To tell the truth, all Magee needed to interpret the true message of the market was the price, volume, and time of transactions—all of which were available from the ticker tape. With price, volume, and time, Magee could create daily charts and weekly charts, then go on to draw trendlines, mark levels of support or resistance, and then, finally, elevate all into a fantastic geometric typology: wedges, triangles, head-and-shoulders, saucers, and so on and on.

But why has the metaphor of the sealed room lingered for so long? Why do the words *sealed room* evoke such warm and knowing familiarity among some technicians and vivid mental images among others?

The answer to these questions lies, I believe, in the allegorical qualities of the story of the sealed room. An allegory is a story in which figures and actions are symbols of general truths. It is a method of indirect representation of ideas as truths. The essence of the story of the sealed room is that *you need your own private space, your own "sealed room,"* free of the noise, interferences, competitions, and expectations of the external world, so that you can do your best technical thinking and trading. You can best organize yourself for effective decision-making by first *creating in your own mind your own version of the sealed room.*

Retiring to the bounty of your own sealed room is important. It promises you an opportunity to shift your state of mind into that zone where superior trading performance is naturally fostered. In his article on "Finding 'The Zone'," Lawrence Shainberg recounted how Denise Parker, a diminutive world-class archer, found her sealed room for her zone of top performance. According to her coach, Keith Henschen, an applied sports psychologist,

> *". . . athletes who are best at this are the ones who get into the zone most easily."*
>
> *Her coach asked her to create for herself what he called a "happiness room," a place to which she could withdraw in her imagination in order to visualize an upcoming meet. Of all the exercises this was the one to which Denise brought the most enthusiasm. The room she created was primarily a replica of her bedroom, but it had its magical dimension, and it was anything but austere. "There's stairs leading up to it and these big doors you go through," she explains. "It has brown wall-to-wall carpet, a king-sized waterbed, stack stereo, a big-screen TV and a VCR, posters of Tom Cruise and Kirk Cameron on the wall, and a fireplace that's always blazing. That's where I go when a meet's coming up. I drive up to it in a Porsche, go inside, lie down on the waterbed and watch a tape of myself shooting perfect arrows. Later, when I get to the tournament, everything seems familiar. Even at the Olympics I was calm as soon as I began to shoot."[2]*

Like Denise's, your sealed room can be your happiness room; like Denise, you can create your sealed room in your mind. Like Denise, you can outfit your sealed room with all the modern gadgetry and wizardry you wish. Like her, you can retire to your sealed room at any time, but particularly before major trading events; you can run movies of yourself making the perfect market calls time after time after time, or, if you prefer, you can run mental movies of those times in the past when you made your best trades, you did your best technical work, and you felt you were in sync with the market.

Only One Client

Within your mind you should have a vision of yourself achieving your defined purpose. Such a vision has magnetism; it has the power to pull you toward its fulfillment. To be most magnetic, such a vision should depict you accomplishing your heart's desire—for example, imagine seeing yourself receiving an award for brilliant trading, feeling the congratulatory handshakes from the big hitters whom you admire, and exchanging messages of trust, respect, and mutual admiration with them. Such a vision engenders commitment, raises standards, and enlivens a creative search for better solutions to problems, be they trading, personal, or monetary. Such a vision generates the creative tension you need to call forth your best efforts, to push forward your frontiers of trading and technical analysis, to create wealthy and happy clients, to make a better world for yourself and those around you. As management guru Dr. Peter Senge relates,

> *Robert Fritz says, "It's not what the vision is; it's what the vision does." Truly creative people use the gap between vision and current reality to generate energy for change. . . .*
>
> *But vision is different from purpose. Purpose is similar to a direction, a general heading. Vision is a specific destination, a picture of a desired future. Purpose is abstract. Vision is concrete. Purpose is "advancing man's capability to explore the heavens." Vision is "a man on the moon by the end of the 1960s." Purpose is "being the best I can be," "excellence." Vision is breaking four minutes in the mile.*
>
> *It can be truly said that nothing happens until there is vision. But it is equally true that a vision with no underlying sense of purpose, no calling, is just a good idea—all "sound and fury, signifying nothing!"*[3]

Let us look more deeply into your purpose and your trading clients. At the bottom there may well be a curious love-hate relationship between you and your clients. You are the expert, they are novices, or so the reasoning goes, for otherwise why should they accept your advice? Your superior knowledge presumably gives you power, yet modern marketing philosophy states that the consumer, your client, is king! You want to be rational; your clients too often are emotional! You want to focus and concentrate your energies, but too many diverse clients are always scattering your attention and efforts. You may have a solid track record and a method for generating reasonable, consistent results, yet potential clients avoid you and current clients leave you to flock around the guru with the latest hot hand and a seductive trading gimmick. You are dependent on your clients, but you may prefer to affiliate with your peers; you may wish to stand tall in the market timing ratings.

Now let us walk into a bookstore and purchase a copy of a forward-thinking management text, *The Fifth Discipline: The Art and Practice of the Learning Organization,* by Peter M. Senge (Currency Doubleday, 1990, 1994, 2006). Between its covers you can find nuggets of wisdom. Take purpose, for instance. The author implores you to extend the boundaries of your ego and the functions of your business, and in the process, widen your circle of compassion. By expanding your compassion you will see more clearly how you and your client are enmeshed in the same system of mutual dependence. Out of this expanded compassion also springs a commitment to the whole, which will make your sense of purpose a genuine motivating force.

As Senge goes on to say, " 'Genuine commitment,' according to Bill O'Brien, 'is always to something larger than ourselves.' . . . The sense of connectedness and compassion characteristic of individuals with high levels of personal mastery naturally leads to a broader vision. . . . Individuals committed to a vision beyond their self-interest find they have energy not available when pursuing narrower goals."[4]

Viewing your technical-trading efforts from the client's perspective is a commitment to the truth. It means a relentless willingness to root out the ways in which we limit or deceive ourselves from seeing what is and to continually challenge our theories of why things are the way they are. It is broadening our awareness; it is expanding our boundaries; it is taking another observation of our work from the outside looking in.

But how do we reconcile what is—the culture of the client-customer relationship on Wall Street—with what should be: a wider, deeper sense of purpose that incorporates your client as a partner in your progress? I propose that you simplify your life down to "only one client." Then incorporate that one client into your personal vision of achievement, and into your statement of purpose.

"You Are the Customer, You Are the Company," exclaimed Paul Hawken in the title of a chapter in his book, *Growing a Business* (New York: Simon & Schuster, 1988). Hawken went on to make the following observations:

> *In order to develop a good business idea and earn the permission of the marketplace, you must be the market. You should want to shop at the store you run, to receive the services you offer. Every expression of the business, its ads, decor, service, packaging, pricing, and selling techniques should be 100% credible, respectable, and acceptable to you.*

And further on, Hawken said:

> *While you "approximate" the customer, you can know only yourself. So stay close to the person you understand, and market products for yourself. This takes the guess work out of it.*[5]

Hawken calls our attention to the fact that we, too, are the clients of our own trading and technical products and that we, too, should shop critically at the windows of our trading and technical enterprises. We should repeatedly ask ourselves, "Would I buy that? Does it meet my standards as a client?" If it does not, then change it.

You yourself are that one client. You yourself or at least the customer-client part of you, are the proxy for all of your other clients. That is a responsibility. Consistently serve that one client very well over the long term and you will serve all of your other clients.

Think of it this way. If you are by yourself, trading for your own account, you are, in the final analysis, doing it for some larger purpose. That larger purpose is fulfilling the needs of the consumption side of your business, the customer. Your larger purpose is inextricably tied to fulfilling broader client needs, be they safety needs satisfied by money in the bank, affiliation needs met by caring for your loved ones, or even philanthropic needs gratified through charitable donations. Cut a corner, cheat your customer, and you cheat yourself.

But your vision of yourself as your best and most worthy client will only enhance your decision making if it becomes an internal part of you. Writing down, "I am the customer, I am the company" as a motto, then placing that affirmation everywhere along your daily path, is not a bad idea. But the really good idea, the idea that will give that motto some punch, is to have it installed in your mind, in one or more of your primary senses of seeing, hearing, and feeling.

Let's do a simple exercise to get this point across. At this moment create a mental picture of an ideal client in your mind's eye. Focus on the head and shoulders. Now center this picture of your ideal client as though it were appearing on a $1 million bill. Can you make the client look a little more like you? Can you place that image of your ideal client in your upper visual field alongside an image of yourself?

If you did this exercise, you were creating an internal visual representation. On the other hand, if you were unable to make mental images or if you were unhappy with this picture-making process, then try words or feelings instead. Develop some words to represent your client (yourself) such as, "He is a jolly good fellow." Those words, like your conscience speaking, will come up to remind you of your purpose, your vision. Or maybe you will be reminded of your vision by how you feel, by a tingling sensation in your arms or a thrill through your solar plexus. Best of all, develop all three internal representations of your "only one client"—see, hear, and feel.

The next facet of your vision calls for constantly, continually maintaining a vivid image of your growing, thriving client or client-self. A hallmark of effective decision-makers and successful people is a capacity to sustain their vision, to have it as a handy reference against which to check their decisions. Their vision is both now in the present and out there in the future; it is focused on ends and results rather than on ways and means.

An effective decision maker is so bound to fulfilling her larger mission that she will make the needed adjustment in ways and means. For example, if reversing a market opinion is needed to fulfill her vision of a prospering client, she will amend her opinion; if abandoning a pet technical approach is required to reach the future vision, so be it; if different time frames or styles of trading or even a bullish bias must be surrendered to fulfill the vision, appropriate change will be made. And the effective, visionary decision maker will take these and numerous other so-called mistakes in stride; she'll accept them as learning opportunities along the path to the fulfillment of her compelling future.

Any important decision you make should be tested against that vision. If the action you are contemplating leads toward the fulfillment of that vision, it is an effective decision; if the action leads away from the fulfillment of that vision, it is an ineffective decision.

Your vision of you and your client on the face of a $1 million bill can serve as the trigger that causes you to generate multiple options of the future. Your vision can be the standard against which you measure those options, and your vision can be the motivator that pulls you into action. The stronger and richer the image of your only client, yourself, the more deeply rooted, the more pure, and the more single-minded your purpose, the more likely it is that this entire decision-making process will become automatic for you. Maintaining the image of only one client will work to harness the immense powers of your unconscious mind to give you a true and enduring trading edge.

Thinking back over these ideas should bring some insights worthy of your consideration. There may be some truth to the picturesque notion of making a habit of slipping away to your own special redoubt, your own sealed room. From there you can sally forth with the foremost technical forces that you can muster. And the direction you choose is determined by the vision in your mind's eye, namely "only one client." The vision I see is you as the best technician or trader or investor you aspire to become. I see you doing this by serving, to your utmost capacity, your client or both of you together.

If you find merit or even hope in the notions of a sealed room and only one client, then you might wish to consider two helpful hints:

1. Identify an exclusive place for yourself that you can call your sealed room. This place can be located a few feet away from your computer screen or several hundred miles away from your city, or both. Remember to have a positive mental attitude; remember to relish the creation of your sealed room.

2. Focus your attention on only one client. Imagine this client growing wealthier and thriving. Commit yourself to the enhancement of this client's welfare. Develop an image of yourself as this ideal client or be-

ing with that client. See you or both of you moving along a path of continual growth and thriving. Use this image as a benchmark for the choices you make. Each day renew this vision until it is there for you always and automatically.

PRINCIPLE 2: LEAPFROG YOUR COMPETITORS

The world of technical analysis for traders has become overcrowded with number crunching that is unguided by conceptual schemes in tune with the true nature of the market. Too often, this results in a muscular but mindless mechanical trading system. Relying on this "information age" path will send the trader's job to a computer-savvy 20-year-old in Sri Lanka.

Leapfrog your competition and capture a first-mover advantage by getting the conceptual edge by trading with your *whole* mind, as explored in Daniel Pink's groundbreaking book, *A Whole New Mind: Why Right-Brainers Will Rule the Future* (New York: Riverhead Trade, 2006). Tom Peters, author of *In Search Of Excellence* (New York: Collins, 2004) proclaims that "[Daniel H. Pink's] book is a miracle. Completely original and profound." According to Pink, we are on the cusp of the Conceptual Age, an age that champions "high concept" and "high touch." Success in this new age will depend on your "capacity to detect patterns and opportunities, to create artistic and emotional beauty, to craft satisfying narrative, and to combine seemingly unrelated ideas into something new."[6] High touch empowers you to get a feel for the market.

While trading for my account, I used high-concept, high-touch techniques long before they were labeled as such by Pink. Later, I wrote articles about these concepts, assembled a book, and designed a course to teach others how to apply these techniques to the market. In all these avenues, my work echoed and incorporated the concepts and empathies Pink declares are foundations for success in the twenty-first century. These high-concept and high-touch gems are available to the trader who studies *The Three Skills of Top Trading*.

You will find high-concept pattern recognition and synthesis tasks and the skills with which to execute them throughout this book. Part One illustrates high concept for the trader with a behavioral finance model, the Life Cycle of Crowd Behavior. Then Part Two continues to develop your high-concept aptitude with discretionary trading and pattern recognition using the Wyckoff method of technical market analysis. Finally, Part Three provides opportunities to deepen your understanding of high touch and develop your aptitude with the help of the Ten Tasks of Top Trading and the concepts of a "sealed room" and "only one client." With the sound logic of modern behavioral finance and the classic pattern recognition skills of technical analysis, the trader and the market analyst will find pathways to trading success in the twenty-first century.

PRINCIPLE 3: LEARN THE WYCKOFF METHOD

The Wyckoff method is a classic pattern-recognition system. Wyckoff relies on bar charts and point-and-figure charts to judge the relationships of price spread and volume between comparative waves of buying and selling.

From his many observations of behind-the-scenes manipulations by the large operators on Wall Street, Richard D. Wyckoff discovered time and again by reading the stock market ticker tape and the charts of stocks that the best indicator of the future price of a security was the relationship between supply and demand. In 1910, under the pen name "Rollo Tape," he wrote the pioneering book *Studies in Tape Reading*, in which he revealed how to read the market and conduct speculative operations. In this classic, Wyckoff covered such basics as stop orders, volume indications, dull markets and their opportunities, and other market techniques that would one day be incorporated into his method that first appeared around 1931.

Wyckoff placed prime importance on the analyst's ability to judge the relative power of the buying and selling waves, and thus to comprehend the dominant forces behind a market move. In essence, this pattern recognition approach predated what Pink labeled the "information age." In fact, the talents Wyckoff deemed important for effective stock market diagnosis, prognosis, and trading foreshowed the now emerging "conceptual age" that Pink asserts will soon become the dominant way of thinking in the twenty-first century. Thus, Wyckoff was both quintessentially classic and utterly modern.

Over the years since 1930, Wyckoff, followed by his associates, formulated a valuable set of rules for the technical trader to follow. These rules appear in Chapter 6 as Wyckoff laws, Wyckoff tests, and Wyckoff schematics. The basic elements of charting, particularly bar charts and point-and-figure charts, appear in Chapter 5.

The essence of Chapters 5 and 6 is summarized by the five-step method of market analysis, often referred to as the Wyckoff method. The five steps of the Wyckoff method are presented in Chapter 4. The Wyckoff method has stood the test of time. Over a hundred years of continuous development and usage around the globe have proven the worthiness of the Wyckoff method for use with stocks, bonds, currencies, and commodities.

The Wyckoff method of technical analysis furnishes you with an almost ideal set of laws and principles that you can use as general guidelines to interpret chart patterns and take action. However, before you can master the Wyckoff method, you must firmly embrace the fact that you need to exercise judgment. Experience in a variety of different case situations guided by accurate and intelligent principles is essential.

PRINCIPLE 4: BECOME THE COMPLETE TRADER

According to Richard D. Wyckoff:

> *The market is made by the mind of man, and all the fluctuations in the market and in all the various stocks should be studied as if they were the result of one man's operations. Let us call him the Composite Man, who, in theory, sits behind the scenes and plays a stock to his advantage. It is to your disadvantage if you do not understand the game as he plays it and to your advantage if you do understand it. Not all of the Composite Man's moves can be detected. Not all of the moves are made by the Composite Man. In fact, it does not matter to the tape reader or the chart reader whether the moves are real or artificial, that is, the result of actual buying or selling by the public and long term investors or by buying and by selling traders. Most of the important trades in the market are prepared, executed, and concluded. It is our business to show you how a large number of these trading and investment opportunities may be spotted in time to take advantage of them.*[7]

Wyckoff instructs us to use charts to study price and volume relationships over time for the purpose of discerning the motives of the Composite Man, or Composite Operator. The Composite Man is the presumed power behind the scenes and thus behind the movements in the markets. The Composite Operator conducts market campaigns on the bull side and the bear side for his own profit, and he executes these campaigns by attracting a public following.

We can get a better understanding, a real feel for the market, by imagining ourselves in the shoes of the Composite Operator. The manipulations (actions) of the Composite Man are possible because market participants are propelled by their own inner drives of fear or greed in an environment of risk and uncertainty.

The Composite Operator is the ideal of the Complete Trader. He grooms a stock for an advance by first forcing out the weak holders by fostering a panicky sell-off, and then keeps stock prices low while he accumulates his line, his inventory of stock, by buying from the tired and fearful public during the accumulation phase. He then leads the charge that creates an upside price breakout on good volume as he begins the markup phase.

By playing the role of the Composite Operator you will sense how to execute the bullish markup phase by attracting a public following of buyers from the sidelines into the market and into the stock, then judiciously offer support along the advancing path to keep up the optimism. Then, just as the advance matures, as the Composite Operator, you will make an about-face and conclude your campaign by selling your inventory of stock to a greedy and uninformed public who has become excited and hopeful about a further advance in stock prices. By placing yourself in the role of the Composite Operator you gain a commanding view of market behavior, seen on the charts, and gain a valuable tool for self-discipline.

PRINCIPLE 5: ALWAYS BE DISCIPLINED

The Ten Tasks of Top Trading presents a trader psychology and mental discipline system with roots in behavioral finance. Through our collaborative research, Dr. Van K. Tharp and I developed this series of discrete contexts for selecting appropriate mental states and providing a logical and comprehensive sequence of tasks for the successful trader to follow. We have both worked with traders who have employed our model with good results. Market wizard Ed Seykota labeled the Ten Tasks of Top Trading model "a significant contribution to the art and science of trading."[8]

Implementing the Ten Tasks of Top Trading helps the trader adopt the most appropriate mental attitude, beliefs, and emotions for each of the principal tasks for trade setup, trade trigger, and follow-through. Indeed, the Ten Tasks reveal that the challenges of following through a trade commence in the heart and mind of the traders well before the actual trade is made. In using the Ten Tasks, you will gain a deep appreciation as to how, where, when, and why to apply such contrasting sentiments as fear, greed, hope, forbearance, courage, and patience in following through on your trades.

Success in system or discretionary trading requires a model of trader psychology for mental state control. Discipline is key.

PRINCIPLE 6: BUILD YOUR TRADING SYSTEMS ON BEHAVIORAL FINANCE

Behavioral finance and technical market analysis are two sides of the same coin. Behavioral finance provides a sound, logical grounding in scientific models for understanding markets. Technical market analysis furnishes indicators for analysis and decision rules for taking action. Hence, the deeper and better the underlying theory about how markets work, the more reliable technical analysis can become.

Behavioral finance is essentially the study of how people *really* behave in markets, not how they are *theoretically supposed* to act according to the random walk hypothesis. Psychology and the social science disciplines of sociology and anthropology provide models for studying how real people actually behave in markets. Scientific research using these disciplines reveals that there are predictable patterns to human behavior.

A behavioral finance framework for systems building provides the structure for integrating and interpreting indicators organized along the key dimensions of price, time, volume, and sentiment. A solid footing on the bedrock of behavioral finance can give the trader much greater fortitude in the pursuit of his market technical analysis and much greater confidence in the setup, trigger, and follow-through of his trades.

What concrete advantages can a trader hope to gain from behavioral finance?

- Models to extract more and better information. Models of market behavior based on behavioral finance economize the number of indicators employed and help to extract more information from each indicator and from the interrelationships of indicators.
- A scientific basis for testing and diagnosis. Behavioral finance models provide a sound, scientific logic for understanding how and why markets work, and therefore a sound guide for the selection, integration, and interpretation of market indicators.
- Creativity. Behavioral finance models help usher forth new ways to view markets and can spotlight overlooked indicators and techniques of great value.
- A confident edge in trading. A scientific rationale underlying a trade gives the trader greater confidence in entering trades, exiting trades, and following trends.
- Self-improvement. Behavioral finance is the solid ground upon which to build an understanding of trader psychology and mental state control.

Model Building

Models drawn from the behavioral sciences, such as behavioral finance, can help the trader-analyst clear away the current underbrush and confusion that have been created by the weed patch of technical indicators and mechanical trading systems without solid foundation. Specifically, behavioral finance can help the trader-analyst avoid the following obstacles:

- Too many technical indicators to select from. "There is nothing more practical than a good theory," goes the saying. Behavioral finance models can help the trader pare down the myriad indicators available on most software programs to a manageable if not ideal number of indicators.
- Systems that look good when back-tested, but blow up when implemented in real time, using real money. Behavioral finance helps traders create more reliable, enduring trading systems based upon proven patterns of human behavior.
- Infinite possibilities. There are endless possible combinations of indicators. Behavioral finance offers models to help you identify the key combinations and shows how they interrelate.

Behavioral finance can also help shed light on dilemmas confronting the trader:

- Complexity versus keeping it simple.
- Setup versus trigger versus follow-through.
- Mechanical systems versus judgmental methods.
- Right-brained, big-picture thinking versus left-brained, analytical thinking.
- Individual psychology versus mass behavior.
- A Life Cycle Model of Crowd Behavior versus computer-driven data mining.

PRINCIPLE 7: USE DECISION SUPPORT SYSTEMS

For market timing, the Life Cycle Model of Crowd Behavior acts as a decision support system for setting up trades with an assortment of mutually reinforcing price, volume, time, and sentiment indicators that can be weighted and summed up for more powerful timing signals. It contains both a visual (right-brained) component and an analytical (left-brained) component to give you a complete or whole-brained approach to analysis and training. Furthermore, the S-shaped curve of the Life Cycle Model fits neatly with and gives a solid scientific foundation to the Wyckoff method's stages of accumulation, markup, distribution, and markdown. You will remember the thorough discussion of the Life Cycle Model of Crowd Behavior in Chapter 3. However, stock selection was left out of consideration until this chapter.

PRINCIPLE 8: TEST YOUR TRADING SYSTEM

According to Walter Baets, "Information is static (and linear) and therefore can be copied and repeated, whereas knowledge is dynamic (and nonlinear) and therefore needs to be created each time over and again."[9]

The Action Sequence

Back-testing a trading system is a good idea when that back-testing exercise involves you in the decision making. You can build your judgment and skills of analysis at the same time you learn about the habits of a stock or commodity. If you put your trading system through the rigors of the Action Sequence method, you can see which trading techniques (for example, Wyckoff principles) work best in the market or stock you are trading. The trick is to put yourself back in history and then go through testing as if you were actually trading that stock in real time. It is a game of paper trading where you cover up the future of the chart and do your trading unaware of what lies ahead. Then you reveal to yourself one section of that future after another, taking action, getting feedback, and making adjustments.

I find that 5 or 10 bars of chart data unveiled at a time is about ideal for testing and learning; you can use either hourly, daily, or weekly bar charts. With daily charts you should do this over a one- to two-year period. These data provide the feedback for you to evaluate how well you are in gear with the stock and whether your trading system is working correctly. If you're not doing well, then you should replay the sequence. Using this Action Sequence process over many trades and with a variety of different stocks, you will discover the trading principles that work best for you. The Action Sequence will also give you valuable feedback regarding your own internal strengths and weaknesses as a trader and what remedial steps you can take to make you a better, more complete trader.

Refer to the Action Sequence sheets in Chapter 9, Appendix A. They present a section of stock data, provide the analytical questions to use, and are followed by a feedback commentary from me.

PRINCIPLE 9: ADOPT A PLANNING AND CONTROL PROCESS

As the old proverb goes, "Having lost sight of our objectives, we redoubled our efforts." Creating a compelling future through visualization is a superb way to keep you on track toward your desired outcome. However, even the best-laid plans are subject to the caprices of nature and man. It is not sufficient merely to develop plans. Plans are not self-fulfilling. You must monitor the results of your trading efforts and make adjustments when they seem warranted. Planning must be matched by control.

Control

Control in trading refers to a series of procedures that ensure that a trader's actual results verge on her desired results. To operate, the trader must have specific results (called *objectives* or *standards*) in mind, and these results must be within a certain range so as not to lead inevitably to dissatisfaction. In preparation, the trader plans and observes the actual results of his trades and compares them to the desired results through daily debriefing, post-trade debriefing, and periodic review. If there is too much deviation, the trader undertakes certain control activities to close the gap.

Control is predicated on the following conditions:

- The trader sets standards or objectives.
- The trader is able to observe actual results.
- Not all results are acceptable to the trader.
- The trader has devices available for influencing the disparity between actual and desired results.

The meaning of control can be clarified by contrasting it to two other processes: *analysis* and *planning*. A trader undertakes market *analysis* to understand where he is in the market, why he is there, and what his opportunities are. Typically, market analysis means applying technical analysis to a specific market juncture in order to come up with a low-risk idea. Market analysis also means scanning the longer-term time horizon to ascertain opportunities and threats, then incorporating these observations into a plan. This plan may seek to exploit intermediate cycle swings.

Traders undertake *planning* to specify a direction in which they would like to go and a means for getting there. A trader's plan is frequently a Wyckoff campaign for exploiting the potential of an imminent move, including initial entry, adding to a position, and then exiting it.

Control is designed to keep the trader in harmony with his plan so that he can maximize his opportunities and minimize his losses. Market analysis and planning campaigns do not necessarily ensure the reaching of desired objectives because the market environment is never perfectly predictable, and also because of random disturbances. In order to secure desired results, analysis and planning must be supplemented by procedures for dealing with unexpected behavior emanating either from within the trader or from without. The body of such procedures constitutes control. Figure 10.1 presents an overview of the plan-control process, with emphasis on the different places where the process might get out of control.

The management-of-trading process is divided into the four processes of analysis, planning, implementation, and control. *Analysis* involves looking for low-risk opportunities. *Planning* involves the choice of a plan, and the construction of standards. *Implementation* consists of both implementing the plan and monitoring the performance. These processes are also expressed in the Ten Tasks of Top Trading.

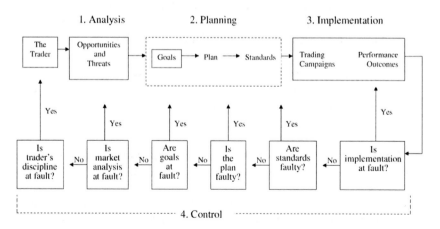

FIGURE 10.1 A Planning-Control Process for a Trading Business
Source: This Planning-Control Diagram was inspired by Philip Kotler, *Marketing Management, Analysis, Planning, and Control,* 10th ed. (Upper Saddle River, NJ: Prentice Hall, 2002).

Analysis   The trader must develop a technical system for identifying opportunities. Opportunities can be classified into two separate categories. For me the most important are the *intermediate* cycle swings of about 5 percent or more in the DJIA. I anticipate approximately six to eight such opportunities during the year. Additionally, there are the *minor cycle* swings of 5 percent or less in the DJIA. Expect approximately 15 to 20 such opportunities during a calendar year. Minor cycles are most often oscillations around an intermediate trend, where either the intermediate is given priority over the minor cycle via a buy-and-hold approach or the minor cycle is used to trade around a core intermediate position.

Planning   Your planning could, for example, contain the following goals:

- Objectives: Make a 100 percent return on beginning capital.
- Plan: Catch at least 50 percent of the minor cycle moves and 75 percent of the intermediate swings. Catch at least four good, 5 percent or more moves during the year.
- Standard: Maintain a profit-to-loss ratio of at least 3:1 during the first six months of 2007. Attempt to trade every minor cycle, but do not miss any 10 percent or greater intermediate swing opportunities.

Implementation   Your next two steps are essential for the success of your planning.

1. Follow through all trades with the Ten Tasks of Top Trading. Execute initial entries and add-ons. Set up and move protective stops. Develop and keep fresh a contingency plan for every trading campaign. Be sensitive to your intuitive self.

2. Measure your performance. Every two months prepare a written review of performance. Appraise opportunities won, lost, or missed. Prepare profits/losses and other ratios of effectiveness and efficiency of your trading. Is the performance satisfactory?

Consistency is the aim of the game. Performance can get out of control with too many losses, too few gains, too much left on the table, or too large drawdowns. Similarly, performance can suffer after a spurt of behavior that is simply too good! Making a giant killing can color a trader's perceptions, leading to a subsequent subpar performance. Remember the old saying, "Over can be the beginning of under."

If the performance is satisfactory, then exit this control review procedure. If not, go to the next step.

Is the Implementation at Fault?   If, for example, you had suffered a large drawdown because the market gapped open beyond your protective stop, was it an error in implementation? Maybe not, if you followed standard operative procedures by moving your trailing stop just beyond an observable technical danger point. Maybe yes, because your subconscious mind flashed a picture of the paper profits earned or you kept forgetting little things that caused you to return twice to your office. Obviously, if errors occur, diagnosis of both person and system should follow. Specify the standards for profit taking and instill skills to such a degree that you can automatically execute the appropriate procedures.

However, in this example, let's say it was not clear that implementation was at fault. Hence proceed to the next question. (Remember to keep a logbook of your trades and a psychological trading diary.)

Are the Standards at Fault?   Maybe the standards are too tight and too mechanical for a loose and entrepreneurial enterprise like trading? Doubtful, but the foregoing assertion could be true. On the other hand, productivity might improve if you stopped attempting to trade every minor cycle, instead conserving your capital and energy by passing up all but the best opportunities. With maximum effort on one or two trades per year, you might easily reach your 100 percent growth objective.

A consideration of changing standards must not be taken lightly. Leave the question for the six-month or annual review.

Is the Plan Itself at Fault?   Has there been confusion or conflict between the intermediate and minor cycle trades? Is there too much stress or burnout associated with trying to catch all the fluctuations? Was it a mistake to add on controls or to wait too long before adding substantially to a winning position?

Entertain these and similar questions during the periodic review of performance. Remember, too, that your plan should vary with the circumstances. There are times to be fancy with a bet; there are other times to rely on a plain commitment and not to pyramid.

Are the Original Objectives at Fault?   Are the standards too high or too low, pressing you into the panic zone or leaving you to slumber in the drone zone? Is your trading style just too far out of gear with your trading plan? Are the objectives simply too ambitious for the current state of the trading and your skill and knowledge level? Rewarding yourself for completing each task step of trading, have you gotten off balance through overly focusing on technical analysis, psychological analysis, or money management?

Is the Opportunity Analysis at Fault?   Here we come back to the
elements of technical analysis. If too many errors are reported, you may
need to revise or rebuild your trading system and/or yourself.

PRINCIPLE 10: INTEGRATE THE THREE SKILLS AND MAKE THEM AN INTEGRAL PART OF YOURSELF

I wanted to wrap up this book with a living case study of someone who
studied basic technical analysis, the Wyckoff method, and trader psychology with me at Golden Gate University in San Francisco, California. Mr.
Weylin Canada fits that bill perfectly.

During September and October 2006, Canada, an experienced foreign
exchange trader at Esoteric Investments in the San Francisco Bay Area,
very kindly donated his time and even interrupted his daily trading activities to interview with me and to make several voice recordings describing
his trades. His account covered his personal growth as a trader, and his
learning and use of the Three Skills of Top Trading, coupled with examples of his technical analysis and trading actions with recent currency
pairs. Canada's own charts accompany the text.

Canada's track record as a trader is very good and his willingness and
ability to report honestly and thoroughly about himself, his own experiences, and his advice to other traders is admirable. What follows was
culled from several hours of recording, using, as much as possible,
Canada's own words.

The purpose behind giving you this report is to demonstrate the practical benefits of integrating the Three Skills of Top Trading into the per-
sonality and life of a trader. I hope it will inspire you also to make the
Three Skills an inseparable part of yourself.

A Report from Weylin Canada, a Complete Trader

To focus my commentary, I reread several of the articles and handouts by
Dr. Pruden that I studied with him and that I've been using. It was a great
refresher for me to read them. On my desk today I have these sets of
notes: "The Ten Tasks of Top Trading," "The Life Cycle Model," "The 3-in-1
Trader," "Chart Reading in the R-Mode," and "Putting It all Together."
Since I consciously use Wyckoff all the time in doing my trading, I didn't
need to refer to my Wyckoff notes.

Please look at Figures 10.2 through 10.9, which represent four different currency pairs around which I'll weave my commentary. I selected
them purposely because they show the full spectrum of accumulation and

FIGURE 10.2 Australian/U.S. Dollar Accumulation Markup
Source: Courtesy of Weylin Canada, Head of Proprietary Trading/Esoteric Investments, LLC.

distribution trading ranges to which I had applied Wyckoff principles at the time.

What's nice about currencies is that they trend. Wyckoff is a choice method to use for seeing the big picture and following the primary trend. I've learned that it is a smart policy to trade in sympathy with the primary trend. Trading ranges, on the other hand, are significant at bottoms and tops. That's where I see the professional interest stepping in. The Composite Man enters to pick up bargains from the public sellers who believe that prices will go much lower and so they are eager to unload. We can see evidence of that in the euro/U.S. dollar and Australian/U.S. dollar charts.

I've made an important observation about currencies that other traders ought to keep in mind. That observation is that the same thing is happening in different currency pairs at about the same time. The Australian/U.S. dollar combo and the U.S. dollar/Canadian dollar pairs revealed much the same tendencies during 2001. Sometimes you can use the clues given in one pair to alert yourself to take a position in a separate currency pair.

Wyckoff distribution patterns are apparent in the U.S. dollar/Swiss franc currency pairing shown in Figure 10.9. That pair tended to add

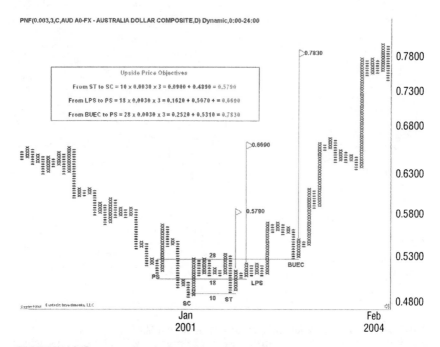

FIGURE 10.3 Australian/U.S. Dollar Currency Pair
Source: Courtesy of Weylin Canada, Head of Proprietary Trading/Esoteric Investments, LLC.

confirmation to my conclusions about the other currency pairs. Breakouts on the charts would cross-confirm. Traders please take note that the Australian/U.S. dollar and the euro/U.S. dollar prices are quoted so that an increase in the value of the Aussie or the euro relative to the U.S. dollar translates into the Aussie or the euro advancing upward on the chart. It's important to remember how a currency pair is quoted because that will tell you whether an advance in price on the chart means that the U.S. dollar is going up or whether the U.S. dollar is going down.

These charts give me a feel for the trade. I sense the Composite Man coming in to buy or to sell the dollar. The Composite Man's preparation for his campaign is a lot like the ideal examples shown on the Wyckoff schematics. I keep the Wyckoff schematics for accumulation and distribution handy with the expectation that the actual trade setups are going to look a lot like the ideal schematic examples. Knowing how charts tend to go directly with the ideal Wyckoff schematics gives me greater confidence in my ability to judge what the Composite Man is preparing and what will logically be his next move as he executes his trading campaign.

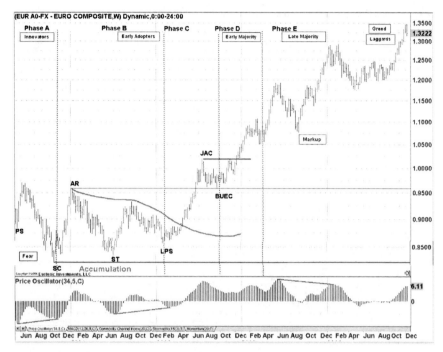

FIGURE 10.4   Euro/U.S. Dollar Accumulation Markup
Source: Courtesy of Weylin Canada, Head of Proprietary Trading/Esoteric Investments, LLC.

When I was first beginning to trade back in Atlanta, I learned firsthand the importance of watching commodities and understanding trading positions for their influence on currency prices over a longer time frame. At the time I was very short-term, looking intraday for quick trades. Then I learned that JP Morgan had a large short position from selling gold contracts when China and India were buyers. I sensed that Morgan would be squeezed to cover when gold prices rose.

Gold did rise in price, but I missed that trade, a big trade, by being too focused on today and not focused enough on tomorrow and the days after. Now I know about the correlation across commodities and currencies. I should have bought the Australian dollar, but both gold and the Aussie got away from me.

The lesson of those missed trades and the correlation between markets made me aware that if you missed a breakout in the euro/dollar, then look for a "jump across the creek" and a "backup to the edge of the creek" in Aussie. There is still an opportunity even after the other currency pair

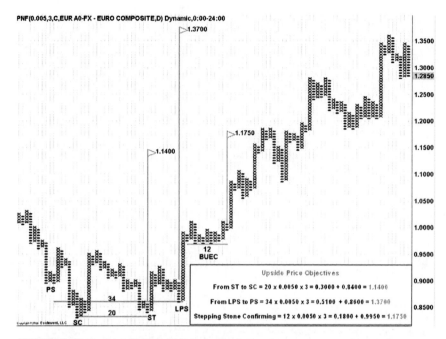

FIGURE 10.5 Euro/U.S. Dollar Currency Pair
Source: Courtesy of Weylin Canada, Head of Proprietary Trading/Esoteric Investments, LLC.

has moved ahead. Another thing I've learned is the importance of symmetry; look for the last point of support (or supply) (LPS) to come in at the same price level as the preliminary support on the chart. I think that reflects the cyclic nature of markets, the kind of thing shown in the Life Cycle Model. Cycles tend to show where you are during trends, trading ranges, and the extent of moves. I find it really helps my trading to overlay the Wyckoff schematics with the Life Cycle Model of Crowd Behavior.

I believe that Wyckoff is most useful for the longer term. Wyckoff has gotten me into the habit of using weekly basis charts. Overlaying the Wyckoff schematic with the Life Cycle Model opens my eyes and brings attention to where a trend might be pausing or reversing direction. Together they help me to get into the right zone. I've found that simply buying breakouts can be dangerous. Instead, I like to enter my trade as the trend gets under way. I've found several spots I can use to enter. On a Wyckoff accumulation schematic those entry spots are ideally the secondary test, or back-up-to-the-edge-of-the-creek, or LPS following the upside breakout at the end of a trading range, or the rally

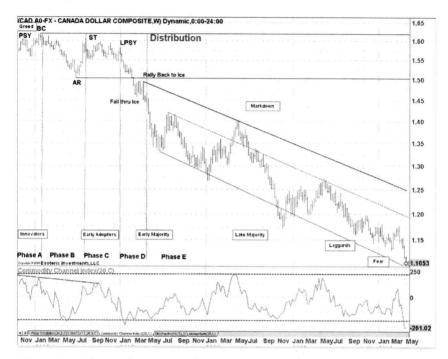

FIGURE 10.6 U.S./Canadian Dollar Distribution Markdown
Source: Courtesy of Weylin Canada, Head of Proprietary Trading/Esoteric Investments, LLC.

back to the ice after a breakdown below the price support level of a distribution trading range.

Once the trend is established it is okay to add to winning positions on reactions or rallies to trend-lines in bull and bear markets. But personally, it is difficult for me to sit tight. That is why the Ten Tasks of Top Trading help me to control myself. There is a reminder: "Don't misread the market, wait for the test." Another trick to help me be patient and to gain perspective is to use the Life Cycle Model of Crowd Behavior. I love that model because it can help predict just about anything. It really helps to tell when the late majority and the laggards are jumping on the bandwagon. Currencies are more popular now and so the reports given on CNBC are useful for taking a contrary opinion.

Canada's Comments on Chart Reading

You can see so much with charts. I like to look at charts as if they were a moving picture. The market is telling you a story. It's telling you where it

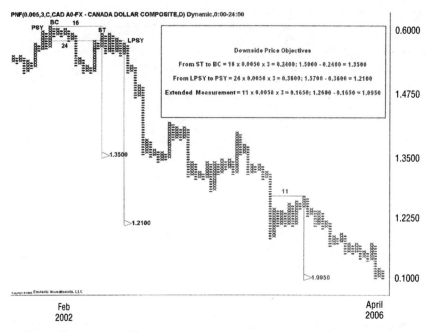

FIGURE 10.7   U.S./Canadian Dollar Currency Pair
Source: Courtesy of Weylin Canada, Head of Proprietary Trading/Esoteric Investments, LLC.

has been and it gives strong hints about where it is going. If it's not telling you anything, then don't force a trade. Don't put on a trade out of boredom or impatience or because you feel you need to earn a living. Rather, stand aside. Better to get away rather than to sit at your monitor anxious to make something happen.

I have increased my ability to step aside, and I find stepping aside to be more and more valuable as time goes by. Early in my career I wanted to pull the trigger all of the time.

These days I spend a lot more time with the first two quadrants of the 3-in-1 Trader Model. With experience I've learned the value of analysis, paper trading to get a feel, scenario building, and role playing, rather than just putting on positions. With experience you'll learn that the mechanics of trading are not that difficult. Currency trades are easy to execute, and currency trades for me usually work out quickly or not at all.

I believe that with $50,000 or $60,000 capital you have plenty enough to allow you to build a three-lot position in each of four currency pairs. Place a protective stop of 100 to 200 pips, and sit with the trend without risking more than 5 percent of your capital. I can't hold a position for four

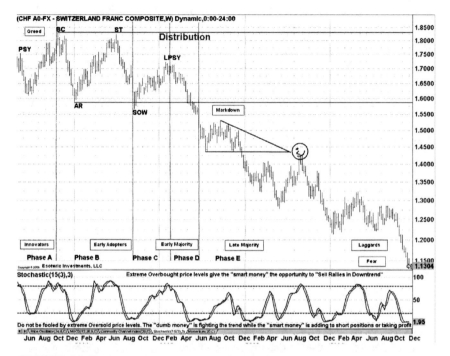

FIGURE 10.8 U.S. Dollar/Swiss Franc Distribution Markdown
Source: Courtesy of Weylin Canada, Head of Proprietary Trading/Esoteric Investments, LLC.

years, but if you could have, you would have made approximately $500,000 or say $100,000 per year. That is good money!

You can set up a position trade using the Wyckoff schematic plus the Life Cycle Model. As I said, I don't like to buy breakouts. I prefer buying on the secondary test after the breakout or, in other words, the "backup to the edge of the creek" after the "jump across the creek."

This brings up the matter of *analogies* that help the trader to judge where we are in the ongoing moving picture of the market. I find the use of analogies to help me explain what I'm seeing on a chart makes a big difference in a sideways market. Telling the story of the market, or rather reading the story the market is saying to you, is easier and clearer when you think of the market with Wyckoff analogies like the creek story or the ice story. I also like to think of a trending market as the path of a general and his army.

The analogy of the general and his army helps remind the trader that consolidations are natural parts of markets. The general needs to

262

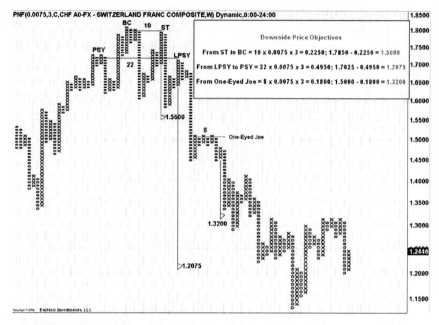

FIGURE 10.9   U.S. Dollar/Swiss Franc Currency Pair
Source: Courtesy of Weylin Canada, Head of Proprietary Trading/Esoteric Investments, LLC.

rest his troops, wait for the arrival of supplies and reserves, and consolidate his gains before pushing forward again. With weekly basis charts in hand, I like to think about the market like it was the general and his army. Then with daily charts I drill down to finer detail using Wyckoff creek and ice stories. These analogies make it easier to take money out of the market and put it back in when the reward-to-risk ratio is favorable.

The point-and-figure chart of the euro/U.S. dollar and the Wyckoff law of cause and effect can orient you to a long-term perspective and help you to trade in sync with the primary trend. The euro/dollar chart shows a base around 90 and a figure chart count up to 137.00. The euro/dollar actually reached 136.25 before reversing its price trend. It is around here, too, that I like to overlay the Life Cycle Model of Crowd Behavior.

The Life Cycle Model alerts me to look for evidence that the late majority of the laggards are joining the parade. Since currency markets have become popular, the news on CNBC and elsewhere reports on the markets more frequently. When you start hearing stories in the news that the Euro is headed to 1.50 or 1.60 and the U.S. dollar has nowhere to go but down, you become suspicious. The news and the sentiment are early warning indicators that tell you when and what to look for on your price charts. You are looking for the dumb money to come into the market.

For me, price always comes first. But indicators might help corroborate key junctures like preliminary supply, buying climax, upthrust after distribution, the fall through the ice, and the rally back to the ice. I particularly look for divergences in the indicators from the price action on the chart. These indicators are a big help because the currency market does not report volume data. For further confirmation of what I'm seeing I consult a parallel but different currency pair on another chart. If I'm thinking of buying the Canadian dollar, I'll consult the Australian chart. Don't expect a one-to-one match-up, but overall, the pictures ought to be the same.

You can short the last point of support and then sell against the rallies up to the downsloping resistance line. I always want to do my buying or selling in line with the primary trend of the market. If the Canadian dollar has topped out and is headed downward, then you should expect that the Composite Man will be selling to the public that thinks it is buying bargains. The Composite Man may continue that sort of campaign all the way down to the price target objective of 135.

Let me wrap up by saying that all three parts of the 3-in-1 Trader Model are designed to work together, and I appreciate having them to help me with my trading. I really like the Life Cycle Model of Crowd Behavior; it is a terrific addition to the Wyckoff schematics for telling me where I am in a cycle. I know that in the first one or two years of my trading I concentrated on trading methodology. But now that I'm growing confident in those areas, I believe that my attention over the next 20 years will be on mental state discipline and the Ten Tasks of Top Trading.[10]

CONCLUSION: LOOKING BACKWARD, GOING FORWARD

It is my sincere hope that you take to heart the 10 principles for a trader to live by. Long ago, Wyckoff characterized the Wyckoff method as a "way of life" for the trader. In much the same spirit, I hope that these 10 principles become an integral part of your life as a trader. The 10 principles in this chapter are in essence a summary, a looking backward, of the preceding nine chapters.

As you practice your craft going forward, I invite you to periodically return to this chapter. Indeed, please return to the entire *Three Skills of*

Top Trading for information and for inspiration. *The Three Skills of Top Trading* is designed to show you how to take a giant step upward and forward in the quality of your trading. Please master its contents.

> *With money in your pocket, you are wise and you are handsome and you sing well too.*
>
> —*Yiddish Proverb*

Notes

CHAPTER 1 Systems Building for the Three Skills of Top Trading

1. Anthony W. Tabell, "Technical Pioneers and the Changing Theory of Markets"(address, Society for the Investigation of Recurring Events, New York, May 15, 1992).
2. Charles Mackay, *Extraordinary Popular Delusions and the Madness of Crowds* (New York: Noonday Press, 1974), Preface to edition of 1852.
3. Edwin Lefèvre, *Reminiscences of a Stock Operator* (New York: John Wiley & Sons, 1994), 134.
4. Ibid., 134–135, 137–138.
5. Daniel H. Pink, *A Whole New Mind: Why Right-Brainers Will Rule the Future* (New York: Riverhead Books, 2005), 141–142.
6. Ibid., 67.
7. Ibid., 65–67.
8. Lefèvre, *Reminiscences of a Stock Operator*, 128–131.
9. Joseph Granville, *New Strategy of Daily Stock Market Timing* (Englewood Cliffs, NJ: Prentice Hall, 1976), 19.
10. Ned Davis, *The J.C. Bradford Market Timing Letter* February 1979 (Nashville, TN: J.C. Bradford & Company), 1.
11. Harvey Krow, *Stock Market Behavior: The Technical Approach to Understanding Wall Street* (New York: Random House, 1969).
12. William S. McFeely, *Grant: A Biography* (New York: W. W. Norton, 1981), 103.

CHAPTER 2 Behavioral Finance

1. Bernard Baruch, Foreword to Charles Mackay, *Extraordinary Popular Delusions and the Madness of Crowds* (New York: Noonday Press, 1974).
2. Pink, *Whole New Mind*, 1.

CHAPTER 3 The Life Cycle Model of Crowd Behavior

1. Theodore Modis, "Life Cycles: Forecasting the Rise and Fall of Almost Anything," *The Futurist* 28, no. 5 (September–October 1994): 20–25.
2. Richard D. Wyckoff, "Volume Studies," in *Basic Course in the Wyckoff Method* (Phoenix, AZ: The Stock Market Institute, 1975), section 14, 6.

CHAPTER 4 Wyckoff: The Man, the Method, the Mystique

1. Richard D. Wyckoff, *Wall Street Ventures and Adventures Through Forty Years* (New York: Greenwood Press, 1968; first published 1930), 186.
2. Wyckoff/Stock Market Institute, *The Richard D. Wyckoff Course in Stock Market Science and Technique* (Phoenix, AZ: The Stock Market Institute, 1995; first printed 1968), Preface.
3. Wyckoff/Stock Market Institute, "How a Campaign Is Conducted—Individual Chart Studies—Part 1," in *The Richard D. Wyckoff Course in Stock Market Science and Technique* (Phoenix, AZ: The Stock Market Institute, 1995; first printed 1968), section 9, 1–2.
4. Ibid., 2–4.

CHAPTER 6 The Wyckoff Method of Technical Analysis and Speculation

1. Lefèvre, *Reminiscences of a Stock Operator*, 125.

CHAPTER 8 Trader Psychology and Mental Discipline

1. Wyckoff/Stock Market Institute, "Market Philosophy," in *The Richard D. Wyckoff Course in Stock Market Science and Technique* (Phoenix, AZ: The Stock Market Institute, 1995; first printed 1968), section 25, 1.
2. David Nusbaum, "Mind Games," *Futures* Magazine, June 1994, 60.
3. John Sweeny, "Van K. Tharp, Ph.D.: Trader's Psychologist," *Technical Analysis of Stocks & Commodities*, April 1987, 7.
4. Van K. Tharp and Henry O. Pruden, "The Ten Tasks of Top Trading," *MTA Journal* 40 (Winter 1992/1993): 25–34.

CHAPTER 9   The Composite Man

1. Richard M. Restak, M.D. *The Brain* (New York: Bantam Books, 1984), 70.
2. Robert Dubin, *Human Relations in Administration*, 2nd ed. (Englewood Cliffs, NJ: Prentice Hall, 1974), 433.
3. Wyckoff/Stock Market Institute, *The Richard D. Wyckoff Course in Stock Market Science and Technique* (Phoenix, AZ: The Stock Market Institute, 1995; first printed 1968), section 9, 5.

CHAPTER 10   Putting It All Together: Ten Principles for a Trader to Live By

1. John Brooks, *The Seven Fat Years: Chronicles of Wall Street* (New York: Harper, 1958), 146–147.
2. Lawrence Shainberg, "Finding 'The Zone,'" *New York Times Magazine*, April 9, 1989, 34.
3. Peter M. Senge, *The Fifth Discipline* (New York: Currency Doubleday, 1990, 1994, 2006), 148–149, 153.
4. Ibid., 171.
5. Paul Hawken, *Growing a Business* (New York: Fireside, 1987), 176.
6. Pink, *Whole New Mind*, 51–52.
7. Wyckoff, "How a Campaign Is Conducted—Individual Chart Studies—Part 1," in *The Richard D. Wyckoff Course in Stock Market Science and Technique*, section 9, 1–2.
8. Taken from a conversation between Ed Seykota and Van Tharp in Northern California/Nevada, spring 1989.
9. Walter Baets, Bernard Paranque, and Henry Pruden, "Interpreting Data from an Experiment on Irrational Exuberance, Part B: Reflections from Three Different Angles," *Journal of Technical Analysis* 62 (Summer–Fall 2004): 6.
10. Weylin Canada, interview by Henry O. Pruden, September 2006, at Esoteric Investments, San Francisco, California. Recording continued by Canada in days following.

Recommended Reading

BOOKS

Bazerman, Max. *Judgment in Managerial Decision Making*, 4th ed. New York: John Wiley & Sons, 1998.

Chancellor, Edward. *Devil Take the Hindmost: A History of Financial Speculation*. New York: Plume Publishing, 1999.

Granville, Joseph. *New Strategy of Daily Stock Market Timing*. Englewood Cliffs, NJ: Prentice-Hall, 1976.

Hartle, Thom. "On a New Market Paradigm: Henry Pruden of Golden Gate University." Interview, *Technical Analysis of Stocks & Commodities* 16, September 1998.

Hutson, Jack K., ed. *Charting the Stock Market: The Wyckoff Method*. Seattle, WA: Technical Analysis, 1986.

Kirkpatrick, Charles D., and Julie R. Dahlquist. *Technical Analysis: The Complete Resource for Market Technicians*. Upper Saddle River, NJ: Financial Times/ Prentice Hall, 2006.

Krow, Harvey A. *Stock Market Behavior: The Technical Approach to Understanding Wall Street*. New York: Random House, 1969.

LeBon, Gustave. *The Crowd*. New York: Viking, 1960; Isis Large Print, 1995.

Lefèvre, Edwin. *Reminiscences of a Stock Operator*. New York: John Wiley & Sons, 1994.

Leonard, Brent L. "Answering the Bell of Sentiment Indicators." *Market Technicians Association Journal* (Spring–Summer 1996).

Mackay, Charles. *Extraordinary Popular Delusions and the Madness of Crowds*. New York: Noonday Press, 1974; Crown, 1995.

Modis, Theodore. "Life Cycles: Forecasting the Rise and Fall of Almost Anything." *The Futurist*. September–October 1994.

Murphy, John. *Technical Analysis of the Financial Markets: A Comprehensive Guide to Trading Methods and Applications*. New York: New York Institute of Finance, 1999.

Peters, Edgar E. *Chaos and Order in the Capital Markets*. New York: John Wiley & Sons, 1991.

Pring, Martin J. *Technical Analysis Explained: The Successful Investor's Guide to Spotting Investment Trends and Turning Points*, 4th ed. New York: McGraw-Hill, 2002.

Pruden, Henry O. "Behavioral Finance: What Is It?" *Market Technicians Association Newsletter and MTA Journal* (September 1995).

Pruden, Henry O. "Trading the Wyckoff Way: Buying Springs and Selling Upthrusts." *Active Trader* Magazine, August 2000.

Pruden, Henry O. "Wyckoff Axioms: Jumps and Backups." *Active Trader* Magazine, January–February 2001.

Rogers, Everett M. *Diffusion of Innovations*, 5th ed. New York: Free Press, 2003.

Rogers, Everett M., and F. Floyd Shoemaker. *Communications of Innovations*. New York: Free Press, 1971.

Schwager, Jack D. *Futures: Fundamental Analysis*. New York: John Wiley & Sons, 1995.

Schwager, Jack D. *A Study Guide for Fundamental Analysis (Schwager on Futures)*. New York: John Wiley & Sons, 1996.

Statman, Meir. "Behavioral Finance." *Contemporary Financial Digest* (Winter 1997).

Thaler, Richard H., ed. *Advances in Behavioral Finance*. New York: Russell Sage Foundation, 1993.

Wyckoff, Richard D. *How I Trade and Invest in Stocks and Bonds*. New York: Cosimo Classics, 2005.

Wyckoff, Richard D. *Wall Street Ventures and Adventures Through Forty Years*. New York: Greenwood Press, 1968; first published 1930.

Wyckoff, Richard D. *Stock Market Technique, Number One*. Burlington, VT: Fraser Publishing Company, 1984; first published 1934.

WEBSITES AND OTHER RESOURCES

Financial Economics Network (FEN), www.ssrn.com/fen/index.html

Investors Intelligence, www.investorsintelligence.com.

Van Tharp Institute, www.vanktharp.com.

Wyckoff/Stock Market Institute, P.O. Box 84227, Phoenix, AZ 85071-4227. smi@abilnet.com, craigschroeder1@cox.net.

Some sites for software:

www.decisioneering.com
www.hoadley.net/options.html
www.nag.com/index.asp

For information and news:

www.fenews.com
www.financialengines.com
www.ssm.com

Please see Chapter 2, Appendix A for additional online resources in behavioral finance.

Bibliography

Bernstein, Jake. "Set Up, Trigger and Follow Through." Presentation, annual conference of the Italian Society of Technical Analysts, Genoa, Italy, April 22–23, 2005.

Cameron-Bandler, Leslie, David Gordon, and Michael Lebeau. *Know How: Guided Programs for Inventing Your Own Best Future*. San Rafael, CA: FuturePace, 1985.

Cato, Ralph. "Buying Stocks That Have Moved Up." *MTA Newsletter* (July/August 1992): 13–14.

Dreman, David N. *Psychology and the Stock Market*. New York: Amacom, 1977.

Edwards, Betty. *Drawing on the Right Side of the Brain*. Los Angeles: Tarcher (1979).

Forte, Jim. "Anatomy of a Trading Range." *MTA Journal* 43 (Summer–Fall 1994): 47–53.

Gould, Edson. "My Most Important Discovery." *Findings and Forecasts: A Vital Anatomy* (1976).

Guyon, Don. *One-Way Pockets*. Wells, VT: Fraser Publishing Company, 1965; first published 1917.

Haas, Albert, Jr. and Don D. Jackson, M.D. *Bulls, Bears and Dr. Freud*. New York: World Publishing, 1967.

Harper, Henry Howard. *The Psychology of Speculation*. Wells, VT: Fraser Publishing Company, 1966; first published 1926.

Hutson, J., D. Weis, and C. Schroeder. "Charting the Market, The Wyckoff Method." *Technical Analysis of Stocks & Commodities*, 1990.

Hutson, Jack K., ed. *Charting the Stock Market: The Wyckoff Method*. Seattle, WA: Technical Analysis, 1986.

Kirkpatrick, Charles D., and Julie R. Dahlquist. *Technical Analysis: The Complete Resource for Financial Market Technicians*. Upper Saddle River, NJ: Financial Times Prentice Hall, 2006.

Krow, Harvey A. *Stock Market Behavior: The Technical Approach to Understanding Wall Street*. New York: Random House, 1969.

Le Bon, Gustave. *The Crowd*. New York: Viking, 1960; Isis Large Print, 1995; first published, 1895.

Lefèvre, Edwin. *Reminiscences of a Stock Operator*. New York: John Wiley & Sons, 1994; first published, 1923.

Mackay, Charles. *Extraordinary Popular Delusions and the Madness of Crowds.* New York: Noonday Press, 1974; Crown, 1995; first published 1841.

Mandelbrot, Benoit B., and Richard L. Hudson. *The (Mis)Behavior of Markets: A Fractal View of Risk, Ruin and Reward.* New York: Basic Books, 2004.

Mathis, David. "Santa Fe: A Classic." Audiotape and charts. Phoenix, AZ: Stock Market Institute, 1978.

Neill, Humphrey B. *The Art of Contrary Thinking,* 4th ed. Caldwell, ID: Claxton Printers, 1971.

Nelson, S. A. *The ABC of Stock Speculation.* Wells, VT: Fraser Publishing Company, 1964; originally published 1903.

Nusbaum, David. "Mind Games." *Futures* Magazine, June 1994, 60–62.

Pink, Daniel H. *A Whole New Mind: Why Right-Brainers Will Rule the Future.* New York: Riverhead Books, 2005.

Pruden, Henry O. "Behavioral Finance: What Is It?" *MTA Journal* 45 (Fall–Winter 1995): 7–9.

———. "Catastrophe Theory and Technical Analysis Applied to a Cal Tech Experiment on Irrational Exuberance." *Managerial Finance* 31, 5 (2005): 38–59.

———. "A Challenge to the Senior Technician: Integrating the Technical Market Analysis Mix." *MTA Journal* 53 (Winter–Spring 200): 7.

———. "Chart Reading in the R-Mode." *MTA Journal* 36 (Summer 1990): 33–38.

———. "Life Cycle Model of Crowd Behavior." *Technical Analysis of Stocks & Commodities* 17:1, January 1999.

———. "Putting It All Together." *MTA Journal* 46 (Spring–Summer 1996): 7–8.

———. "A 'Sealed Room' and 'Only One Client.'" *MTA Journal* 39 (Spring 1992): 35–38.

———. "Trading the Wyckoff Way: Buying Springs and Selling Upthrusts." *Active Trader* Magazine, August 2000, 40–44.

———. "Wyckoff Axioms: Jumps and Backups." *Active Trader* Magazine, January–February 2001, 46–51.

———. "Wyckoff Tests: Nine Classic Tests for Accumulation; Nine New Tests for Re-Accumulation." *MTA Journal* 55 (Spring–Summer 2001): 50–55.

Pruden, Henry O., and Bernard Belletante. "Wyckoff Laws and Tests." *STA Market Technician* 51 (November 2004): 9–10.

Pruden, Henry O., and Bruce Fraser. "The Wyckoff Seminars." Golden Gate University, San Francisco, Fall 1992 and Spring 1993.

Schultz, Harry D., and Samson Coslow. *A Treasury of Wall Street Wisdom.* Palisades Park, NJ: Investor's Press, 1966.

Selden, G. C. *Psychology of the Stock Market.* Wells, VT: Fraser Publishing Company, 1965; first published 1912.

Shiller, Richard. "Stock Prices and Social Dynamics." In *Advances in Behavioral Finance,* edited by Richard H. Thaler, 167–218. New York: Russell Sage Foundation, 1993.

Smelser, Neil J. *Theory of Collective Behavior.* New York: Free Press, 1962.

Tufte, Edward R. *The Visual Display of Quantitative Information.* Cheshire, CT: Graphics Press, 1983.

Wolf, H. J. *Studies in Stock Speculation.* Wells, VT: Fraser Publishing Company, 1966; first published 1924.

Wyckoff, Richard D. Schematics and charts in "Basic Lectures: 2, 3, 7 and 12." *The Richard D. Wyckoff Course in Stock Market Science and Technique.* Phoenix, AZ: Stock Market Institute, 1995; first printed 1968.

Wyckoff/Stock Market Institute. *Introduction to the Wyckoff Method of Stock Market Analysis—Text.* Phoenix, AZ: Stock Market Institute, 1983.

Wyckoff/Stock Market Institute. *Introduction to the Wyckoff Method of Stock Market Analysis—Text Exhibits and Illustrations.* Phoenix, AZ: Stock Market Institute, 1983.

Index

Lightning Source UK Ltd.
Milton Keynes UK
UKOW050707120613

212095UK00001B/66/P